CHURCHILL
COMES OF AGE

CHURCHILL
COMES OF AGE

CUBA 1895

HAL KLEPAK
PHOTOGRAPHY BY GLEN HARTLE

Cover illustration: Churchill in 1895 in the full dress uniform of the 4th
Hussars; Martínez Campos' headquarters in Santa Clara (Glen Hartle).

First published 2015

by Spellmount, an imprint of The History Press
The Mill, Brimscombe Port
Stroud, Gloucestershire, GL5 2QG
www.thehistorypress.co.uk

British Library Cataloguing in Publication Data.
A catalogue record for this book is available from the British Library.

ISBN 978 0 7509 6225 4

Typeset in 11/14pt Bembo by The History Press
Printed and bound in Great Britain by TJ International Ltd.

To the Memory of
Sir Winston Churchill, KG, OM, CH, TD, DL, FRS
(1874–1965)

Winner of the Red Cross of Military Merit for his comportment
in Cuba in 1895, long before the rest of these honours but already
emblematic of them all

The 'Greatest Briton who ever lived' and the greatest inspiration to
Britain and the Commonwealth they have ever had

CONTENTS

Acknowledgements   9

Preface   13

Chapter 1   1895: A Year and a Context   21
Chapter 2   Cuba? An Idea and a Plan   43
Chapter 3   The Multifaceted Adventurer   73
Chapter 4   Cuba: Arrival and Deployment   85
Chapter 5   Oh Bliss! Coming of Age and Coming under Fire   107
Chapter 6   The Sequel: Immediate and Long Term   143
Chapter 7   Myths and Realities: '*Se non è vero è ben trovato*'   168
Chapter 8   The Young Churchill as Political Analyst   179
Chapter 9   The Young Churchill as Military Analyst   191
Chapter 10   The Impact of the Cuban Adventure   222
   Conclusion   236

The Cuban Adventure Chronology   240
Notes   243
Bibliography   273
Index   282

ACKNOWLEDGEMENTS

The research for this book took place in many places as did its drafting. It was necessary to travel to Cuba on several occasions, to Spain on one and to the United Kingdom three times. In those countries much time was spent in a variety of cities. In Cuba it proved worthwhile to visit the archives and historic sites Churchill would have seen not only in Havana but on the way to the war zone – Colón, Santo Domingo, Santa Clara and Cienfuegos – and in that zone Tunas de Zaza, Sancti Spiritus, Arroyo Blanco, Jicotea, Ciego de Ávila and Júcaro. Many other sites of interest to the story were also visited. It will not be possible to thank as they deserve the many average citizens of Cuba who assisted me and my graphics designer and photographer, Glen Hartle, in our work of discovering the route Churchill took in Cuba and the kinds of things he saw and faced there, but we thank them here.

Travelling in the modern Europe of the EU is of course much easier. But in Spain it proved important to visit not only Madrid but also the historic town of Segovia to the north. And in England the trail led not only to London but to Cambridge, Hove, Oxford, Blenheim and Churchill's beloved Chartwell in Kent. While drafting the volume could be done mostly in Havana and Ottawa, the research effort produced considerable strain at times, complexities only confronted successfully because of the number and commitment of many people along the way, again far too numerous to mention as they deserve. But Churchill's name opened doors throughout these countries and made the adventure a delight overall.

In Canada, my thanks must go to Glen Hartle, the photographer and friend just mentioned who, investing his own time and money, has been a wonderful boon to the project. It is beyond me to express how central he was to producing the present book because of his vast knowledge of graphics, computers and photography and his love for Cuba and admiration for Churchill. It is also a pleasure to acknowledge the enormous assistance of my friend Gordon Vachon who, as often in the past, offered his tireless efforts in reviewing the manuscript with his formidable editorial skills and knowledge. Also I thank Gord's wife, Linda, who yet again patiently kept the home fires burning while I worked for part of the time on drafting and reviewing this book out of their home in Ottawa. The inspiration and assistance of Ronald Cohen, MBE, with his vast knowledge of Churchill and devotion to his memory, was essential for success. Also more than supportive there was Paul Durand.

In Britain, my thanks go out to a number of scholars. That list is headed by Maxine Molyneux, director of the Institute of the Americas, who arranged for me to use that institute as a base for my research at Kew, the British Library, Hove and Cambridge, and to her staff, especially Abi Espie and Oscar Martínez. The words of encouragement, practical guidance and friendship of Tony Kapcia, Head of the Forum for the Study of Cuba, were also helpful beyond measure. At Cambridge, Allen Packwood, Director of the Churchill Archive, could not have been more welcoming and supportive of me and the project. Mark Bunt and others at the Hove Library, home of the Wolseley Papers, were also efficient and welcoming and deserve much thanks. As always at the National Archives the personnel were efficient and ready to help at all times. Major David Innes-Lumsden, regimental secretary of the Queen's Royal Hussars at Regent's Park Barracks in London, allowed instantly complete access to the regiment's archives and book collection as well as its valuable photos and sketches, and supplemented this with thoughts of his own. He arranged a visit to the regiment at Sennelager in northern Germany, where Captain Mark Cubitt, the adjutant, Second Lieutenant Sebastian Durrant and the highly knowledgeable Warrant Officer II Arran Bevington-King received me graciously and helped me through their collection of useful documents and photos not only of Churchill but also of General Reginald Barnes.

Celia Sandys, far from jealously guarding her turf where her grandfather's memory is concerned, was attentive and supportive from the start, and meeting and working with her has been an honour and an inspiration. At Chartwell, Wayne Thornton leapt into the breach more than once to assist. The British ambassador to Cuba, Tim Cole, opened doors and showed a keen interest in the project, kindly answering my appeal for assistance for the work Lourdes Méndez was doing on Churchill in her village.

In Cuba, a place where it is not easy to do research without local support, I had it in large quantities. I have pleasure in acknowledging the ideas of Lourdes Méndez Vargas, whose first thinking on Churchill's visit to her beloved village of Arroyo Blanco stimulated both her work and mine. Her friends at museums in Arroyo Blanco and in Jatibonico were also willing to assist in many ways including the difficult task of discovering exactly where key sites from the time were to be found. Gustavo Placer's guidance and steadiness were essential to success in ways too many to cite. Also of great help was the Director of the Institute for the History of Cuba, Colonel René González Barrios, who knows the Spanish Army in the Cuba of 1895 like no one else, and who generously shared his knowledge with me.

Nancy Machado at the José Martí National Library of Cuba smoothed things for me in my use of that essential place. My friend José Abreu Cardet in Holguín kept me on the straight and narrow more than once, as he has done often in the past in my sojourns into Cuban history. The city historian of Sancti Spiritus, María Antonieta Jiménez, guided me through the history of her town and province despite her being terribly busy with preparations in 2014 for the 500th anniversary of the founding of the town. Similar help was provided by Hedy Águila Zamora, a historian of the city of Santa Clara, who not only provided much useful information but also introduced me to the journalist Arnaldo Díaz who was equally willing to share his often intriguing stock of photos and documents with the author.

In Spain, Captain Agustín Pacheco, Esperanza Vega Morán and Luis Mateo González at the Servicio Histórico Militar bent over backwards to assist me in going through that vast and invaluable archive in Madrid. Their colleagues at the Archivo General Militar in Segovia were also welcoming and a great help. Staff at the Biblioteca Nacional and the Archivo Histórico Nacional likewise were more than willing to be of assistance despite the difficulties through which Spanish diplomatic archives are currently passing.

In the United States I benefitted not only from the constant interest and support of Lee Pollock, the Executive Director of the Churchill Centre, but through him from an anonymous donor who provided invaluable assistance to a project that until then was funded entirely from my own pension. Others who helped more than they may know are Clara Adorna Peña, Yuniesky Álvarez González, Gilbertico de la Torre Peña, Israidel Espinosa Arias, Captain Paul and Jamie Dempsey, Ricardo Guardarramo, John Kirk, Emily Kirk, Librada Morales, Emily Morris, Odalys Gorcias Durán, Ian Kemp, Colonel José Pardo de Santayana, Neriberto Pérez Valdés, Alberto Prieto, Chantal Quinn, Jesús Ramos, Marilú Uralde and Roman Jarymowycz. Without the inspiration of the late Francisco Pérez Guzmán, this book might never have seen the light of day.

To all these people my sincere thanks.

PREFACE

In the review of a recent book on Winston Churchill the *New Statesman* reviewer advised readers, and doubtless any writers who proposed to work in the field of the study of this great man, that 'Of books about Winston Churchill there is no end ... Newcomers to this field need either to bring with them a reputation already made or else to happen upon a theme that has so far escaped notice.'[1] His conclusion about the book he was reviewing was that the author had done both. In the case of the author of the book you have in your hands no such claim can be made. Whatever reputation this author has is as a historian and political and military analyst of Latin America and not as a student of Churchill. On the other hand, he certainly has a firm belief that he has happened upon a theme that has so far escaped serious notice.

A keen reader of works on and of Churchill for many years, I had never ventured before into a field which had for obvious reasons attracted the attention of some of the greatest historians of the age. Sir Winston's status as 'The Greatest Briton of All Time' according to a BBC poll at the beginning of the new millennium, and as at least 'Man of the Half Century' if not 'Man of the Century' according to *Time* magazine, was such that his story was the focus of the life's work of several eminent historians, not a few psychologists and many other aficionados of all ages and from all climes. As a Latin Americanist, even one keen on Churchill, I could not see how I could do anything that would add in an important way to what was known of him. After all, he had shown little interest in my region and, great traveller though he was, had never spent any real time in the area. While I, like many people who work on Cuba, had a vague recollection that he had done something on the island during the wars for independence, I did not go into it any further than that.

My interest in the British connection with Cuba did exist, however, and I have studied for many years the nineteenth century, a period when British influence on ex-Spanish colonies was significant. Britain captured Havana and much of the western part of the island in the 1762 campaign of the Seven Years War as part of its exceptionally successful series of amphibious operations during that conflict which gave it Quebec, Manila and Saint Lucia as well as Cuba's capital. And of course this war was not the first time the British had set their sights on this rich prize.[2] In addition, the use by moderate Cubans of the Canadian model of 'Dominion status' as their goal short of full independence in the years before the 1895 war of independence ensured my interest in at least that aspect of the British imperial connection with Cuba in the second half of the nineteenth century.

I could not help but come across occasional mentions of Churchill and his time in Cuba but, other than knowing vaguely that he had come as a war correspondent and stayed at the city's famous Hotel Inglaterra, I did not know much more. And I certainly had no idea of the exceptional moment, and formative experience in Churchill's life it had been, including the preparation for it and the sequel to it, as well as the visit itself.

That interest, however, did bring me to a conference in 2002 for the 240th anniversary of the capture of Havana, the Cubans having a taste for commemorations that goes far further than the usual northern idea of celebrating only half-centuries or centuries, and certainly nothing less than quarter-centuries. There I listened to Celia Sandys, Churchill's vivacious and engaging granddaughter, speak at the Hotel Nacional on the subject of her relative's visit and what little we knew at that time of the subject.[3] I was very interested in what she said but saw little connection between what I heard and the work I was then doing on Cuba in its first independence war of 1868–78.

A decade later, however, and after publishing my own first books on Cuban politics and history, there was another conference on Britain and Cuba, again focussed on the 1762 fall of the capital but dealing with many other elements of the bi-national story, and there Lourdes Méndez Vargas, the unofficial but no-less-real historian of the village of Arroyo Blanco in central Cuba, came to see me and told me about the work she was doing and on which she was speaking that day. She was interested in the stay of the then 20-year-old Winston in her village in the last couple of days of November 1895 and she was a source of considerable knowledge on those days and on what local lore has done with the story in the 117 years or so since. She was writing a book on the subject and was certain that, with full access to Cuban archives and a visit to those in Spain, she could find out much more than had hitherto been known about his visit.

I suggested it might be possible to work together and, after her book on the local context, attempt to do a second volume telling the full story of the visit, from the preparation to the sequel, and do so by gaining access to British archival sources as well as working thoroughly through the Spanish archives, military and diplomatic, in Madrid and Segovia. Ms Méndez does not have English so I could do the British part of the effort, she could do most of the Cuban with my helping out on the more strictly military issues, and we could both do the Spanish portion of the work. Regrettably, it did not prove possible to find the financial resources to work together on the larger book, which I had reluctantly to do by myself and which is the volume readers have before them. Since at that time my pension from the Royal Military College of Canada was covering all the costs of research, it was simply not feasible to cooperate and for me to pay for her trip to Spain and associated costs in Cuba. Hence she continued with her work on the more local story in Arroyo Blanco and I began to seriously deploy my efforts to the wider theme.[4]

The excitement I felt at delving into something which was clearly so new was palpable. I did the usual literature search to discover that, as I had expected, there was virtually nothing known on the subject. Biographer after biographer had run up against the same problems and short shrift was inevitably given to the visit with only the occasional slight hint produced of its likely importance in Churchill's development. Most biographies included only a page or two on the adventure and several not even that. The importance of Churchill's visit to New York on his way to Cuba, relatively easy to research and certainly of value to do, took the limelight away from the strictly Cuban part of the trip. Churchill's admittedly significant meeting with Bourke Cochran in New York often took much more space than did the whole of the nearly three weeks on the Caribbean island covering Winston's first war. This induced me even more to engage in a serious treatment of the subject especially as it became ever clearer the role the experience had in the forging of the Churchill we were to know and for what it told us about who he was even at this very young age. This was not just about eighteen days on a Caribbean island but rather at least five months of Churchill's life during which Cuba dominated his thinking, his work and his movements, from late September/early October 1895, when the idea of the trip first struck him, until March 1896, when his last major article on the war there was written. The list of 'firsts' in his life that the visit represented was soon revealed to be a very long one, little known even among the most serious of historians studying his life.

But why was this the case? What had made research into this subject so fraught with problems and meant that, even as late as 2012, this was still almost totally virgin territory for any historian trying to tackle the subject? It might have been expected that both British and Cuban historians would have had an avid interest in addressing the first overseas adventure Churchill had ever had. And historians of other countries might also have shown the same keen interest in this aspect of his life as they have in so many others.[5] The reasons are both complex and actually in the end rather easy to understand.

In the first place, of course, Churchill's life covers such a wide canvas, is so varied and is so important to the history of the twentieth century that there is an *embarras de choix* seemingly unending where subjects of interest to historians and the public are concerned. His actions on the North-West Frontier of India, in Egypt and the Sudan, in the Boer War, in politics before the First World War, in government and in the field in that massive conflict, in political life between the wars, and as a member of, and then leader of, the wartime coalition government of 1940–45, and hero of the free world in the downfall of Hitler and Nazism, has given more than ample scope for the work of many historians and writers over many years. This is attested to by new titles that continue to be published on his life, even after the 50th anniversary of his death in January 2015. Cuba simply did not seem like a major or perhaps even very interesting part of the wider story and this acted to stymie what little interest there might have been.

It is entirely clear too that without access to Cuban and Spanish archives, there is very little to go on in order to understand the whole picture of that adventure of late 1895. British archives and other sources in the United Kingdom help a great deal as of course do his own 'letters from the front' (articles for the press), his letters to friends and family at home, material from his regiment, private papers of those involved and the like. But it is only through the archives and published literature of Cuba and Spain that one can complete the picture.

This means access of course but also knowledge of the languages in question. English-speaking historians working on Churchill have rarely had Spanish and, especially since the rupture of relations with the United States and the rise of Soviet influence in Cuba after the victory of Fidel Castro's Revolution in 1959, Cuban historians more and more rarely had English.

In addition, in Cuba, Churchill's reputation for visceral anti-communism made study of him if not taboo at least hardly easy or a priority. And, though many Cuban historians would agree that he was the most famous visitor to Cuba of all time, they would have for many years been less than sure that they wanted to give him much praise or even close study of his time on the island. The Cuba of today has changed markedly, but for most of the period since 1959 academic freedom had been noticeable by its absence. Likewise candidates from abroad coming to study Churchill in Cuba, if they came from an English-speaking country, were often hamstrung, at least to some degree, by the poor relations existing between their countries and the island. US authors in particular found study of the island a challenge since both US and Cuban governments often seemed to do their best to make such efforts flounder. Often such permission as was needed was not forthcoming from either Washington or Havana, or even both. But even British academics do not find studying Cuba easy. Suspicions of London's close links with the United States have at many times coloured Cuban governmental views of British academics to a considerable degree. Only the Canadians, with their relatively understanding approach to the Revolution since the beginning, and their refusal to bow to US pressures to break with Cuba or to join its embargo of the island, seemed to avoid most obstacles of a political kind, especially after the friendship between Prime Minister Pierre Elliott Trudeau and President Fidel Castro blossomed in the 1970s.[6] However, Canada until recent years did not have many historians working on Churchill at any stage of his life.

There was also, of course, the usual vital question of funding. There is essentially no money available for Cuban researchers to spend long periods abroad. Especially since the beginning of what is called the 'Special Period' in the summer of 1990, that period after the collapse of the Soviet Union,

COMECON and the 'socialist division of labour' from which it benefitted so much in trade, investment and even defence terms, Cuba has been in the midst of a deep economic crisis and the most stringent belt-tightening imaginable. It has been unthinkable to do research on anything not deemed essential and Churchill's visit to the island more than a century ago would not have qualified for such an assessment of its centrality. Add to this that much of the research would have had to be done in London, a city in which it is expensive to pass much time, the idea of such a research project would have been a non-starter entirely for Cubans. And even for researchers from Britain and other countries, the expenses of sustained periods in Cuba and Spain would have been daunting.

Most of all, however, I suspect, the reason why it was not done is that no one actually thought of doing it. This was certainly the case for this author, whose gratitude to Ms Méndez is all the greater as a result. And, even if others had considered doing the research, they would have been dissuaded by the questions above and by the fact that seemingly what could be done had been done. This was especially true after the publication of a book by Douglas Russell in 2005 with a chapter on Churchill's visit to Cuba.[7] But even his excellent work is based essentially on the already known articles from Churchill in the press of the time, the letters he wrote to family, and other material in the Churchill Archive at Cambridge.

In my own case, I have had several advantages others have not enjoyed and these alone have allowed me to engage in this project. First, I was honoured to be made a Member of the Academy of History of Cuba, a privilege few foreigners have enjoyed, on the basis of other works I have done on Cuban history in the past. This credential opens many doors not easily passed through in facing and overcoming Cuba's formidable bureaucracy.

Secondly, studying and working on and in Latin America for so long has meant that I speak fluent Spanish and have had to deal with archival material in that language all my working life. It has accustomed me to dealing with the often demanding Cuban academic and governmental maze, usually a challenge for even the most determined academics.

My previous books on Cuba were on themes potentially much more politically charged than this one and they have not brought down the wrath of the Cuban government, even though I was made to know that a variety of things I had written had not gone down well with some high authorities. Cuba has been a nation 'under siege' for well over half a century and that siege is conducted by a nation that is the greatest power in the history of the world, a country with a long tradition of military intervention on the island and in the region, and a source of hostility a mere 90 miles away from Cuba's northern shores. And, while direct military attack and sustained economic warfare have been parts of the US strategy to unseat the Revolution, subversion has been even more constant and all pervasive. Little wonder then that the Cuban government takes foreigners who work on Cuba's history and politics very seriously indeed. If these foreigners, like me, come from a proud country, a founding member of NATO and a close friend of the United States, and also work on defence-related affairs, the concerns in some governmental circles can be greater still.

In the end, in my case, books on such hot topics as the Cuban armed forces' difficulties in the Special Period, and a military biography of Fidel Castro's brother Raúl, the new president as of 2006, ensured the government would be wary of what I wrote.[8] This worked in my favour in the long run, however, in that, seeing that the two books were hardly anti-Cuban and both attempted to be fair, bureaucratic patience with me seems to have grown. Thus I found that when I was proposed for membership of the Academy of History of Cuba, there were no objections, and when I began work on the Churchill in Cuba project, I found only good feelings and a desire to help whenever I needed assistance from members of the state bureaucracy.

In addition, I had the enormous advantage of having several senior and respected Cuban historians and other analysts who were friends and who had assisted in many ways in my previous endeavours and were willing to do so again. Especially important in this sense I had a very serious naval and military historian more than able and certainly willing to assist in the lengthy and sometimes tedious business of searching for newspapers, books, pamphlets, published speeches, documents, and other elements of this story. Gustavo Placer Cervera, my colleague in the Academy of History, a major force on the Cuban military history scene (and Cubans take their military history, like their history in general, very seriously), kindly offered from the beginning to help out with some of the more challenging areas of research, especially in the search for relevant Cuban periodicals of the time.

My doctoral research had taken me to the Spanish archives and to the then Public Records Office in London; later research obliged me to return on occasion to those places to work. London and Madrid had each been my home at one time or another and a large part of my adult life had been in the United Kingdom, as student, army officer, professor, and simply visitor and theatre and opera buff. This meant that the friendship of many academics and others smoothed the way in myriad ways in capitals where Cuban historians find many significant challenges to successful research efforts not the least of which is financial. I was able to get some limited financial support, unlikely to have been forthcoming for a Cuban national, from a US donor keen on Churchill as well as from other sources to face those challenges.

Thus very few Cubans scholars have been interested in working on such a subject and few British ones were either. And those who might have been knew well that the difficulties of such a project might make its success unlikely. As a historian, a Canadian, speaking both English and Spanish, an academic equally comfortable in London, Madrid and Havana, and reasonably well seen by all the national governments whose archives I would need to consult, I alone seemed well placed to carry off the research required and, given the obvious importance and relevance of the work, I quickly chose to do so.

Hal Klepak
Academy of History of Cuba, Havana

CHAPTER 1

1895: A YEAR AND A CONTEXT

So little time, so much to do.

This story is a complicated one, full of many of the surprises that seem to almost always accompany Churchill's life. It is important to set the scene for this discussion in order to fully understand the context for this formative experience of the man we later come to know so much more fully and who, in William Manchester's delightful phrase, showing the traits that would make him famous and a hero for countless millions around the world, 'saved civilization'.[1]

The year of Churchill's visit to Cuba, 1895, began as one more or less typical of the period of the Pax Britannica, which had dominated the global political scene since the victory over Napoleon eighty years before in 1815. That political context had seen a series of arrangements reinforcing European peace that had passed through what was known as the Concert of Europe and, after the great revolutions of 1848, subsequent alliances and balances of power, was moving steadily into the seemingly firm peacetime blocs of the 1882 Austro-German-Italian Triple Alliance and the 1892 Franco-Russian Alliance.

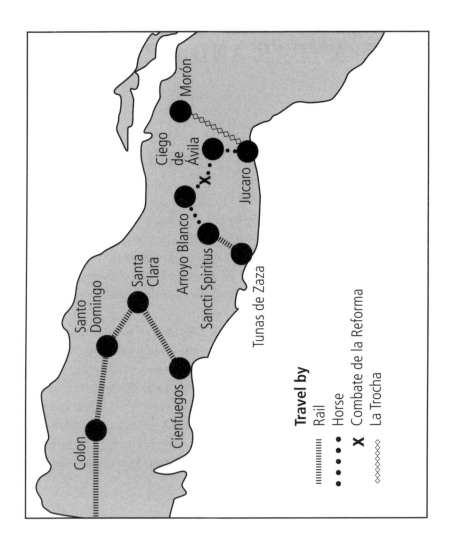

Britain

Just as important to world peace as the balance of power in Europe was, as the name Pax Britannica implies, the unmatched power and strategic reach of Great Britain in the century following Waterloo and Trafalgar, and the opposition of London to the outbreak of regional conflicts in Europe that might damage British trade, and increasingly British investments in Europe and in the growing colonial empires of several of the countries of the continent. In a quip of the time, 'Britain wishes to keep the rules in Europe so she can break them everywhere else.' That is, British policy aimed generally, but with exceptions, over time, at measured expansion outside its already established empire, joined to diplomacy and military influence aimed at peace in Europe.

British naval power, unequalled in the history of the world at that point, ranged over the world's oceans, made and broke governments, assisted some governments and political movements while stymieing others, pressured reluctant governments to move in directions sought by London, brokered peace treaties, established blockades, ended piracy and helped massively in ending the international slave trade. With improvements in communications, especially the telegraph after mid-century, the Admiralty could increasingly coordinate those efforts with its worldwide deployments based on the major naval bases along eventually all the world's major seaborne trading routes: Halifax, Bermuda, the Falklands, Simonstown (South Africa), Gibraltar, Malta, Cyprus, Aden, Suez, Singapore and Hong Kong, and of course greater India and the British Isles themselves. The resulting 'All Red Route', named thus after the red colour usually used to portray the British Empire on maps of the time, meant a maritime empire with its solidity and communications assured by the might of the Royal Navy, a force able to best those of any other two naval powers combined, if war did come. If it had been the lands of the seventeenth-century Spanish Empire that were first termed 'the empire on which the sun never sets', it was the British Empire of the nineteenth century to which that term has best applied.

Wars had nevertheless broken out in Europe during the course of the Pax Britannica in the period 1815–1914. Some, such as the Italian wars of national unity, the Austro-Prussian War of 1866, the Franco-Prussian War of 1870–71 and the Crimean War of 1854–56, had been major struggles involving more than one great power. But no war had engaged the full efforts of all or even most of the great powers over that 100 years, which was novel in the context of the constant warfare on that continent in previous centuries. This relative peace was what made the period so special and such a 'golden age' for those who were soon to face the horrors of twentieth-century warfare in geographical scope, weaponry employed, frequency and scale of destruction.

The British Empire seemed to many to epitomise this era of peace, leading as it did so many of the advances of the age in government, industry, science and the arts. London was a vast metropolis, the largest the world had seen, and Britain's cities and their industries produced the finished products of the empire and much of the rest of the world. Britain was by far the greatest trading nation in the world, its biggest investor, its most important centre of international finance, and the home of its greatest merchant navy, as well as its greatest fleet. The Union Jack and British subjects were almost guaranteed respect in most of the world and British influence, and, often enough, pretentions, seemed boundless.

While in some key areas of industrial production there were reasons for concern, such as the growth of German steel production in the immediately preceding years, or the rise in the importance of the Paris Bourse for international development and loans, the splendid overall dominance of Britain went largely unchallenged. Indeed, the peaceful context for world commerce provided by the Royal Navy was most welcome to other trading nations such as France, Germany, the United States, Italy and Japan, and even more so to smaller trading states such as the Netherlands or the Scandinavian countries.

Germany's challenge to Britain on the high seas was still in the future. And, though its financial and trading competition was beginning to be felt, that challenge was hardly central to British concerns of the time. France remained suspicious of Britain but was so engaged in its deep difficulties with a united Germany that it could spare scarce time or effort to think of competing. Russia's ambitions in Asia, to be sure, could conflict with Britain's but there too British naval power allowed for powerful force to keep those elements of Russian landward expansion into that continent at bay.

Britain's empire included protectorates or informal arrangements, such as those with the emirates of the Persian Gulf, as well as formal territorial domination. Even more striking were dominant commercial and other connections with important developing states such as Argentina, the 'informal empire' as it was often called. The end of the 'first British Empire' with the independence of the United States in 1783 seemed a far-away memory compared with the often thrusting expansion of the 'second Empire' especially after mid-century. Australia and New Zealand became new settlement colonies on something of the model of Canada, the administration of India, the 'jewel in the crown', was regularised after the mutinies of 1857, real expansion to obtain the 'Lion's Share' of Africa had begun, South East Asian colonies such as Malaya and Hong Kong saw truly modern development trends come into play, and Britain seemed to be top of the pack in most valued fields. Churchill was a classic product of this empire and of this era of peace. But this visit was to be to a colony of another European empire – that of Spain.

Spain

Spain of 1895 could hardly have presented a more contrasting picture to that of Britain. The once greatest empire in the world, defender of Catholicism at home in Europe in the face of the Reformation, standard bearer of that faith outside Europe, its dominions included the Low Countries, Portugal, including for a time (1580–1640) its vast empire, large parts of Italy and Germany, the majority of Central and South America, with, in name at least, North America, and the islands of the Caribbean Sea, the Philippines, the Marianas and Guam. It had by now fallen on hard times indeed.

The gold of Peru, silver of Mexico, and other precious metals, woods and high-value goods had for long ensured the access of the Spanish Crown to power, and to vital loans as well. For two centuries the great treasure fleets had assembled in Havana, waiting for the Spanish Navy to escort them to Cádiz in one of the famous *flotas* (fleets). And, though corsairs and pirates, usually from England, Holland or France, were only occasionally able to seriously disrupt the arrival of the fabulous wealth of the Indies, Spain had to spend vast sums to deter or defeat them.[2]

But all this was a thing of the past. Spain in the eighteenth century went from one disaster to another. The century opened with a war over the Spanish royal succession. It was not only largely conducted by foreign forces but Spain itself became a battlefield instead of being, as it had been for well over two centuries, the source of invading forces heading for other lands.

Its new dynasty, a branch of the Bourbons, tried to establish the closest of links with its northern neighbour and such 'family compacts' brought great advantages to Spain, which needed the modernisation and new ideas of a France then dominating European politics, military affairs, thought and culture. But those connections also helped to bring new wars which almost always ended with Spain being on the losing side. Indeed, the rise of British and, before that, Dutch naval power was largely at the expense of a Spain unable to find an effective reply to the challenges Britain and the Netherlands posed to its imperial status. Soon, as the American naval thinker and strategist Alfred Mahan pointed out in the 1890s, the Spanish Empire was transformed into a maritime empire, but with insufficient naval power to support that status, a combination doomed at some time to extract a high price.[3]

By the end of the eighteenth century, though Spain had lost much of its island empire in the Caribbean, it had at least been able to hold on to most of its continental possessions in the southern part of the Americas. Even this was not to last and the new century was to prove even more disastrous. Madrid tried everything it could to stay out of or at least profit from the Revolutionary and Napoleonic Wars, but instead found itself at various times an ally or even a vassal state, and was further humiliated by French occupation and the imposition of one of Napoleon's brothers on its throne. Its honour was only saved by national resistance of epic proportions, which caused unending grief to the occupiers and was crucial in assisting the British, eventually under the Duke of Wellington, in driving the French out. The *guerrilla*, or guerrilla warfare, the Spanish waged at this time became the model for others including much of what came to be seen in Cuba later in the nineteenth century.[4]

As if this were not enough, that usurpation of the throne and invasion gave the opportunity, over the years after 1808, for some of the once deeply loyal colonies of Spain in the Americas to be taken over by less loyal elements of the local aristocracies and militias. Anti-Spanish revolutions were soon sparked in much of the region and no metropolitan forces were available to quell them: Spain needed to drive out the French invaders before even thinking of countering separatist movements thousands of miles away. While local royalist forces were initially very effective at dealing with the rebels, with time and a combination of Madrid's bad government and the metropolitan army's incompetence, the forces of independence eventually got the upper hand. By 1826, after some three centuries of colonial rule, all of Spain's continental American possessions had become independent and Madrid proved powerless to reassert its rule anywhere. Spain in the Americas retreated to its bastion, long-time base and 'always loyal' colony of Cuba, with its small and dependent island territory of Puerto Rico, sole places where the colours of the Spanish 'bicolor' still flew in the western hemisphere.[5] Elsewhere the vast empire was reduced to the Philippines, some smaller island neighbours in the western Pacific region, and tiny posts surrounded by Morocco in North Africa.

Spain for decades then went from one system of government to another, reactionary absolute monarchy to constitutional monarchy, from one dynastic pretender to another, and from one civil conflict to another. Modernist and traditionalist forces vied for power with no decisive victor until the civil war a century later. The economy, weak at the best of times, suffered the consequences. The Spanish Navy ceased to be a serious force, and the army became almost totally engrossed in politics and thus the arbiter of the national destiny. Under such circumstances little attention was paid to good colonial government or reform, and the general conclusion from the Spanish-American revolutions seems to have been that Spain had been too gentle to the locals and should have adopted an even more intransigent line than the one which had largely brought about those risings.[6]

In the decades before Churchill's visit to Cuba, Spain had had a series of unstable governments, none of which could grasp the nettle of real economic progress, significant governmental reform, including of colonial administration, or military modernisation and depoliticisation. While the country would still know some economic progress in the boom times of the second half of the nineteenth century, it tended to be minor in comparison with other large European states.

Frustrations with its decline also led to often ill-conceived attempts to relive former glories. In the 1860s, Spain sought to take advantage of the essentially suspended status of the Monroe Doctrine caused by the United States Civil War to regain some influence in the Americas. This doctrine, issued by President Monroe in 1823, and more importantly backed by the power of Britain and its fleet, stated that the region was no longer available for further European colonisation. Spain defied this ban, in order to back France in its ill-starred attempt to establish a European monarchical regime in Mexico, by briefly re-establishing Spanish rule in the Dominican

Republic on the advice of particular political elements in that troubled country, and by creating a context in which a rogue Spanish admiral was able to range the Pacific coast of South America bombarding Chilean and Peruvian ports in a contemporary but preposterous attempt to re-establish Spanish influence.[7]

Such moves brought little prestige and no profit to the Spanish Crown. The monarchy was actually abolished following the 1868 September Revolution, though re-established under a different dynasty three years later. That dynasty likewise soon succumbed and, in the face of a weak Republican movement and a discredited Republican experiment, the Bourbons were soon back on the throne having, once again in that dynasty's history, 'forgotten nothing and remembered nothing'. Socialism invaded key sectors of the growing mining and industrial parts of the economy, and anarchism became a force to reckon with, including serious terrorist actions in many places over the last years of the century with attempted and sometimes successful assassinations of both politicians and members of the royal family. In 1895 Spain had a population of 18.5 million of which 64 per cent was illiterate and 65 per cent of the labour force was in agriculture, figures among the highest in Europe.[8]

Cuba

The Cuba of 1895 was greatly changed from the '*siempre fiel*' garrison island of seventy years earlier. Several generally small conspiracies, often similar to slave risings of the past, had taken place in the years between the achievement of independence by continental Spanish-American states and the outbreak of revolution in Cuba in the latter year. More troubling, a real independence movement had been developing as Spanish abuses had continued, no autonomy or even colonial dignity was granted to the island for its past loyalty, and taxation grew to unsupportable levels.[9]

Successive sugar booms of the decades prior to 1895 had, however, done much to cool such separatist sentiments. The west of the island in particular was peaceful and little inclined to revolution, though disgust at Spanish rule was widespread even there. In the poorer east, dissatisfaction was almost generalised. The differences between the two halves of the long island had been meaningful and deep-seated almost since initial settlement in the west had followed close upon that of the east. Oriente, as the east was called, had known much less sugar-related development and continued to have a more varied economy, one more dependent on other products such as coffee and tobacco. It had likewise been hit not only by more hard times but also by more destructive hurricanes than the west in the years immediately preceding Churchill's visit.

Repeated promises by Spain to reform colonial administration, and especially to grant a special status within the empire to the island, had resulted not in progress but in backward movement. Cuba had always been governed by a military governor, never therefore knowing civilian rule, a situation with no parallel among the major colonies of Spain. In addition, despite its loyalty, large and sophisticated white population, and massive contributions to imperial finances, Cuba was never allowed any sort of status in the empire beyond that of a simple colony and military base. And all attempts to have a government on lines similar to what was known in the British Empire, and especially in nearby British islands and even in Canada, were met with stony rejection by Madrid.

When the latest attempt to find a way forward failed in the mid-1860s, what followed was what in Cuban history is known as the *Guerra Grande*, the Big (or Great) War, or the Ten Years War for its duration from 1868 to 1878. This conflict took thousands of lives and divided the country terribly with enormous destruction in the war zones. However, it should be noted that the west was hardly affected as the rebels, strong in the east but almost unnoticeable in the west, were unable to bring the war to the more prosperous regions and were eventually defeated in 1878 in a carrot and stick campaign led by General Arsenio Martínez Campos, Captain-General of Cuba, of whom we will hear more. While the Cuban rebel forces, known as *mambises*, held much of the countryside of the liberated zone of Cuba Libre, they were not able to take and hold any towns, nor were they able to establish a capital with a functioning government.[10] But it is important to note that there was a 'Republic in Arms', often mobile, but always able to maintain some semblance of order in its territory and keen to receive the recognition of any power so that it could obtain more easily the arms and material needs of war, without which victory proved impossible.

There followed a brief interregnum where the promises made by the general in order to bring the rebels to lay down their arms were to some extent implemented. These included the right to form political parties and

freedom of the press. At the same time steady movement towards the abolition of slavery, always a complicated issue in an economy so dominated
by sugar production, culminated in the complete end of the practice in
1886.[11] The result of this reformist atmosphere was for the first time the
consolidation of a political party (the Liberal or Autonomist Party) which
soon represented majority opinion among Cubans born on the island.
Newspapers and magazines reflecting its views were founded in many cities
and the debate on what kind of regime Cuba should have in the future was
active and constant. In general, the call was for the 'Canadian solution': a
government where complete autonomy would be enjoyed by the island
but where defence and foreign affairs remained in the hands of an imperial
government in Madrid. This, for the Liberals, had many advantages. Spain
could have more success in deterring US tendencies to acquisition of the
island, ensure that rebellions by the large black portion of the population
had no chance of success, and continue to add prosperity through military
spending in many parts of the colony's territory. This call for what would
have been essentially 'dominion status' was backed by a majority on the
island but mattered little because of Spanish manipulation of the electoral
rules. Those related to being accepted as a voter ensured that the minor-
ity intransigent movement in favour of the status quo, termed *integrista* in
Cuba, almost always had its man elected in the political contests from the
1878 peace up to 1895.[12]

   This possible way to avoid another bloody independence war and the
likely total loss of the island to Spain did not prosper. As the main historian
of the movement puts it in the conclusion of her book on the autonomist
movement, the problem was that 'Cuba was not Canada and Spain was not
England'. Instead, a Spain accustomed to 'tax Cuba dry' was little inclined
to grant it any status whereby it would no longer be contributing in a major
way to the imperial treasury. Even Spain's military adventures in the region,
such as the interventions in Mexico and the Dominican Republic, were
paid for in large part by the Cuban colonial treasury. The fact was that Cuba
was a milch cow of great importance to the Spanish state and in many ways
a captive market for several major Spanish industries, as well as essential for
the prosperity of the merchant marine.[13]

   The years of what in Cuba is called the 'the profitable truce', 1878–95,
saw enormous change on the island. The sugar boom in the west continued
but slowed in intensity especially in the serious slump of the early 1890s,

while the economy of the east continued to decline steadily, and the arrival of tens of thousands of freed slaves into a free labour market was a dramatic change. In addition, prosperity in the west attracted tens of thousands of Spanish immigrants to Cuba, usually young and poor bachelors in search of bettering their lives by working in the cities' many shops and small industries or starting their own farms, while other immigration schemes founded new agricultural villages especially in the centre of the colony. In 1882–92 almost 100,000 Spaniards came to Cuba to stay, with a prosperous economy stimulating demand for them. All this meant a whiter population with all the political consequences that such a new situation implied. Already by 1862 the white population had grown larger (54 per cent of the total population) than the black and multiracial, but by 1887 their percentage of the population had reached almost 68 per cent.[14]

Another major trend was that towards US dominance of the Cuban market. While Spain might try to control the commerce of its colony, the power of the US attraction, joined to the fact that Spain could not provide from its own industries and agriculture all the goods Cuba needed and the US was so near, meant a natural involvement of the northern country in providing Cuba's imports. While not as central in receiving Cuba's exports, even in that area the US was very important indeed. The US began soon after the end of its Civil War to rank high as a destination for Cuban exports but by the 1880s was far and away more important than Spain in Cuba's international trade.[15] In effect, the island had one political metropolis, Spain, but quite another economic one, the United States.

Finally, the period saw the continuing trend towards unstable conditions for the export of Cuba's major crop of sugar. In what has been termed the 'sugar revolution', the whole context for production changed over these years. The destruction caused by the first war, the formation of ever larger sugar complexes (*centrales*) to replace the smaller 'estates' (*ingenios*) of earlier years, the abolition of slavery and the arrival of a free labour market, the utter dominance of the US market, the beginning of significant competition by beet sugar, and other tendencies transformed the sugar industry.[16]

During this whole period of seventeen years the Cuban independence movement continued to build its strength. Shattered by defeat in the Ten Years War, and especially the causes of the defeat, which were largely disunity in the insurgent ranks and the inability of the Cuban exile community abroad to provide enough men, weapons and ammunition to those fighting on the island, the various groupings were slow to garner their potential again. The movement was numerous enough with branches in New York, Tampa and Key West, these last two with the participation of the large number of Cuban cigar workers who immigrated there, and in Jamaica, the Bahamas, Central America and Paris. But the membership was divided on many central issues, including the value of incorporating Cuba into the American Union – an idea termed in Cuba 'annexationism' – the place of blacks in an independent Cuba, the direction for future immigration, the conduct of the war, the timing for its renewal, its leadership and a host of other matters.

In this context it fell as a priority to the aspiring leader of the movement to bring unity and provide better communications among all its branches. José Martí Pérez, born in 1853, had been too young to fight at the beginning of the previous war for independence but had written letters and articles urging rebellion against Spain. For that he was arrested and deported. In exile in New York and in a variety of Latin American capitals, Martí became by 1880 a central figure in the movement, founding newspapers supporting the cause of independence, writing and speaking in public, and planning its new phase.[17] In 1892 he created the framework of the constitution of the new Partido Revolucionario de Cuba (Cuban Revolutionary Party) and was elected as its head with the title of Delegate after it was proclaimed by Cubans in exile in Key West, Tampa and New York.

In December 1894, he planned with military commanders the next rising on the island, moving to the Dominican Republic to recruit the services of Máximo Gómez, the key general from the previous war, an excellent ex-Spanish Army officer and Dominican citizen who had commanded *mambí* forces in that conflict, and to issue a joint call for rebellion from the Dominican village of Montecristi. The revolution broke out in late February 1895 and, in stark contrast to the first rebellion twenty-seven years earlier, had some quick success in spreading outside the immediate area of Oriente. But to a great extent the lack of leaders with prestige from the first conflict, but not actually present on the island, meant that relatively few answered the call to arms. It was only in April, with the arrival of Martí, Gómez, the great multiracial commander Antonio Maceo, amongst others, that the rebellion gained steam. The seventeen further years of Spanish misrule and intransigence, the seeming defeat of the Liberal autonomist more moderate and peaceful option, economic disorder and problems especially in the east, reductions in the perception of a threat from the blacks as a result of the smoothness of the emancipation process all combined to make this rebellion more successful.[18]

The Spanish moved quickly to try to control the situation. Martínez Campos was almost immediately recalled from his post as recently appointed Captain-General of Madrid and sent out to Cuba for another tour as captain-general there. Reinforcements were quickly despatched from the metropolis to the island. The revolution, once again strongest in the east, spread rapidly now that it had both political and military leadership of high quality. Gómez, now 58 years old and looking his age, showed, however, that he had lost none of his former tactical and strategic sense and Spanish forces proved entirely unable to crush the rebels, even after Martínez Campos took over effective command in mid-April. Refusing, as he had done in the previous war, to meet the Spaniards in open battle, Gómez carried on with the harassing raids, lightning attacks and general wearing down of the enemy that had been his hallmark in the earlier conflict. Though he spoke of a 'Cuban Ayacucho', referring to the decisive victory of the Spanish-American rebel forces in the wars for independence in South America, his approach was rather different. He said that, since the Spanish Army in Cuba was so large, reaching eventually more than 200,000 men and the largest European force ever sent to the Americas, it would be necessary to defeat it bit by bit, day by day, and not by a major pitched battle on a single occasion.[19]

In that slow wearing down of the Spanish Army, his main weapon was disease. Of course many European armies had over the years of colonial conflict in the region learned to their cost of the dangers of campaigning on any Caribbean island. In the seventeenth and eighteenth centuries, mothers, wives and sweethearts would take news of their loved one's departure with the army to the Caribbean as essentially news of his death. In the 1762 campaign to take Havana, the British Army lost 4,708 men to disease, out of a total of 5,366 dead, with yellow fever being the most fearful of several diseases.[20]

While service in the region had become more salubrious by the mid-1890s, it was still highly dangerous. Spanish forces suffered terribly and certainly much more than the insurgents, although it must be said that the insurgents' claim to be invulnerable to these diseases is belied by statistics and personal accounts from the field and the rebel camp.[21] Yellow fever, the infamous *vómito negro* (black vomit), was the main killer, though acute dysentery, smallpox and typhoid also thinned the ranks of both young and old soldiers sent from the peninsula to preserve what was called 'national unity' or the territorial 'integrity of Spain'.

The other main enemy was the climate, even beyond its links with disease. The heat of Cuba in summer is intense and in winter it can still be beyond the imagination of a Spaniard, especially one from the north of Spain. And that heat is often and for long periods joined with levels of humidity even more rarely felt in the old country. In addition, the long rainy season makes conditions for marching extremely unpleasant with the tracks and roads of the island, never in particularly good condition, even worse. Long marches on these terribly rutted and often almost impassable routes exhausted the troops, and the fearfully powerful sun, endless swarms of mosquitoes and short but sharp rain storms soaking men, animals and equipment were the incubators of diseases of all kinds.

These challenges must have seemed, at least to the majority of the troops most of the time, much more of a hazard than the occasional if vicious attacks of the enemy in the field. It is surprising, and a compliment to the qualities of these soldiers, that morale was really quite high in the field army and that loyalty to country, regiment, and above all comrades was palpable.

The Lead-up to 1895 for the Young Winston

Long before his trip to Cuba began 1895 was a deeply marking year for young Winston Churchill. The young man he had become was the result of what must be described as an unhappy childhood, marked by parental indifference, dreadful experiences overall at a variety of schools, few if any real friendships and, at least until his recent experience at Sandhurst, neither intellectual nor physical prowess in most of his pursuits.

He settled at Harrow in the spring of 1888, but this was only after several attempts to find him a school where he would feel more at home instead of having a troubling time emotionally and educationally at places he hated and where he advanced only slowly while causing major disciplinary problems for his masters. Forced to study the favoured subjects of the day, classics and especially Latin, he had shown rebellion and obstinacy from the beginning. While enjoying English, History and at times French, he disliked almost all the others and showed his dislike openly.

Only at Harrow, one of the two truly great English public schools, was he to feel slowly a bit more comfortable, particularly after September 1889 when he was allowed into the army class. At the time many such schools had a separate stream for students who wished to eventually join the army, or at least whose parents so wished. The boys could then concentrate on subjects which would be helpful in passing the examinations for the two military academies of the day, Woolwich for the artillery and engineers, Sandhurst for the cavalry and infantry. He had already joined the Harrow Rifle Corps, a typical nineteenth-century cadet corps, shortly after arriving at the school. But now, in addition, he would take part in field days, be more active in the army cadet corps and engage in basic musketry, field craft, map reading, military history, army organisation and other elements of army training. He was also able to begin the sport of fencing in which he soon did very well, winning important prizes within the school and beyond. It was clear that military pursuits fitted in well with his personality and deep-set interests.

Winston, who had hated school with such a passion, began to like at least those parts of the curriculum which were finally more suited to his interests. Early on in his childhood he had loved playing with toy soldiers with a keenness and seriousness which surprised many. Indeed, the discovery of this passion by his father, Lord Randolph Churchill, on one of his rare visits to where his son found himself in their home, led to the question as to whether Winston would like to go into the army. It seems that this short exchange led to Winston's long journey to public life through military service.[22]

It was not to be an easy trip. Winston did well in the subjects he liked but continued to be recalcitrant when it came to those he did not. Attendance at Woolwich was out of the question, given his marks in several subjects and given not only its demands in mathematics and the hard sciences, but also the unromantic army branches, from Winston's perspective, for which its students were destined. It is unlikely that it would have suited Winston in any sense and it is difficult to imagine him in one of the more intellectual and less dashing technical corps instead of the infantry or the even more splendid cavalry

Be that as it may, he failed in his first two attempts to get into Sandhurst and only scraped by in his third. Even then, his success, such as it was, was due to the hiring of a crammer, specially brought in for his third attempt at the examination. But once there, for the first time in his life, he simply flourished. He had found an atmosphere in which he was thoroughly at home, studying subjects he enjoyed almost exclusively and at which he did well. His favourites were tactics and fortification but he also studied military law, map reading, drawing, explosives and army administration, some of which he had already dabbled in at school. Entering the college for the sixteen-month course in September 1893, he could expect to graduate in December 1894. His time there passed quickly and his passion was soon to extend to horses. He excelled at riding and won prizes for his equestrian prowess, which gained him a respect among his peers utterly absent from his previous life, except for his Harrovian fencing exploits. His father arranged for him to have extra riding lessons and it paid off. Even more telling, he began to make friends and enjoy having them.[23]

In the end he passed out (graduated) from Sandhurst 20th out of a class of 180, a very respectable result especially in view of his arriving there 92nd out of the intake of 102.[24] The question then became choice of regiment, a task which has bedevilled the life of many a cadet moving into the 'real' army after the college.

His father had been very keen for him to join the 60th Rifles, an infantry regiment of considerable flare and influence going back to the days when rifle regiments had duties requiring many more individual skills and knowledge than line infantry units. The Rifles had an extremely impressive history especially in the North American wars of the eighteenth and early nineteenth centuries and as a result a reputation of weight in the army that attracted to them many bright young men who would do very well in the service. The Duke of Cambridge, not only Commander-in-Chief of the British Army but also honorary colonel of the Rifles, and a friend of Lord Randolph, had been pleased to support Winston's bid for a place as a junior officer there despite the high demand for such an honour.[25]

As usual, however, Winston had other ideas and, perhaps with his keen love of horses, this was natural. But those ideas were also stimulated by exposure to an exceptional officer of whom we will see more in Churchill's life, Colonel (later Major-General) John Palmer Brabazon, known in the army as 'Bwabs' for his difficulty in pronouncing his Rs. This dashing and efficient officer commanded the 4th (Queen's Own) Hussars and was an old friend of Lord and Lady Churchill. The regiment was stationed in nearby Aldershot having just returned from an extended posting in Ireland. Thus it came about that Winston was invited by the commanding officer of the 'Fourth' to the first of several regimental officers' mess dinners which he would attend while at the college.

A regimental mess dinner in a British cavalry regiment even now is a splendid affair and at the time doubtless more splendid still. Churchill was impressed. He wrote years later:

> In those days the mess of a cavalry regiment presented an impressive spec-
> tacle to a youthful eye. Twenty or thirty officers, all magnificently attired
> in blue and gold, assembled round a table upon which shone the plate
> and trophies gathered by the regiment in two hundred years of sport and
> campaigning. It was like a State banquet. In an all-pervading air of glitter,
> affluence, ceremony and veiled discipline, an excellent and lengthy dinner
> was served to the strains of the regimental string band.[26]

Winston was captivated. His reception among the officers, the glittering splendour of it all, being hosted by a commanding officer like Brabazon, cavalry life surrounded by horses, and being sought after for himself and not for anything else, cast a spell over the whole experience. He was soon peti-tioning 'mamma' for support to go into this regiment rather than his father's choice of the Rifles. His father was having none of it. After all, while the family was hardly poor and had always lived beyond its means, service in the cavalry was far from inexpensive. No officer in a British cavalry or infantry regiment of the 1890s expected his dismal army pay to cover his expenses and it was assumed that his family would help him keep up appearances and live as a gentleman in uniform; and the cavalry was a much dearer prospect than service in any other corps. Army pay was then £120–£150, generally considered to be the equivalent of several thousands in today's money, but the average annual costs for a cavalry officer were £600.

A cavalry officer was in the first place expected to keep horses – never a cheap enterprise – and also to hunt (riding in fox hunts as opposed to shooting game), which was also a fearfully expensive pastime. In addition, his uniforms were much more glamorous and grand and thus much more expensive than those of other branches of the armed services, themselves usually very striking indeed. His father reacted as one might imagine, tell-ing Winston he should be grateful that, despite his past marks in school and generally disappointing behaviour, he was still able to enjoy the Duke of Cambridge's support and could get into a regiment like the Rifles, which would be expensive enough without imagining one could tackle the financial demands of a cavalry officer's life. He was also miffed that his old friend Brabazon had sought Winston out, complaining that Brabazon 'had no business to go and turn that boy's head' by inviting him over to the regiment for special events.[27]

His father, however, was dying and faded quickly from the scene as these issues were actually coming to the fore. When he died on 24 January 1895, Winston was able to convince those around him that his father had given verbal consent to the change to cavalry before his passing. In any case, his arguments in letters to his mother showed that he was not going to be easily put off. Showing her the advantages of a cavalry versus an infantry regiment in terms of living conditions, prospects for promotion, interesting postings, prestige and the comfort of riding rather than walking to war, he pressed home his arguments with the sheer determination she was soon to know in spades.[28]

At this key juncture of his life, Winston was left essentially as arbiter of his own fate. Brabazon wrote to his mother advising her to write to the Duke of Cambridge to ask for the change and giving her the arguments to use with him. The duke, himself mourning Lord Randolph's passing, was in no mood to refuse his widow's request and spoke highly of the 4th Hussars and of Winston's prospects therein. In the British Army of the time, a regimental choice was made, both by candidate and by unit, only after graduation, and all fell into place nicely as by 18 February the newly graduated second-lieutenant had arrived at the 4th Hussars at Aldershot to take up his first post in the army, and was gazetted (formally commissioned) two days later.[29]

The 4th Hussars were a fine regiment with a glorious history. Founded in south-western England in 1685 as an independent troop of cavalry, they had, like almost all regiments, seen many name changes and until as late as 1861 had been designated as light dragoons instead of hussars. They had served all over the empire and in several parts of Europe, distinguishing themselves on many occasions. Their last major war had been in the Crimea in 1854–56.

Churchill was to serve with them as a regular officer for only four years, resigning from the army in 1899 to write and to go into politics, but he became their honorary colonel in the exceptional days of 1941 and remained in that position until his death, although by then the regiment had been amalgamated with the 8th King's Own Royal Irish Hussars to become the Queen's Own Royal Irish Hussars. Later that regiment was again amalgamated and became the Queen's Royal Hussars, the name they have to this day.

Sandhurst transformed Winston. He seems to have found himself finally. Thoroughly at home and happy with the curriculum, if not with the hard work of the college, he came through nicely and was not only successful with horse and weapon but perhaps equally importantly with real friends. As he sadly remarked many years later, most of them were to die either in the dreadful battles of the Boer War (1899–1902) or in the horrors of the First World War. And those that returned were scarred forever. But in 1895 they were numerous and real friends, and this new sense of belonging could not fail to make him feel that the cavalry offered much to him. It is worth noting, however, that even then the stirrings in his thinking that would take him into public life and politics, rather than have him remain in uniform, were not far away.

The regiment was safely tucked away at Aldershot in rural southern England, conveniently close to London, and was soon to move to Hounslow, even closer to the great metropolis and centre of the political and economic life of the empire. It had, however, been 'told off' for India: advised that it would be going to the vast subcontinent for the usual extended stint in the 'jewel in the crown' that cavalry regiments could expect in the peaceful Raj of the 1890s. There were twenty-eight regiments of cavalry in the British Army of the time, made up of some 17,000 men, and at any one moment six to nine of these regiments would be in India. That posting would be a comfortable one, in all likelihood, but initially Winston was to know the fate of many new 'one-pip wonders': he would have to undertake normal trooper's training for the first few months of his time and not know the more relaxed life of an officer fully until such training was done.[30] The training was rough with many a fall from the saddle, often accompanied by the laughter of troopers all round him, many a sore joint and much hard work into the bargain. But Winston thrived and got through it smartly enough and was once again entirely accepted, as he had been at Sandhurst, instead of being the outcast as at school and in a sense even at home.

The year continued, however, to be marked by deaths among people close to him. His grandmother Clara Jerome, his mother's mother, died in April. She had never been close to Jennie, Churchill's mother, and she did not leave her daughter anything in her will. Winston was not overly affected although he had received kind attentions from her from time to time and had even received at least one visit from her at school.[31] He was, however, to be greatly affected by the third major death of the year.

In July, his former governess, and the woman he may well have most loved in his childhood, Mrs Elizabeth Anne Everest, died of peritonitis. Mrs Everest, who was much more than just a nurse, was devoted to Winston and his younger brother Jack, and for Winston she had been friend, confidante, main support and chief shoulder to cry on during those sad and lonely days of his childhood. He was permitted to go to her funeral, and he paid for her headstone and inscription, writing sadly to his mother about the event. It is tempting to conjecture on what might have happened if this passing had occurred before Winston had found his legs in college, army and regiment.

Thus, as summer turned to early autumn, 1895 had already been an extraordinary year for Churchill. Out of Sandhurst, commissioned into the regiment of his choice, welcome and happy therein, a fully fledged if very junior officer in the army, Winston was now the senior male in the family and thus at least formally its head in the way of things of the nineteenth century. He was not in any way able to keep up the lifestyle of a cavalry officer without significant help from his mother or other family sources but that support was forthcoming. He thus was able to buy the vast range of uniforms and civilian clothes required of an officer of the day, and even horses, thanks to his aunt, the Duchess Lily, who gave him the money for one charger and loaned him another £100 for polo ponies.[32]

The uniforms and obligatory new civilian clothes were very expensive indeed. Regimental headquarters today are unaware of a regimental tailor existing as such in 1895. Many regiments had one by that time but others preferred to leave it to individual officers to choose their own. Winston approached Messrs Tautz & Sons, Breeches and Trousers Makers, of 485 Oxford Street, for his. They were specialists in clothes required for the colonies and especially India. He ordered seven pairs of trousers and breeches over his first eight weeks of service at a cost of nearly 40 guineas each, if we are to believe Randolph Churchill's account. Martin Gilbert gives a smaller though still very high figure for these items of dress suggesting the real price was £144. In either case they were from a very high-class tailor who advertised in the regimental journal for many years.[33] And he was able to take a full part in the life of the regiment supplemented by the kind of social activity into which he was thrust by his mother or by his own thirst for experience over those months of service close to the capital. He met or re-met many influential people, and his mother's beauty and vivacity combined to ensure him access to social circles only a rather pampered member of the aristocracy could imagine reaching while still a second-lieutenant. His father's death ensured him, and his mother, some further attention within many influential groups, and life must have seemed to have changed very much for the better despite the real loss that his father's passing represented for him.

What Was Churchill Like at the Time?

There are so many biographies of Churchill that we have a good idea of what his personality was like at virtually all times in his life, but there is not much on what he was like at the age of 21. One person who was to know him well met him shortly after the trip to Cuba and gives us a description that will help us in thinking about this young man as he set out on his first international adventure.

Churchill's close observer was one of the most important adventurers, soldiers of fortune and war correspondents of the age, Richard Harding Davis, who, as a 34-year-old, covered Cuba with the US Navy three years after Churchill. He wrote in 1910 perhaps the best known contemporary account of the soldiers of fortune of his day, with a long chapter for 'Winston Spencer Churchill', whom he had met when Winston was still a second-lieutenant. He wrote of a 'slight, delicate-looking boy', 'with blue eyes, many freckles, and hair which threatened to be a decided red', who did not look his age of 21. We can only imagine what the older swarthy Spanish officers and troops on campaign would have made of him, much less the usually much darker-skinned Cubans.

The two men had something in common when it came to frustratingly telling reporting as war correspondents. Just as Churchill later so annoyed senior military staff that he was largely responsible for the ending of the arrangement whereby serving officers could at the same time be war correspondents, so Davis did the same with the US fleet after its actions off the Cuban port of Matanzas in 1898, ending the permissions for war correspondents to accompany the navy's ships. Churchill was of course to infuriate more than one senior officer with his later books on the Malakand Field Force, the war in the Sudan and even the Boer War.[34]

Harding Davis later reserved high praise for Churchill calling him a 'real' soldier of fortune in the best sense of the word. But when they first met, in 1895, he described his 'manner of speaking as nervous, eager, explosive', and that, in contrast to other British people, Churchill 'spoke constantly' of his father. And, as so many others of the age have said, he asked many and frequent questions, often embarrassing ones. He summed up his chapter on Churchill saying, 'Of the many of his years speaking our language, his career is probably the most picturesque.' For Harding Davis, this was an adventurer indeed. And if it is the later wars that have got most of the attention in ensuring his prominence as such an adventurer and soldier of fortune, it all started in Cuba. This young man, pale, slight, delicate-looking, blue-eyed, freckly, nervous, talkative, with nearly red hair, was about to show just the sort of stuff of which he was made.

CHAPTER 2

CUBA? AN IDEA AND A PLAN

Difficulties mastered are opportunities won.

With regiments being sent to India for long periods, and postings probably lasting some nine years or more, officers were given extended leave before embarkation and were also less heavily tasked so that arrangements could be made for such an extended absence from home. Thus Winston was to have some five months of leave including a period of ten full weeks in which he would have no army duties whatsoever.[1] It was in these circumstances that the idea of embarking on some sort of adventure of real style germinated in his mind.

The main option open to cavalry officers of the time was to spend these months enjoying the 'season' in and around London, with its seemingly unending range of balls, opera, concerts, theatre, social outings and, of course, hunting. Hunting was considered by the infantry as useful for officers and that it gave them a very much needed 'eye for country'; the cavalry, as might be expected, was even more convinced that this was the case. Thus for many hunting was felt to be the ideal way of spending such a long leave.

The Motives for the Cuba Trip

Winston was not keen on emulating other officers. He remarked to his mother on the expense of such a use of time and also his desire to do something different. But it is clear that the idea of an adventure of this scope came suddenly. He wrote to ask his mother how she would be spending her time in the near future as he wanted to spend time with her, yet four days later he wrote to tell her of his decision to go away.[2]

As Winston explained later in life, his wish was to see action and to use this special time to do so. His motives were very mixed but not without a relationship among them. He wrote during the summer that, while he was greatly enjoying the army, the regiment, the new camaraderie in his life and the military life in general, he felt that the military was not really his métier.[3] More and more his mind was turning to a life in the public eye, of service to Britain and its great empire, a life in which he could exonerate his father, who had had a major fall from grace in the years before his death, and yet despite all was Winston's undoubted hero. He was reading a great deal about politics now, much more than previously, but his interest had long been visible.

The army must therefore be a means to that end, and not the end itself. Luckily, at least in his view, the best way to public notice and acclaim was in doing great deeds in the interests of great causes and thus attracting the attention of the new mass printed press then so much a part of the nineteenth century's urban life. But this was only part of the story. Like most young officers, Churchill wanted to know how he would behave in that most important of events for a military man, the first time under enemy fire. This is of course in military terms 'baptism of fire', and the term is well chosen: it is a life-changing moment when you see if you have the stuff of a soldier and whether your courage and calm under great stress is up to the test. Churchill wrote without shame later on that he wished to have a 'private rehearsal' of this event rather than finding himself in the normal context of being part of a regiment in action when such a test occurred. He wanted to find out in this way, as he put it, if his personality was 'suited' to war and its exigencies. No young officer today or then would find such reasoning odd and Churchill's circumstances permitted him to consider such a course of action as a real possibility.

It is perhaps worth noting here that most officers tend to find it reassuring, if potentially disastrous, to be surrounded by their commanders, their peers and above all their troops, at such a testing time. They feel that they are much less likely to let down the side as a whole than they might be just in letting down themselves, and that the presence of others will buttress their courage at the key moment. But Churchill clearly felt that the advantages of a private rehearsal far outweighed those of facing the challenge in the midst of others.

In addition, Churchill wanted deeply and personally to be acknowledged as having personal courage of a high order. Like many boys unhappy at school he had been bullied and it is almost certain, given his letters to his brother, that he was not always able to find the courage to face down the bullies. Winston is only one of countless men who, later in life, wish to know that those highly unsatisfactory school memories will not affect their subsequent behaviour. He wrote to his brother Jack, 'Being in many ways a coward – particularly at school – there is no ambition I cherish so keenly as to gain a reputation for personal courage.'[4] And there is no better way of finding out than testing yourself under fire, that moment when you are facing the immediate presence of the threat of death or maiming of a serious kind, when you can finally see the level of your real mettle. Winston wanted this experience and only a real adventure of a military, and warlike, kind could provide it. The time seemed propitious for such an adventure and, with the prospect of several years before him in what seemed to the young officer as an excessively peaceful India, the need was to take up the call of adventure then and there and not imagine that it might come his way automatically in an India that had not known widespread conflict in four decades. He was particularly aware of the danger of sinking into slothful complacency and a lack of stimulating life experiences. He wrote to his mother in late August that he was 'getting into a state of mental stagnation … a state of mind into which all or almost all who soldier fall'. And since his father's death he was keenly aware, or had come to the conclusion, that Churchills die early.[5]

Thus a combination of a drive for notoriety and a need to know himself set the scene for the rapid germination, initial planning, obtaining of permissions and overcoming of obstacles to the adventure that was to follow. If you did not know that the person doing all this was the future Winston Churchill, you might doubt its reality.

If Churchill was to set out on a real adventure, test his courage and begin to be known by the public, he would need to do something striking, dangerous and probably far away. The logical thing would be to go and find a war and try to see something of it from close at hand, but there were precious few wars during the flourishing Pax Britannica. To be sure, China had been attacked by Japan the previous August in what was to be known

as the First Sino-Japanese War and that conflict had captured the head-
lines until April 1895; it even briefly looked like it might engage the other
great powers in a mediation or show of force over what were viewed as the
excessive demands of Tokyo in the Treaty of Shimonoseki. But with the end
of that war the world seemed again at peace.

It was only on the island of Cuba that there was open conflict since
Martí's call in late February for a rising against Spain had been answered.
This then would have to be considered as the logical destination for an
adventurer with the objectives in mind that Churchill had. There were
advantages to such a choice if indeed his decision was made, and the requisite permissions could be had, to finally undertake such a trip. Cuba was
a great deal closer to Great Britain than China and, while it was possible to
get to Cuba via British territories such as Jamaica and the Bahamas at the
time, Churchill could also travel via the United States, in which he logically
had an interest, given his family connections and his interest in politics. He
would thereby have a chance to get to know this new power with which he
was to become so familiar over a lifetime.

The United States at the time was undergoing rapid economic expansion
following its successful re-establishment as a united nation after the years of
division and reconstruction before, during and after the Civil War of 1861–65.
In addition, it had already begun to engage in not just territorial conquest
but also overseas expansion with its acquisition of Alaska from Russia in 1867,
thereby cutting off British imperial expansion from the north-west Pacific
and further hemming in the new Dominion of Canada, created that same
year; and its subsequent seizure, in all but name, of Hawaii in 1893 and its
incorporation into what was to become in reality by 1898 a US 'empire'. It
had, of course, expanded by war and treaty ever since independence but it had
never grown by territorial expansion overseas before this period. Indeed, a
huge body of American opinion opposed the very idea of empire, given the
country's perceived negative experience within the British Empire.

Both options, travel through the British Caribbean or through the United
States, held some appeal and he considered both for a time. However, long
before travelling the obstacles to the adventure had to be faced and overcome, and potentially they were many and serious.

He would need a companion for a start. Cuba was at war and he would
be going into a war zone in that colony. He was 20 years of age, had never
been outside north-west Europe and even in his schoolboy trips to France

and Switzerland had never travelled alone. He had not even been to other parts of the British Empire closer to home. He had absolutely no Spanish, and, while familiar with French, the international language of gentlemen of the day, it was not a language he spoke fluently. He knew nothing of Cuba, of the Spanish Empire or of the troubles on the island. He had no operational military experience of any kind and held the lowest rank in the officer corps of the army. He was also, by his own admission, rather spoilt and had no knowledge of fending for himself. An older and wiser companion would be vital if he was to be able to go.

He would also have to win over his mother who might well find the whole idea not only silly but dangerous. And Jennie, now a widow, was taking an active interest in her boys, especially Winston, instead of showing the marked indifference of so many previous years. He would crucially need his commanding officer's permission to undertake such an adventure. And, given the nature of the conflict, and Britain's position as officially supportive of Spain as a friendly government but with British public opinion largely sympathetic to the rebels, he would need army permission in order to go. It was also quite likely that there would be a requirement for acceptance by the Foreign Office of such an idea. In any case, he would need the acquiescence and goodwill of Spanish governmental and military authorities in order to get close to the action, which would mean having to enlist British diplomatic assistance.

Thus a series of potential or very real challenges and obstacles opened up to the young subaltern which would surely have daunted anyone, much less someone as junior and as yet untested as the young Winston. But he plunged into the outfacing of all these obstacles one by one with the energy, drive, determination and cheek that were to become hallmarks of his style for his whole life.

Since he obviously overcame all these obstacles, we might ask why his request was eventually granted by all these levels of authority. It is usually easier to refuse such requests and there were certainly many levels of concern which would have permitted a fellow officer, a mother, a commanding officer, a commander-in-chief of the army and a senior diplomat in a sometimes awkward position, and a foreign government and army, simply to deny permission for such a venture. Yet they did not. All in the end agreed to the request, however much they might have had doubts about its wisdom or ease of achievement.

Lieutenant Reginald Barnes: Why Did He Say Yes?

Winston's first choice for a travelling companion seems to have fallen immediately on a senior subaltern of the 4th Hussars, Reginald Barnes, almost always referred to by him as 'Reggie'. As we have seen, Churchill had finally, after so many failures at school, made many friends at Sandhurst and seems to have done so in the regiment as well from the very first dinner he attended, as Colonel Brabazon's guest, while he was still at the college. But Barnes was special and was to remain so for life. Winston referred to him as 'one of the best friends I shall ever have – perhaps the best'.[6]

Very little attention has been paid to Reggie in accounts of the trip, which is unfortunate because he was obviously a very good choice, stuck with Winston to the end, and is in his own right worthy of study. Reginald Barnes was born, the son of a prebendary, at Stoke Canon, near Exeter, in April 1871, making him three and a half years older than Winston. He attended school at Winchester, which was already well known for its great contribution to the officer corps of the army and where the army class was honoured and numerous.

Like Winston he seems to have been greatly attracted to the army early on. He joined the King's Shropshire Light Infantry in September 1889 at the age of 18 and was, following the procedures of the day, appointed lieutenant at that time in the reserve battalion of the regiment. This subsequently illustrious cavalryman thus began his military service as an infantryman. Slightly over a year later, in December 1890, he transferred to the regular force, 'losing one pip' in so doing, that is, reverting to the rank of second-lieutenant. His regiment was the 4th Hussars where it was to be well over two years, May 1893, before he got his full lieutenant's second pip back again.

Barnes was, even by this stage of his career, clearly seen as an excellent officer. He was already assistant adjutant by the summer of 1895. The adjutant in a regiment of the British Army is the regimental staff officer, working directly for the commanding officer on staff matters such as administration, discipline, coordination of regimental activities, supervision of junior officers and a host of other matters. He is the CO's mouthpiece and speaks with his authority. He is usually a captain with some seniority but especially one with writing skills, a gift for administration, stature among the officers and the confidence of the 'colonel', as the commanding officer is usually referred to, even though his actual rank is lieutenant-colonel. His assistant, if he has one, is normally a senior lieutenant who shares the aptitudes described for an adjutant. Being chosen for either job at the appropriate rank level is an honour for a young officer even though many colleagues will see the work as bureaucratic drudgery and not as appealing as actually commanding a troop or platoon, the lowest hierarchically that officers command in a unit. It is worthy of note that Barnes was actually promoted captain and appointed adjutant in May 1896, a few months after his return from Cuba.

Barnes was later, like Churchill, often to be in the right place at the right time and, given his skill and good service, rose rapidly in the ranks. Posted as adjutant to the Imperial Light Horse for the Boer War, he was severely wounded at the Battle of Elandslaagte but subsequently commanded the 2nd Imperial Yeomanry in 1900–02. By the end of that war he had been awarded the Distinguished Service Order and mentioned in dispatches.

It is curious to note that Barnes became aide-de-camp in 1904–06 to the Commander-in-Chief India, Lord Kitchener, Churchill's bête noire in so much of what he wanted to do during his army days. Alas, no correspondence between Winston and Reggie on the subject of the great man seems to have survived.

The First World War found Barnes commanding the 10th (Prince of Wales' Own) Royal Hussars, another highly prestigious cavalry regiment, in South Africa, from whence they returned in September 1914 in order to hurry to the front. The rapid expansion of the army for war service, the beginning of the huge casualties of that conflict, and his own impressive command skills ensured that he did not remain as a regimental commander long and he was given command of a brigade, the 116th Infantry, in April 1915, thus returning to his initial corps, the infantry. He took the brigade to the Western Front in early 1916 and while commanding it took part in the ghastly Battle of the Somme, the blackest day in the whole history of the British Army.[7]

Even as a brigadier he did not last long as headquarters promoted him to major-general and named him to command the 32nd Division in November 1916. At the Battle of Lys the division was nearly destroyed in the heavy fighting and was subsequently used in part to train arriving US troops from April 1917, receiving high praise from the Americans for work done.[8] But Barnes moved on again soon after, taking over the 57th (West Lancashire) Division in July of that year. With that formation he fought in such actions as the 2nd Battle of Passchendaele, the 2nd Battle of Arras and the fighting which took the famous Hindenburg Line. He had thus faced and succeeded with the challenges of commanding both a 'New Army' and a territorial division and had done excellent work in both, being decorated with the Companion of the Distinguished Service Order and becoming Knight Commander of the Order of the Bath (KCB). He was also awarded two French Croix de Guerre. If it had not been for the fact that the armies of the First World War were so massive, and their divisional commanders so numerous that their actions were often lost in the broad sweep of the history of the war, Barnes would doubtless have become better known to the public. Churchill later described Barnes' commands in that conflict thus: 'His career is one of the most sound stories of British control and fighting in the Great War.' His medals in the regimental museum in Sennelager in Germany belie the idea, held by some, that he was a mere hanger-on with Churchill and not worthy of further study for himself. He most clearly is worthy of such study, and he was of course the sort of officer who would have much appealed to Churchill.[9]

Equally, Barnes appears to have been as keen on horses as Winston. Indeed, Reggie had been a pillar of the polo team in Ireland, just before the 4th Hussars return to England on the eve of Winston's getting to know the regiment. He would almost certainly have had something to do with Winston's joining the team and becoming himself one of its pillars. And, on Winston's frequent absences from regimental duties on his later adventures on the North-West Frontier and in North Africa, Reggie seems on more than one occasion to have replaced Winston for important matches.[10] The boot would be on the other foot for more important matters when Barnes, made honorary colonel of the 4th Hussars in January 1919 on return from the war and in honour of his distinguished war record, handed over that position to Churchill in 1941.

It was this young man, four years his senior in age and in the service, a senior subaltern in the regiment when Winston was about the most junior, like Winston a fine horseman, a man enjoying the confidence of both the adjutant and the commanding officer, and by all accounts a fine man generally, whom Churchill asked to accompany him on an adventure which doubtless Barnes would not have conceived of without Winston's prodding but which might well appeal to an officer keen on more action in his life. Luckily we have a good idea of how the conversation went between the two officers due to a speech made by Barnes at a regimental dinner many years later. Churchill began, after clearly remarking on the prospects for doing something special during the leave, 'After all, Reggie, we are soldiers and should see some fighting.' This was a golden opportunity to do something of note and Cuba was the only war going on at the time. Churchill pressed his friend, 'Come on out there with me. It might be better than hunting and polo.'[11] Winston had once said about Reggie, 'he was a bit older than I, and consequently I did not always see eye to eye with him', but on this matter Barnes soon acquiesced and agreed to accompany Winston on the trip. Churchill later described the moment of acquiescence as being one where when he laid out the plan to Barnes and 'found him keen' on the idea.

Mamma: Why Did She Say Yes?

Winston's mother, however, was not greatly taken with his scheme. She referred to it in a letter to Winston's brother Jack as this 'foolish business', although initially it was the way it was brought to her attention which most bothered her.[12] For Winston had not thought to ask for permission but rather, characteristically as his self-confidence increased more and more in the months after his father's death, had merely informed his mother of his decision, already taken, to undertake the adventure, with the curt words 'I have decided to go.'[13]

He wrote on 4 October that he would be going to Cuba in order to see some action and how pleasant it would be to visit the Caribbean at that time of year; he also mentioned visiting Haiti and Jamaica while on the journey. But the key point was money: he suggested that the ticket for the journey would be only £37 and that he could do the whole trip for £90, with the whole adventure costing less than a season of hunting while being much more useful and interesting. He did not ask for Jennie's financial support but certainly would have hoped to have it. His army salary was very small, the costs of keeping up in the regiment vastly more, and this trip was clearly a luxury seen from any angle. His suggestion therefore that the £90 was 'what I can afford to spend in 2 months' rings a bit false.

Jennie was clearly shocked and a bit hurt. She wrote back that she always wished to support him in his search for interesting things to do but that she would have preferred being asked rather than told, and told in such an abrupt manner, especially since the degree of danger was not slight. Her letter tells us much about their relationship at the time:

> You know I am always delighted if you can do anything which interests & amuses you – even if it be a sacrifice to me. I was rather looking forward to our being together & seeing something of you. Remember I only have you and Jack to love me. You certainly have not the art of writing & putting things in their best lights but I understand all right – & of course darling it is natural that you shd want to travel & I won't throw cold water on yr little plans – but I'm very much afraid it will cost a good deal more than you think … Considering that I provide the funds I think instead of saying 'I have decided' it may have been nicer & perhaps wiser – to have begun by consulting me.[14]

The annoyance in her tone is palpable. The use of terms such as 'sacrifice to me', 'little plans', 'nicer and perhaps wiser' points to considerable frustration with the idea and the way it was presented. Doubtless Ralph Martin is correct in his biography of Lady Churchill when he suggests that, not only did she have a mother's concern for her son, but also had doubts about his 'unnecessary exposure to combat'.[15] Nonetheless she offered to pay for the trip as a birthday present (his birthday was only a few weeks away) and would do what she could to provide introductory letters to key people along Winston's path.

Interestingly, and surely this was hardly surprising, her main concern was who Winston's travelling companion would be. Barnes received as much attention from her as you would expect when agreeing to allow your eldest son and heir to go to a war. She asked for more information on him and must have been pleased to hear who he was, what position in the regiment he held, and perhaps chiefly his age. She had written, 'I must know more about yr friend. What is his name? Not that I don't believe you are a good judge but still I shd like to be sure of him.' There was of course little reason for concern. Here was a man in whom the regiment had great confidence and so might she. Winston knew the importance of convincing her on this point and described him to her with the words, 'Everyone likes him', 'a great friend', and 'a delightful companion who is one of the senior subalterns and acting adjutant of the regiment & very steady'.[16]

In the end, Jennie may merely have decided that, knowing Churchill's mind at the time and that he had set his mind on going, it was simply easier to agree and make the best of it. Be that as it may she did not in the end oppose the trip and paid the bulk of its cost as a birthday present. The family hurdle was overcome.

The Commanding Officer: Why Did Colonel Brabazon Say Yes?

The power and influence of a commanding officer of a British regiment, of cavalry or any other arm, was impressive. He had the power to try under army law and to convict on many charges in a soldier's life, his was the last word on a very large number of issues in the lives of the soldiers under his care, and reversing his decisions was something headquarters were reluctant to do. Commanding officers were somewhat sacred people whose command years were supposed to be, and usually were, the crowning moments of their military careers. Nonetheless, it is perfectly easy to imagine Churchill's CO feeling some unease at the departure of such a young and junior officer, the elder son of good and influential friends, with no operational experience whatsoever and no knowledge of either the language of the country or the political or military situation on the ground. He would no doubt have been thinking the wiser course was to refuse the request from these two young men. Cuba was also infested with disease and its struggle for independence got surprisingly good if only occasional coverage in the national press, as well might this visit.

Churchill's commanding officer was, as we have seen, no less than Colonel John Palmer Brabazon, an old friend of the family. Brabazon, born in 1843, had had an extraordinary career marked by many unusual events and changes of fortune. He was from a rather impoverished branch of the minor Irish aristocracy and joined the army twice, first being commissioned into the 16th Lancers in 1863. He moved on to the Grenadier Guards as a lieutenant, later captain, in 1869. In 1870, in one of the last cases of such a move, he retired by selling his commission in order to dedicate himself more fully to running his Irish estates.[17]

But, unsatisfied with such a stationery existence, he took the highly unusual step of asking to join up again, this time as a special service volunteer for the Kumassi expedition to West Africa with General Wolseley in late 1873. He had written to the War Office saying he was willing to go as a mere trooper if necessary but the army gave him the temporary rank of captain and he was very successful on that campaign. He was therefore offered a commission in the 10th Hussars and joined them in time for their departure for India in 1874. There he took part in the Afghan War of 1878–79 and came to the notice of Sir Frederick Roberts, destined to be one of the best-known British military commanders of the era. Roberts made him brigade-major (staff officer to the commander of a brigade) for the march on Kandahar and he was repeatedly mentioned in dispatches on this campaign.

On return to Britain in 1889, he was made aide-de-camp to the Queen and given the temporary rank of colonel, although his substantive rank was only that of major. He became a regular and rather gallant star on the London social scene with his stature and fine moustache, of which Winston would write admiringly. Indeed, Churchill had nothing but good things to say about his first commanding officer. In his book *My Early Life*, he gushed admiration for Brabazon. He was, for Winston, 'always charming' and Churchill later wrote of his 'friendship, warm and unbroken, through the remaining twenty years of his life'. Certainly, as Carlo d'Este says in his biography of Churchill, Brabazon was 'one of the very few who could take him [Churchill] to task and still retain his friendship and esteem'.[18] He had done such a good job as commanding officer of the 10th Hussars that he was sent in the same role to the 4th Hussars in 1892 and stayed for five years, an unusual tenure given him for his excellent work with the regiment.

As we have seen, he had taken a shine to Winston at Sandhurst, perhaps earlier, and had made possible his coming to the regiment rather than going into the infantry. Few people could have been better placed to get the commanding officer's permission to go on such a trip than Churchill. As a subaltern Brabazon himself had been something of a cheeky lad, in his own search for adventure, and must have rather liked the idea of Winston wanting to do something different and adventurous at this stage of his career. Brabazon's adjutant, too, Barnes' immediate superior Captain Frederick Wauchope Eveleigh De Moleyns, was not only fond of his assistant but also of Winston. Indeed, when Winston had arrived at the regiment earlier than expected that February, De Moleyns had lent him his room in quarters and his servant, and seems to have befriended him as early as Winston's dinner visits to the regiment in 1894. He was also to be a key player in support of the young subaltern during the scandals that lapped close to Winston following his return to England after the Cuban venture.[19]

De Moleyns was an old Harrovian and doubtless one of the ones to whom Winston paid credit in one of his first letters home to mamma upon arrival at the regiment. He had enjoyed a steady but certainly unexciting career, including a long stint in Australia on the staff of the Governor and Commander-in-Chief Victoria, not a post known for its glamour or military challenges. Indeed, it may well have been Winston's adventure in Cuba that prompted him to ask for leave the following year to go to Matabeleland. There he was to see active service for the first time and to distinguish himself in action, consequently winning the DSO.[20]

Thus Brabazon had a panoply of much appreciated officers, including key regimental players, in favour of the adventure and perhaps a few who, envious of the two prospective travellers, held back short of keenness. Brabazon with alacrity, if not without some concern regarding Winston's youth and the obvious political sensitivities of the trip, agreed to the leave.

The Commander-in-Chief: Why Did Lord Wolseley Say Yes?

It was of course one thing to get the permission of a friend of the family, a commanding officer who was fond of him and who had support of his adjutant and assistant adjutant, to permit Winston to go. And the fact that the assistant adjutant wished to go as well must have helped Winston's case at the regimental level. But it would be quite another story to get the approval of a commander-in-chief who Winston did not really know and who was so enormously far up the military ladder. As so often in Churchill's life and in this particular story of a part of it, exceptional circumstances, you might almost say fate, intervened or was at least present in what now took place.

Lord Garnet Wolseley had a distinguished career after joining the forces in 1852, including active service in Burma, Crimea, the Indian Mutiny, China, Canada, the Red River Expedition and the Ashanti Wars. He had also served in Natal, Cyprus, South Africa (1879–80), and as Quartermaster General in Egypt prior to and during the ill-starred attempt to save General Gordon in 1884–85. He had always shown the greatest of courage in the field and was known as a model officer in time of war. But he also had a sharp mind and it is difficult to agree with Carlo D'Este's characterisation of him as merely another typical general officer of the age in that he 'distrusted officers who read too many textbooks'.[21] Most books dealing with him, and certainly that of his only biographers, suggest just the opposite, that he felt strongly that officers did not read enough about the service and that they should take a keen interest in all matters touching their profession.[22] In any case, Wolseley was a reformer as he showed when he was posted to the War Office in Whitehall for the first time in 1885–90 as Adjutant-General. This tended to pit him against the Duke of Cambridge, who as commander-in-chief of the army, distrusted reform and reformers. While the duke was keen on changes that improved the lot of the common soldier he was suspicious of such ideas as promotion by merit instead of social status and length of service, and selection boards for nominations to general rank, both ideas Wolseley held dear.

Wolseley had written on professional subjects as early as the US Civil War and continued to write on related matters throughout his career and into retirement. His constant service in the field gave witness of his desire to be near the action as often as possible but his experience with the nineteenth-century British Army convinced him of the urgent need for reform as the great European land powers formed alliances, gained massively in armed strength, and all adopted conscription as the basis for the mobilisation of hitherto unheard of numbers of men in time of war. Only Britain, supposedly invulnerable behind the might of the Royal Navy, retained a small army based exclusively on voluntary service. And this situation could be made tenable, felt Wolseley, only if that army was greatly improved professionally. Large-scale annual manoeuvres, established annual training programmes for units and formations, a large reserve force and the acquisition of major training areas were essential parts of any such reform and Wolseley pushed hard for them but usually from outside Whitehall, and therefore without great effect. He was equally interested in intelligence, which he felt would be vital in future warfare and preparations for it. As Adjutant-General he worked hard to extend and increase the importance of the Directorate of Military Intelligence and achieved major progress by having its head of department granted automatic major-general rank and hence a much greater status than predecessors in the rank of colonel.[23] But away from the corridors of power there was little he could do.

Posted to command in Ireland in the early 1890s, he remained far from centres of decision making. In 1895, however, he knew that he was close to having his moment if only events could be made to turn in his favour. For in the summer of that year pressure steadily built up for the Duke of Cambridge to finally resign after his record-breaking tour as commander-in-chief. The duke was now 76 and had held that post since 1856, some thirty-nine years. He was the grandson of George III and his term of service had been so long that he had actually joined the Hanoverian Army, not the British, in 1819, at a time when the two kingdoms, Britain and Hanover, were joined under the Hanoverian dynasty, on the British throne for over a century by that time.

The duke had commanded the 1st Division of the British Army in Crimea and had shown personal courage more than once. But he was definitely of the old army and found adjustment to the new circumstances of mass armies and rapid technological advance difficult in the extreme.[24] His relinquishing of command was announced in the House of Commons on 23 June, with effect from 1 October. Wolseley remarked in a letter to Lady Wolseley on that early summer day, 'the same day my time ends in Dublin', adding that 'the next week or fortnight ought to tell me if I am to be reemployed when the duke goes'.[25] With Cambridge gone from the position of commander-in-chief, as Wolseley's biographers have suggested, his successor's 'great opportunity had come at long last'. It was not, however, immediately clear that the opportunity would actually be given to him. Other candidates existed and there were some in high places who wished to see the post of commander-in-chief abolished altogether. In addition, the Kaiser had been delighted when the idea that Wolseley might be the new British ambassador in Berlin was raised with him in the summer of that year.[26]

Wolseley of course knew Lord Randolph. There are several letters between them over the years 1885–90 in the Wolseley Papers at Hove Library, although, interestingly enough, none from or to Lady Randolph.[27] They were clearly not close friends even if the letters include invitations to dinner with the Prince of Wales as well as military matters of interest to both men. It was far from self-evident that Winston would receive a positive reaction to his request. The timing could not have been more problematic for Wolseley or perhaps more favourable for Winston.

Yet, difficult as it is to believe, everything fell into place in ways that almost beggar belief. In the first place Wolseley was sensitive to the passing of

Winston's father, largely due to his spending a great deal of time studying the life of Winston's great ancestor, the First Duke of Marlborough, and having only the previous year published a biography covering the duke's early life, a work that had made Wolseley's name in literary circles well beyond the army. Wolseley's interest in the Churchill family dated back to at least 1885 and perhaps even earlier.[28] Even as he was waiting for news of his next appointment, and anxiously working towards the coveted commander-in-chief position, he was busy on the second volume on the Marlboroughs, though he was to publish his autobiography, of his life in the service, first.[29]

Wolseley had friends in very high places including Colonel, later General, Sir John Ardagh, a very close friend of the new minister for the army. The summer of 1895 saw a major change in British politics, and not just in Winston Churchill's life, as Lord Salisbury became prime minister yet again and Lord Lansdowne Secretary of State for War. Wolseley thought Ardagh was 'for so long the truest friend of Lansdowne's [that] he will be able to find out for me if I am to be passed over'.[30] On 7 August Wolseley received a secret letter from Lansdowne saying he wanted Wolseley as 'my principal military adviser during my term of office'.

Seeing his perceived value to the new government, Wolseley played for high stakes. He sought from Lord Lansdowne conditions as to the responsibilities of the post that he was being offered fearful that it would be either abolished or emasculated in changes then in the air. This nearly proved his undoing as the new Secretary of State for War made clear in blunt fashion that there would be no preconditions to the job offer but that he still wanted Wolseley as his chief adviser.[31]

All this was going on just before and indeed while Winston was considering how best to use his long leave. Even more extraordinary, Wolseley was not sent for in order to perform the traditional kissing of hands until very late in October. This is the event where the sovereign, who was then at Balmoral Castle in Scotland, hands over command of her army to the new Commander-in-Chief. It was fairly clear in the midst of the Duke of Cambridge's departure, the debate on the retention or reform of the post itself, and the settling in of the new Salisbury administration that Wolseley would be the man retained. But the formal achievement of the dream was not yet his. Instead he returned to England from Ireland at the beginning of October without formal confirmation even though he had already received some congratulations on his appointment from people in high places.

He was therefore waiting for such confirmation when the request arrived from Winston. While he had written to Ardagh on 4 October that he had been named as C-in-C, there was no clear date for his taking over or indeed of what the position of C-in-C would be by the time he occupied it.[32] At this juncture Wolseley was sometimes asked to come into town but was usually left to his own devices while others did the routine work of his office. And herein came what must have been yet another stroke of luck for Winston for in this interim Wolseley was asked if he would like to come to Blenheim Palace to continue his work on the First Duke of Marlborough and his family. He accepted immediately and went on 21 October to stay in the nearby village of Woodstock while doing the work, expecting to stay there until the end of the month 'if I am not wanted at the War Office'.[33] He then wrote to Lady Wolseley asking her to join him on the invitation of the Marlboroughs suggesting they would both enjoy themselves there and 'everyone' wanted her to come.[34]

Queen Victoria finally wrote to him on 20 October congratulating him on his appointment, discussing plans for the future, and adding that it would be 'difficult to follow as popular a C-in-C as the Duke of Cambridge'.[35] We can imagine Wolseley's reaction to that phrase but also his delight that finally it was all official. He forthwith travelled up to Balmoral for the kissing of hands.

Thus Churchill's request could simply not have come at a better time in terms of Wolseley's likely disposition to agree. He would in any case naturally have been somewhat disposed to accede to the request from an officer who clearly wanted to see action and improve his professional skills. He would also doubtless like to do something for Lady Randolph only a few months after her husband's death. And he would be disposed to concur with the request on the basis of Winston's commanding officer's clear support for the scheme.

At the same time, he had always followed international events with care. He knew very well that the Spanish attempt to suppress the rebellion in Cuba was not going very well and that the trip could be interpreted as British support for Spain. A keen reader of the newspapers, especially at this juncture of his own life and prospects, he also knew that British public opinion tended to favour the rebels even though official support for the established government of Spain was a reality. Little surprise then that he would have preferred Churchill to have simply gone without making an official request to do so, which could cause problems in the future.[36] But he met with Churchill nonetheless and it is fascinating to think of this meeting of the 20-year-old very junior subaltern and his Commander-in-Chief, three times his age, with military experience spanning well over four decades. It must have taken place at Horse Guards, the army commander's headquarters on Whitehall, on one of Wolseley's days in the office and, from a note Churchill received from a J. Duncan Daly dated 19 October saying that his application for leave would be considered, it appears to have taken place on 19 or 20 October.[37] Winston described the senior officer in the army as 'most amenable' and said that Wolseley 'quite approved' of the venture.

This could not, however, be as difficult a decision as many others at the time and was certainly not at all far up the list of things to do as October moved along. About to be submerged in the Marlborough papers at Blenheim, he had much more on his mind even than command of the army. But it is easy to imagine that it would have been impossible to have that very month accepted the proffered hospitality of the Marlborough's at their seat at Blenheim, in support of his project of nearly a lifetime, and to have said no to the request of a close relative of his hosts. The speed with which the wheels of army headquarters turned, even without his as yet being formally at the helm, was impressive and Winston could write to his mother on the 21 October that the 'Cuban business is satisfactorily settled'.[38]

Two days after his meeting with Wolseley, Churchill was sent to see Major-General Sir Edward Chapman, Director of Military Intelligence, at the War Office. Chapman was by then an old hand at military intelligence, having been appointed to this post in 1891, and would serve there for another year before he was replaced by Wolseley's old friend Ardagh. He was a recognised geographer of considerable fame, and much sought after as a speaker on international issues, especially those related to the colonial expansion of the great powers.[39] Here there were no inhibitions about Churchill's going, although doubtless considerable surprise at his very young age. Many of those who served at the time in military intelligence had themselves been military observers with foreign armies in conflicts. This was standard fare for the Directorate of Military Intelligence, which was usually keen to have any information it could get on new weapons, ammunition, equipment, organisation, tactics, strength of foreign forces and the like.

The Foreign Office was helpful in this and forwarded information obtained by embassies as a normal procedure; the War Office, of course, like the Admiralty, had its own staff in major diplomatic posts in the form of military and naval attachés. But an officer on the ground with the forces in contention was seen as a particularly good way of knowing what was actually going on and officers had gone to observe the Franco-Prussian War of 1870–71, the Russo-Turkish War of 1877–78 and a great many other conflicts in recent years. Chapman had not done so himself but he had been on active service many times including Abyssinia 1867–68, China 1878, the Afghan War 1878–80 and the Burma Expedition of 1885–86. He was likely to take a positive view of Churchill's idea, although it is important to remember that such an observer would have been in his thirties or even forties and the usual rank would have been lieutenant-colonel. In addition, such officers would normally have had considerable active service under their belts and certainly not have been recently commissioned second-lieutenants under 21. Perhaps here again Barnes' presence helped reassure Chapman since Churchill's companion, as we have seen, was four years older, a senior subaltern and acting adjutant of a prestigious regiment. He also looked a good deal more mature than Winston.

What we do know is that Chapman concurred when sent Churchill by Lord Wolseley. He not only gave him advice, maps and information on Cuba and the campaign, but also asked Winston and Barnes to 'collect information and statistics on various points' and particularly to look into a new rifle round the Spanish were using, especially its striking power and penetration characteristics. As Winston remarked in a letter to his mother, this 'invests our mission with almost an official character & cannot fail to help us in the future'.[40] Chapman's interest in the round in question is thought provoking given the fact that it was soon to be used in vast numbers against British imperial troops in the Boer War. But it has not been possible to find any record of any report Winston might have sent to the War Office on his return.

Although we cannot be absolutely certain on this point, Churchill was probably asked to look into the Mauser 7x57 cartridge designed by Wilhelm and Paul Mauser. The Spanish Army had adopted the 1893 Mauser chambered for the 7x57 round, appreciated as it was for its accuracy and moderate recoil and called 'one of the best balanced cartridge designs ever made'. The 175-grain bullet used smokeless powder and had a speed of flight of more than 2,300ft per second and the cartridge's accuracy and power were 'widely acknowledged'. It was reported to have 'produced vastly superior aerodynamic performance in comparison to other cartridge designs of the day'.[41]

The 1891 and 1893 Mauser rifle types were in general use by the Spanish Army by the time of the outbreak of the 1895 rebellion although there were still many older Remington rifles in the arsenals or issued specially to volunteer units even at this late date. The 1893 Mauser used by the Spanish was produced on the Argentine model for the rifle but was not, despite some reports to the contrary, built in Argentina. Its five-round clip made it particularly appreciated and the army was very satisfied with the rifle, so much so that 250,000 of the rifles were ordered and designer Paul Mauser was awarded the Grand Cross of the Order of Military Merit. Given British difficulties over these years in getting a smokeless powder round and a new rifle into service, Chapman would have been very keen indeed to get information on such a rifle and such a round.[42]

Why Did the British Embassy in Madrid Say Yes?

Winston of course did not wish merely to go to Cuba. His desire was to directly experience the war there as fully as possible. The necessary contacts with the Spanish government and military authorities would of course require the direct assistance of the British embassy in Madrid. And Winston was well aware that here he had one of his key allies in the project. The ambassador was yet another old friend of the family of very long date and a former close political collaborator of Lord Randolph.

Sir Henry Drummond Wolff had been ambassador to the court of Madrid since 1892 and knew everyone. Dean of the Madrid diplomatic corps, his easy ways and charm had ensured him, here as elsewhere, access to everyone who mattered at the seat of what was left of the Spanish Empire and the power of his country did the rest in making him a force to be counted on the diplomatic scene in Madrid. He was nearing his 65th birthday when approached directly by Winston in early October 1895. A professional diplomat since joining the Foreign Service as a mere clerk at 16, he had first left Rugby School to study foreign languages before beginning his diplomatic work deciphering messages at the Foreign Office. Cosmopolitan and polished, his background was unusual, to say the least, for a Victorian diplomat. His father was born Jewish but converted to Christianity and became a Christian missionary who went to a series of extraordinary places around the world. He himself was born in Malta.[43]

While frequently on leave to engage in politics later on in life he remained a diplomat until 1900 when he retired. He also had a stint as a journalist from 1864 to 1870 when he wrote from a variety of places on the continent. Keen on pretty women, he included among those of interest the sister of Lord Randolph Churchill. But she was far from the only connection he was to have with the Churchill family.

Member of Parliament for Christchurch and later Portsmouth from 1874 to 1885, Drummond Wolff's great desire was to rejuvenate the Conservative Party, especially at the local level. In this he shared the key political objective of Lord Randolph. Together they took part in the '4th Party', composed of the four backbenchers in the 1880–85 Parliament who attacked both the Liberal government and the Conservative opposition.[44] They also formed the Primrose League, a movement with the objective of reformed conservatism in mind which from 1883 admitted all Christian denominations including Catholics, a striking step for the age, and women. It is said that the idea for the League, and for its motto, *Imperium et Libertas* (Empire and Liberty), was Drummond Wolff's. The relationship with Lord Randolph became a close one with Joseph Chamberlain referring to Drummond Wolff on one occasion as 'Lord Randolph's lackey'.[45]

Drummond Wolff, despite his connections and central role, was never offered senior office. But his diplomatic career continued to flourish, when he had time for it. He had an important role in the administration of Egypt and he came to be a much respected expert on Middle Eastern questions. He wrote his autobiography in 1908 in which he praised the young Winston Churchill on two occasions.[46]

He had known Winston since the boy was at school and is credited with giving him some of the first toy soldiers which were to have such an impact on his fate. There was real affection between them and Winston wrote to him directly, not through any intermediary, asking for help with his Cuba project. In a fashion similar to that of the War Office, things were arranged in double-quick time.

Drummond Wolff was a Hispanophile and constantly worked for better relations between Madrid and London. Indeed, he was troubled by the British press' impact on British public opinion on the rights and wrongs of the Cuban rebellion. He likewise felt that Britain needed to understand that, while the rest of Latin America might like to see a Cuban republic join their ranks, they did not want Spain to be humiliated by the

United States or generally to be hurt by the dénouement of the troubles on the island.[47]

British investment in Cuba had been important since the early nineteenth century and peaceful Spanish rule of the island was generally welcome to the British government. As Christopher Hall shows us, British support for Spain in the rebellion, and indeed to some extent in the war with the United States that the rebellion spawned, while something which could have been imagined as quite likely at the time, was not as forthcoming as it might have been:

> On the face of it, Britain might have been expected to support Spain. The sympathies of confirmed aristocrats belonging to Britain's ruling class – such as Prime Minister Salisbury – were predisposed towards traditionalist monarchical regimes. Furthermore the Queen Regent was Queen Victoria's niece. She wrote to her aunt in May 1896, beseeching the monarch's advice and her 'powerful friendship' Salisbury advised the Queen to offer only her deepest sympathy in reply. A month later the United States embassy in London requested Salisbury's views on the Cuban conflict. Britain's interest was purely commercial, the prime minister replied, adding 'It is no affair of ours, we are friendly to Spain and should be sorry to see her humiliated, but we do not consider that we have anything to say in the matter whatsoever may be the outcome [and] whatever may be the course the United States may decide to pursue.'[48]

This was slight support indeed for Spain and this sort of stand would not have been welcomed by Drummond Wolff, but he knew Britain was preoccupied with other issues elsewhere; in particular it wished no further complications with the United States in Latin America as it was having over Venezuela at this time. In July relations between the two great English-speaking democracies had soured even further over the question of a United States *droit de regard* and the applicability of the Monroe Doctrine in the issue of the British Guiana–Venezuela border dispute. Indeed, Churchill felt it possible in late 1895 that he might be back in the Americas fighting the United States if things continued to worsen. Washington mattered a great deal more to London than did Madrid. And so Drummond Wolff had little choice but to be content with continuing his quiet work to smooth bilateral Anglo-Spanish relations and to hope for the best for Spain.

He would have been happy with the task set him by Winston as an opportunity to show the interest of a British aristocrat in Spain's problems, to help create what would be in his view correct British assessments of the nature and significance of the fighting, and to help out the son of his recently deceased friend. Of course his affection for and admiration of Winston were already clear and it is likely that his main desire was simply to help out.

The Spanish Authorities at Home: Why Did They Say Yes?

The one place where it should not surprise anyone to see a favourable reply to Winston's wishes was Madrid. While there was some pro-Spanish sentiment in the aristocracies of Europe and their governments, in fact such feelings were noticeable by their nearly total absence in other spheres of European life, especially in the democracies. In Britain, Scandinavia, the Netherlands and the few other democracies of the old continent, Cuban independence from Spain's bad governance seemed morally a proper goal and this was reflected in public sentiments and the press. In the autocratic governments of more eastern Europe, where a free press was just about unknown, government views tended to prevail and the rebellion was seen from a racist and anti-liberal angle. In France the need to keep focused on the issue of recovery of Alsace and Lorraine, lost to Germany in 1871, meant that, whatever French liberals might think, Spain had to be kept as pro-French as possible to ensure Paris would never face a war on two fronts if a new conflict over the lost provinces ensued.

With the United States totally anti-Spanish on these matters, or at least in general seen as such, Madrid needed any friends it could get. War with the United States was always more than a distant prospect and, while not formally isolated, Spain could look to precious few friends and no potential allies if war with the new behemoth in the west were to come. Britain, the greatest power in the world, the architect through its policies of Pax Britannica, and the 'ruler' of the very waves that separated Spain from its ramshackle but still extant insular possessions in the Caribbean and the Pacific, would be sorely needed as such an ally, or at least as a benevolent neutral, in any such context.

Spain also needed British direct assistance against supply and reinforcement missions mounted by Cuban exile groups in the United States,

Central America and the British West Indies. These could come directly from British territory or pass through British sea space on their way to Cuba. Britain showed time and again that it could often stop such expeditions from making it to Cuba and this was obviously important to Spain and much appreciated by it.

Indeed, the request from Sir Henry for approval of Winston's request came just as Britain was getting thanks from Madrid for a recent effort of this kind, one quite costly to Her Majesty's Treasury but part and parcel of its responsibilities as a sovereign state. Even before London had been crystal clear in its stated determination not to allow foreigners to pass through its territories and territorial seas with the intention of attacking another state, as early as June 1895 the British authorities in Jamaica had seized Cuban rebel weapons in a raid and were thanked by Spain for this.[49]

In October, only days before Churchill and Barnes set sail from Liverpool, HMS *Partridge* had intercepted the *Delaware*, a US-registered merchant ship carrying twenty-three armed Cubans on board, in the Bahamas, a British colony. *Partridge* brought the Cubans to trial in Nassau and stayed in the area for four days. HMS *Mohawk*, another ship on the Royal Navy's North American and West Indies Station, had also moved to Fortune Island in the Bahamas on 20 October following rumours of the movement of anti-Spanish groups on the British islands. Complaints and suspicions of the Spanish consul-general in Kingston resulted in Jamaica alerting the Royal Navy, which rapidly moved to do its duty.[50]

This was of course only days after the initial request was made by Sir Henry to the Spanish foreign ministry for permission for Churchill to visit the island and see for himself the conduct of the war and while the Spanish were still sorting out the arrangements. Also in October there were rumours reported by Spanish consuls-general in both Montreal and Toronto of a 'filibustering expedition' by anti-Spanish Cubans off the French colony of St Pierre et Miquelon near the tip of southern Newfoundland, itself a British colony.[51] The Royal Navy rushed into action again after the Royal Newfoundland Police were declared insufficiently well manned to undertake the investigation.

The offending vessel, according to reports by HMS *Cleopatra* sailing out of Halifax, was the *Pouyer Quertier*, a steamship of the French Compagnie Française des Cables Télégraphiques, now leased, or so the Spanish diplomats complained, by a Florida-based US citizen. The Spanish consul-general in Montreal, José M. Pérez, reported that it was 'likely to take shelter in Lamaline or one of the Western Ports of this island [Newfoundland]', and asked for British assistance. Vice-Admiral Sir James Erskine, C-in-C North America and West Indies Station, a no-nonsense officer, later to be Admiral of the Fleet and only recently posted to command the Royal Navy's assets in the Americas, now sent out HMS *Buzzard* to do a thorough search of the area in question, which it did over a four-day stay off the island but reported 'no trace' of the French vessel.[52]

While the Spanish continued to advise the British of suspicious move-ments of Cuban insurgents throughout the rebellion, and did so with a not always veiled suggestion that Britain could do more to help, the records are in fact replete with Spanish thanks for what the Royal Navy was actu-ally doing. These colonies were far away and not densely populated and it was an expensive business to keep warships on station over such large sea spaces. Nonetheless Sir Thomas Sanderson, the tireless under-secretary at the Foreign Office, asked the Colonial Office to 'inform the Spanish Ambassador that both our Colonial and Naval auth[oritie]s. have been instructed to use the greatest vigilance to prevent breaches of the Foreign Enlistment Act [the law which forbids such activities on British soil]'.[53] All in all, the Spanish were content with what Britain was doing. At least two reports from the Minister of Overseas Affairs (Ultramar) to the colonial authorities in Cuba spoke in April 1895 of the '*actitud amistosa de Inglaterra*' (the friendly atti-tude of England) on the Cuban situation.[54] The British may have felt a bit embarrassed by the fact that General Antonio Maceo, the great multiracial commander, had taken command of much of the rebel army after reaching Cuba in March 1895 from Fortune Island, yet another British possession.

At the same time there were irritants in the relationship, as the ambas-sador reported to Lord Salisbury from the northern port of San Sebastián in August where the Queen Regent was seeing off troops embarking for Cuba. Showing an exceptional lack of understanding, for a granddaughter of Queen Victoria, of the control the British government could exercise over a free press, Sir Henry was spoken to by her and the Duke of Tetuán, the Foreign Minister, 'in a very pressing manner of the accounts in *The Times* from Cuba, calling them "an encouragement and even a material assistance to the Insurgents"'. The Queen Regent told Sir Henry she knew personally Sir Donald Mackenzie Wallace, the director of the Foreign Department at *The Times*, and felt she could 'rely on his good feeling to see that justice was done' but 'urged me in the strongest terms to beg Your Lordship to endeavour to obtain some change in the course adopted by *The Times*'.[55]

Mackenzie Wallace was an extraordinary person, even for the times. Born in 1841, he was educated at Edinburgh, Berlin, Paris and Heidelberg, picking up several languages on the way. He became a great traveller and linguist, and after four years in Petrograd in Russia writing for *The Times* he wrote a classic book on the country. From Petrograd he went as correspondent to Berlin and to Constantinople and a variety of war correspondent missions. He was close to both Queen Victoria and the Prince of Wales but was known for his modesty and unselfish approach to life. At the time of his visit to San Sebastián two weeks after Sir Henry's note to Lord Salisbury, he was a force to be reckoned with in international relations with a deep knowledge of the realities of international politics.

Sir Henry was advised that the Queen Regent would see him straight away when he arrived in the port, something which turned out not to be necessary. It is not known what passed between Her Majesty and Mackenzie Wallace but the ambassador was asked to thank Lord Salisbury for his 'valuable assistance'. Keen on knowing more on the Cuban situation, Mackenzie Wallace saw not only the Queen Regent, but the head of the military household and the Duke of Tetuán as well.[56]

A further irritant came from a source well placed in the British aristocracy which might have had a worse impact on Churchill's plan. Charles James Stanley Howard, the 28-year-old son of the Earl of Carlisle, at that time Viscount Morpeth but on his father's death in 1911 becoming the tenth Earl of Carlisle, was a clear sympathiser with the Cuban rebellion. The ninth Earl, George James Howard, was a friend of Gladstone, a Liberal of some note and a former MP for Cumberland East. By the time his son began to favour the Cuban revolution, however, Carlisle had succeeded his uncle in 1889 as earl and thus could not sit in the House of Commons. He kept up an active interest in politics, however, and was widely well regarded on both sides of the House.

In September 1895, Viscount Morpeth (also known as Howard) took the decision to go to Cuba and see the war for himself, like many nineteenth-century sons of aristocrats had done to one war or another since the end of the Napoleonic Wars in 1815. He had asked, through F. W. Ramsden, British consul-general in Santiago de Cuba, for the British consul in New York to get the Spanish ambassador in Washington to 'facilitate matters' for his trip.

Sir Julian Pauncefote, however, the highly professional British ambassador to the United States, quickly put a stop to any such ideas. Ramsden wrote to Pauncefote saying Howard had 'conversed with Cubans belonging to the Revolutionary party; the Spanish Detective Agents there have probably ascertained this … this must have been the cause of the [Spanish] suspicions aroused'.[57] The excellent Spanish spy and informer network had once again done its work and neither Pauncefote nor Ramsden was going to support to any great extent the adventures of a man so clearly partisan in favour of the rebels where the conflict was concerned.

Howard's father soon got word of what was happening and asked the Foreign Office if it could find out where his son was and whether he was all right, given that he had heard nothing from him for some time and his adventure was hardly without risk. Ramsden and the British consul-general in Havana, Alexander Gollan, worked hard to find out what was happening and Ramsden received further requests from Howard, this time to arrange safe-conducts from the Spanish up country to places very near rebel-infested areas. The Spanish, not surprisingly, were not keen but it is interesting to note that they did try not to annoy the British and did so by offering safe-conducts instead for places not so far from Santiago and not so close to rebel territory. Ramsden advised both Howard and his father that not only was such travel dangerous in a very active war zone but that yellow fever was rife there as well. Under such British diplomatic pressure, Howard agreed to sail for New York on 26 October yet did not do so.[58]

Here was yet another British aristocrat's young son wishing to move around the country more at less at will, someone whose views on the conflict were unknown or unsavoury from a Spanish point of view, yet someone to whom they had no wish to be seen as being rude. And this was just as Churchill and Drummond Wolff's request was going to the Spanish authorities for approval.

Indeed, just as Churchill was moving into the field with the Spanish Army, yet another potential irritant came up in the bilateral relationship. On 23 November the Foreign Office advised Gollan that the Spanish ambassador to London had complained that the son of the British vice-consul in the small northern Cuban port of Nuevitas, Bernabé Sánchez y Adán, 'has joined the insurrection' and that this will make relations with the authorities 'difficult'. Salisbury was firm. If the report were confirmed, the vice-consul 'must be induced to resign'. The report was found to be true and Gollan indeed prevailed on Sánchez y Adán to resign but not before he wrote that he had no control whatsoever over his son's political activities.[59]

There was no call for alarm, however. As far as we know the Spanish senior officials who looked at and approved the request were not concerned about the Churchill visit; rather they welcomed it. The Duke of Tetuán was a seasoned politician and a nobleman. As Foreign Minister he was close to the Queen Regent and responsible for the conduct of all relations with other powers and for keeping an especially close eye on Great Britain. He was well aware of the potential propaganda value of such a visit if it could in any way be made to look like some degree of British official support for Spain over Cuba. But, in addition to this, he wished to please Drummond Wolff whom he had known for several years and who was influential in so many circles in Madrid and elsewhere. He also wished to be cooperative with a country which, as we have seen, had much opportunity to cause mischief in Cuba but was so far holding a very fair and impartial view of things there, at least at the formal governmental level.

Finally, and perhaps of some importance, the duke was an O'Donnell. His ancestors had settled in Spain by the late seventeenth century as loyalists to the Catholic and Stuart cause who wished to serve a Catholic prince and not one of the new solidly Protestant line reigning in Great Britain. These 'Wild Geese' were recruited in significant numbers by the Habsburgs in both their Spanish and Austrian branches and gave a number of generals and even one field marshal (Count Maurice O'Donnell of Austria) as well as several senior statesmen to their adopted countries over successive generations.

The First Duke of Tetuán, the current duke's grandfather, was ennobled after winning the Battle of Tetuán (a small town in northern Morocco near the Spanish outpost of Ceuta) against the Moroccans in the war of 1859–60. He himself had been the son of an infantry officer and it seems almost all male members of the family had some military connection. He was in and out of government until he died and the next duke, Drummond Wolff's contemporary, was Foreign Minister from March 1895 to January 1896 but served in several governments over these years in the usual nineteenth-century Spanish *danse des ministères* as well. Drummond Wolff had first met him when he arrived in Madrid as the new British ambassador while O'Donnell was Foreign Minister from June 1890 to December 1892.[60] The duke had ties to the O'Donnell clan in Ireland that persist to this day.

The Duke of Tetuán clearly wrote immediately upon receipt of Sir Henry's request to the Spanish War Minister, asking that favourable attention be given to the request. The duke had also known Marcelo Azcárraga, the War Minister, for years. They had been contemporaries in the army before the duke had gone into politics. Azcárraga was an unusual minister of the Spanish government as well as an unlikely officer of the Spanish Army. He was the son of a Spanish general and a Philippine *mestiza*, although the latter came from a very good family in Manila.

Azcárraga had studied Law at the University of San Tomás in Manila but his father sent him to Madrid to become an army officer. It is said that he was the only Spanish general or minister to have ever been born and raised in the Spanish colony of the Philippines. He knew Cuba well having served there after the Mexican intervention of 1861 and the Santo Domingo war in 1866, and knew very well the prestige Britain enjoyed on the island especially among native-born Cubans who often saw that country as the fount of democracy, with a free press, good government and modernity. His first military unit had in fact been a Havana militia regiment which he joined at 18. His wife was a wealthy Cuban whose connections with the island's aristocracy were firm and helpful to the general in his rise to prominence. She had come from a slave-owning family as well, which would not have helped with creating an affection for Britain since London had been so active in curbing the slave trade on which the island and its sugar aristocracy were so dependent.[61] But Azcárraga was a shrewd politician as well as a soldier, something very common in the Spanish Army of the late nineteenth century. He knew well the value of a Britain, or at least a Churchill, well disposed towards Spain and its armed forces. He was later to become Provisional President of Spain following the assassination of President Cánovas in 1897.

Azcárraga had been War Minister this time since March 1895, knew Drummond Wolff and clearly agreed with the Foreign Minister's assessment of the potential gains to Spain of such a visit. He advised the colonial authorities in Havana of the planned visit and that it had official backing from the Spanish government. Thus the permissions were all obtained with great speed and almost without effort, with Sir Henry able to write to Churchill as early as 8 October from San Sebastián that both ministers would be writing introductions for him.[62] To put icing on the cake Drummond Wolff also asked the prime minister himself, Lord Salisbury, to

write a letter of introduction for Winston. This was sent to the young subaltern on 31 October by the prime minister of the greatest power of the
day and, though it proved unnecessary to elicit Spanish approval, it cannot
have done any harm for him to have had a letter from the highest political
authority in the British Empire in his pocket as he embarked on such an
adventure into the unknown.[63] It was a testimony to Churchill's determination that, though knowing that there were many obstacles to overcome, he
went about getting over them with speed and intelligence.

The Duke of Tetuán's rapid contact with his colleague at the war ministry ended with both quickly issuing the letters to the captain-general that
Drummond Wolff sought, advising headquarters in Havana of the visit of
the two officers and asking that they be afforded all possible assistance for
their trip. Aldershot, London, Madrid and Havana were all now properly
aligned to permit Churchill's first march into the limelight he so craved.

CHAPTER 3

THE MULTIFACETED ADVENTURER

Twenty to twenty-five! Those are the years!

Winston had been busy for the month of October getting all these permissions in place and in seeing how he could get the most out of the trip and the time spent on it. As we have seen, he wanted to have his first real adventure, his first proper military operational experience, his first test of his personal courage on a private rehearsal basis, and his first fling at becoming a better known public figure through exposure to danger and engaging in what all observers would agree was true adventure, even by the standards of what was an exceptional era of adventurers.

By the third week of the month, with 28 October as the preferred date of departure from England, he had so arranged things that he was going on the adventure with all his own personal objectives but also in a semi-official role as a military observer of a foreign army, a position that had become part of standard procedures by the end of the nineteenth century. He was authorised to wear his uniform, carry a regulation army pistol, although only for personal defence in case of danger, actually accompany a foreign army in the field, and be assured by his position and his letters of introduction of the very best attention by British and Spanish officials during the journey and campaign.

In the nineteenth and early twentieth centuries, British subjects were invariably felt to be the most protected nationals of any country when travelling abroad and especially when going to dubious locations in the world. The vast presence of British diplomats overseas, unmatched by any country then or at any time in history prior to then, ensured that Britons seldom felt entirely without support from the home country when they travelled. In Cuba, for example, there were no fewer than nine British diplomatic offices on the island, including the two consulates-general in the port cities of Havana and Santiago, and seven vice-consulates in the shipping centres of Baracoa, Cárdenas, Cienfuegos, Matanzas, Nuevitas, Sagua la Grande and Guantánamo. Thus few places in Cuba, other than the extreme west of Pinar del Rio province, were further than 100 miles from an agent of the British Crown. In addition, the extraordinary presence of the Royal Navy's vast fleet also meant that help was often close at hand for subjects of Queen Victoria who got into trouble. British retribution could be swift if those subjects were mistreated and the resulting pride of Britons in their status was understandable if often deeply offensive to governments and even individual citizens of other countries. The Spanish authorities on the island had learned in the previous war that treating British subjects as they did others was fraught with danger and more than once British warships had intervened to save these people, usually engaged in support of the rebel cause, merely by their presence in Cuban ports or by the threat, implicit or explicit, of bombardment if such Spanish mistreatment, as viewed from London, did not cease. Churchill of course knew this, as did his mother, adding to their relative lack of concern over what was still a highly risky venture.

In addition, the semi-official status of the young officer as a military observer for the War Office would have been assumed to be the case by the Spanish authorities and perhaps even welcomed by them. In any case it ensured that his activities, at least in so far as they were along the lines of normal military observer duties, were acceptable. Or were they?

Was Churchill a Spy?

It is perhaps worthwhile now dealing with the question as to whether Churchill at this time can be considered to have been something of a spy, as is often asserted even by very serious analysts.[1] In a way, of course, all officers posted abroad to observe and report on what other militaries are doing, could be considered spies. Indeed, diplomatic political analysts, usually first secretaries of embassies, can be thought of as spies as well. After all, they are there to find information of value to the home country, much of which is probably not that favourable to their countries of responsibility, and to do so with or without the consent of their hosts. The old saying that 'a diplomat is a man sent abroad to lie for his country' might also as credibly replace 'lie' with 'spy'. And, needless to say, military and naval attachés posted to embassies are there with the main purpose of finding out what is actually happening militarily and not what the armed forces of the host country say is happening. But this is to miss a very major point.

In the case of all three – military observers, diplomats and military attachés – they are there with the understanding of the host government, which accepts their arrival and their activities as a matter of course. The practice of exchange of such persons is almost as old as modern diplomacy itself. Indeed, they are often seen as what is, in modern defence and conflict-resolution parlance, 'confidence-building measures' and, the more they have freedom of access to the militaries and defence-related issues of their host countries, the more it is likely that their home government will come to trust the host nation.

Churchill was of course neither a diplomat nor a military attaché and was not posted to another army or country for a specific time when he would be responsible for observing and reporting on the military situation in which Britain, and the War Office in particular, were interested. He was, at most, a semi-official military observer under the situation and rules of such an office. Military observers had served with several armies in the series of wars for Italian unification in 1848–70, the wars of German unification in 1864–71, the Crimean War of 1854–56, the US Civil War of 1860–65 and by 1895 were entirely standard. And for some time prior to this period young officers who were members of European royal families could gain some experience of war by attaching themselves, or having their parents attach them, to the armies of allied or at least closely linked countries on campaign. And even for more modern military observers, the status of such officers would always be that of military men coming from friendly states. The nature of Pax Britannica, as a period of overall peace, meant that, with fewer wars occurring, military observers were the only available means to evaluate and keep abreast of changes in equipment, tactics and especially weaponry, and the need for them was greater than at any time for centuries.

In Churchill's case none of the above was true. He was certainly an aristocrat and from an influential family. But he was not from the nobility, much less a member of a royal family. And he was coming from a country where, as we have seen, while formally pro-Spanish in the sense of complying with Madrid's wishes where international law and custom obliged London to handle questions of foreign enlistment and the passage of rebel troops or weapons through British territory, British public opinion was anything but favourable to Spain. And Britain had not been an ally of Spain for some eighty years, when during the Napoleonic Wars Spain and Britain had been on the same side.

This situation was odd but hardly unheard of. What was unheard of was a military observer of Churchill's youth and inexperience in the army. The whole point of sending real military observers to foreign campaigns was to have them report on their conduct with a view to their own armies learning lessons from which they could draw conclusions useful for training, weapons acquisition, needed changes in tactical doctrine and the like. For this role they needed experienced officers of a generalist kind, such as that for general staff officers of the sort Germany had begun to produce as the nineteenth century wore on. Winston was a second-lieutenant almost straight out of military college with no military experience other than a very junior command in the cavalry and no exposure to artillery or even infantry practices.

Almost all military observers of the era were lieutenant-colonels or colonels, and, while a few were majors, a fair number were actually generals. Winston seems to have simply found himself in, or rather manoeuvred himself into, a position where all these rules were not to apply. It is difficult then to see him in the role of spy in any normal sense. He had certainly not received any training in such a role and the informal task set him by General Chapman seems far from the grand ideas of modern spy novels or even instructions given to their agents by intelligence agencies.

It is equally true that if he was thought by anyone to be anything like an agent or a spy, it was not by the British government beyond the War Office. There is virtually nothing in the Foreign Office archive on the visit of Winston Churchill to Cuba in 1895. But there is a highly interesting note to Sir Thomas Sanderson, Permanent Under-Secretary at the Foreign Office, of 9 November from a junior member of his staff, seemingly signing 'A. Laveron'. This was the day that Winston and Reggie docked in New York, a week after they had sailed from Liverpool. The note speaks of a visit that day by Major Wilson of the Directorate of Military Intelligence, who called to let the Foreign Office know 'unofficially' and 'on behalf of General

Chapman', that Churchill and Barnes had 'gone to Cuba' and 'on their own account'. The note adds, 'They have I understand been furnished with letters of recommendation to the Spanish authorities by Sir H. Wolff', ending with 'This information was merely given that we might know who they were in the event of any difficulties arising'.[2]

Thus it is clear that the Foreign Office must have known nothing officially of the trip before this date and that Drummond Wolff had been acting in a private and personal manner with the Spanish foreign and war ministries, not keeping London informed, much less asking its permission to act in the manner he did in the matter of arrangements for Winston's visit. It seems thus to have been a classic example of things done in the best tradition of 'old school tie' and family and personal connections little related to matters of state. It is nonetheless of interest to note that the War Office did not feel that there were sufficient reasons for concern as to inform the Foreign Office before the officers' departure, much less to consult with them about the wisdom of the visit or ask permission from the diplomatic authorities of the land. After all, Chapman knew and approved the venture in mid-October, three weeks before Major Wilson's call at the Foreign Office. It would have been a simple thing to have checked with the Foreign Office earlier. He may have simply not wished to put his colleague at the Foreign Office on the spot by telling him of an activity that both Brabazon and Wolseley saw as potentially difficult.

In any case, intelligence in the Foreign Office of the day, run by Sir Thomas Sanderson, was in a special situation. Sanderson was an exceptional person on any number of scores.[3] Born in 1854, he had only been appointed Permanent Under-Secretary for Foreign Affairs the previous year. But he was hardly a new boy, as he had been assistant permanent secretary for the previous five years 1889–94 and had been working in the Foreign Office since 1869 when he joined as a junior clerk.

This veteran already had a tendency to be a one-man show, with his vast knowledge of foreign affairs, his deep intelligence and analytical capacity, and his dedication to his work. On the intelligence side, he did not have the then usual cypher-making experience of professional diplomats, especially junior ones. And, while he defended the key need for intelligence, and good intelligence, he did not believe it was there 'to dictate policy' but rather to be its 'handmaiden'. Neilson and Otte, in their valuable work, suggest he was 'curiously aloof' from intelligence work and did not interest himself overly in it. Sanderson, who would go on to be the longest serving permanent under-secretary of foreign affairs in history, would perhaps not have been deeply concerned over the War Office's slowness in informing his ministry of the Churchill and Barnes visit. In any case, he like others did not know that Churchill's articles would soon be appearing in the national press.

There seems to be only one possible conclusion: this was no official spy mission or anything of the kind. And Churchill can in no serious way be considered to have been a spy. However, he may be considered deeply in what David Stafford calls the British tradition of the 'amateur spy sent overseas with instructions to keep his eyes and ears open'.[4] While this is almost certainly much of the truth in this case, it is still worth remembering that the word only applies so far because Churchill was in no real way 'sent overseas'. He had decided to go on his own account and dealing with the War Office was a necessary step in getting away, not the principal reason for going.

And a War Correspondent too?

What Brabazon, Wolseley, Chapman, Drummond Wolff and thus the Spanish authorities did not know, and perhaps even Lady Churchill as well, was that Winston, having obtained their approval, had also entered into contact with friends and acquaintances in the press to sound them out as to the possibilities of acting as a war correspondent while on the island.[5] Winston was well aware of the power of the popular press, that exceptional product of the mass urban societies of the late nineteenth century. And perhaps the very best way to gain public notice was not just to be at historic events but also to report on them.

There were other reasons as well. While mamma had said she would pay for the trip as a birthday present, Winston would still hardly be wallowing in money while abroad and was already, as he was to be for almost all his life, in debt and facing significant financial challenges. Writing for the press was something which could help here as well and not just assist in bringing his name to the notice of the public with likely political gain accruing at least in the long run.

Be that as it may, Churchill's connections with the press were brought into service and, through the good offices of a number of people in that profession or connected to influential men who were, he was commissioned to write a series of 'letters' from Cuba analysing the war while he was present with the Spanish Army. He was to write five of these and be paid 5 guineas each with a total of 25 guineas for the series.[6] These were to be for *The Daily Graphic*, Britain's only daily illustrated newspaper at the time and a paper for which his father had written when he dabbled in journalism in 1891 following his fall from grace politically.

The *Daily Graphic* had been founded in 1889 by William Luson Thomas of H.R. Baines and Company, founder of the Thomas newspaper chain. Thomas was born in 1830 and was an engraver and artist who had formerly worked for the prestigious *Illustrated London News*, but personal and professional reasons had driven him to wish to compete with what he himself called the 'most successful and firmly established paper in the world'.[7] He had therefore founded a weekly newspaper in 1869, *The Graphic*, which with great daring he sold for 6*d* a copy at a time when *The Illustrated London News* sold for 5*d*.

Thomas was keen on social reform and scandalised some people by placing images of London's poor and scandals in the empire in his paper. Churchill's father himself had played a part in this by denouncing ill doing in South Africa during his three months there reporting for the paper.[8] Thomas was, however, a much appreciated gentleman whose high artistic and professional standards led to much praise from artists not only in Britain but from abroad, including Van Gogh. The two papers attracted much attention among their rivals too and even *The Times* admitted that Thomas had, with these initiatives, done 'more than improve illustrated journalism, he influenced English art, and that in a wholesome way'.

Under Thomas at the time of Churchill's Cuba trip was Thomas Heath Joyce, a man thirty years younger than Thomas who had taken over the editorship in 1890, in cooperation with Thomas, and was to hold that position until 1906. Neither man apparently knew Churchill well at this time although both were to get to know him well later in life. It is not clear who acted as intermediary between the future war correspondent and these newspapermen. Because of his father's connections, Winston himself may have been able to open discussions with them. Be that as it may, the young officer was now a commissioned war correspondent with a major newspaper as well.

Peter Clarke may perhaps be somewhat unfair when he suggests that Winston subsequently sought other newspapers for which to write because

the *Daily Graphic* was not as good a paper as he would have liked to write
for. Clarke called the paper 'undistinguished'. This seems unlikely given its
status at the time and the reason for his later preference is more likely to
be the simple fact that illustrated journals did not have the same space for
written work as others of a more traditional kind, and of course he wanted
to try his hand at many more papers and be paid much more in the future
as Clarke rightly suggests. In the paper's defence, the comments of Peter
Harrington may be of use:

> nothing could compare with the *Daily Graphic*, the sister publication of
> the *Graphic* ... 'the only illustrated morning newspaper in the world'.
> With 16 pages and occasional supplements, and with the full resources
> of the *Graphic* behind it, the paper brought the news of the day, 'illus-
> trated by rapid sketches from the pencils of the cleverest artists ... [with
> editors] paying artists astounding fees for their services ... sketches were
> mailed back to London where teams of staff artists set to work redrawing
> the rough pictures using black and white ink and wash on white board
> [grisaille] ... Several weeks might elapse between the actual event and the
> publication of the image but this was the accepted practice.'[9]

Striking in all this is that there does not seem to have been any attempt by
Winston to advise those who might be affected by his war correspondent's
status of this state of affairs. While, as other authors have pointed out, it
was not forbidden for serving officers to write for newspapers in the way
Churchill was to do, it was still far from a usual practice, especially for a very
junior officer. Nonetheless, there is no evidence to suggest that, before the
first article came out, Churchill told his colonel, his army commander, his
friend the ambassador in Madrid or anyone in the Foreign Office, or indeed
the Spanish authorities most likely to be concerned, of his new status or
even of the fact that he was seeking such status for his trip. But no less a
person than Mackenzie Wallace backed him in his effort by writing to *The
Times* correspondent in Havana, a Mr Akers, and asking him to support
Winston in any way he could.[10]

The Preparations Go Forward and the Trip Begins

Now, armed with money, the approval and support of a more senior companion, permissions from his commanding officer, his army commander, his mother, more or less the Foreign Office or at least a very senior official who worked for it abroad and the appropriate Spanish military and diplomatic authorities, and with the status of a military observer, a legitimate traveller and a war correspondent to boot, Churchill could move forward with the plan. The date of 28 October had slipped slightly by the time Winston had everything of this complex jigsaw puzzle in place and the idea of taking a steamer from New York to the West Indies had given way to taking the train to a port in Florida from which the two officers could easily sail the last leg of the journey to Cuba. So the plan slowly settled and they were to sail from Liverpool on the posh Cunard steamship *Etruria* on 2 November for New York, arriving on 9 November, spend a very few days there, and travel on to Havana by train to Tampa, Florida, and sail from there to Cuba.[11]

It is not known how Barnes paid for tickets. His salary as a full lieutenant would not have been that much more than Winston's and, as we have seen, he was the son of a clergyman. But he never seems to have had any problems paying the bills associated with being an officer in as chic a cavalry regiment as the 4th Hussars, in keeping horses or in taking a full part in the 'sport of kings', as polo is often called. Jennie meanwhile had got in touch with Lord and Lady Tweedsmouth, family friends who, thinking that the journey might still include Jamaica, were preparing letters of introduction to the Governor of Jamaica for Winston and his companion.[12] All of the papers and most importantly, letters of introduction, were in Churchill's hands and it was now a question of merely travelling.

The First Leg: The United States

Churchill and Barnes spent their first few days in the United States in New York as guests of William Bourke Cockran, a recent former lover of Winston's mother.[13]

Cockran was born in 1854, and was therefore the same age as Jennie. He was born in Sligo in Ireland and went to the United States with his family at the age of 17. He was educated in the US and in France and was admitted to the Bar in 1876. He joined the Democratic Party and ran for Congressional office for New York, winning several times. But in 1896 he broke with the party and concentrated on his highly successful legal practice in New York. He was a noted political orator and repeatedly interested himself in the cause of Cuban independence, although mostly after Churchill's visit.

There is virtually nothing to add about the Cuban side of the adventure in this first week. This could be considered odd because New York was the principal location for rebel activities in the world outside the island itself. The insurgent leader José Martí had lived and worked there as a journalist for much of his life, had conspired there, and there was a large group of Cuban insurgent political figures there at the time of the rebellion of 1895. The propaganda centre for the movement was also in New York, having as its main goal, as in the earlier struggle of 1868–78, the recognition of the Cuban insurgency by the United States or European powers and thus easier access to weapons and other supplies for the insurrection and wider legitimacy for its actions. In fact, New York had been the actual site of a quasi-government in exile during the Ten Years War, and more than one independence movement newspaper had seen the light of day there.

It would seem logical that, at least as a journalist, Winston would have wished to discuss the situation in Cuba with some of these leaders. Almost entirely ignorant of the realities of the Cuban political context as Churchill was, however, this seeming lapse should not really surprise us. It would also have seemed logical for Cockran, who knew who the Cubans were in New York and what they were doing, to have suggested seeing some of them. The truth is probably that he and Churchill discussed the idea but felt that, since Winston was to be a guest of the Spanish Army in Cuba, and that the Spanish spy ring in the United States was so effective, involving even agencies of the famous Pinkerton company, it would be best not to risk disaster by seeing any dissident Cubans. And, although it is unlikely that he already knew of the impact of just such meetings on Viscount Morpeth's attempts to get to the front two weeks earlier, these considerations probably weighed on the two men's thinking.

In any case, Winston and Reggie were far too busy to see themselves as idle on this front. Cockran was extremely influential and in no time had the two young men visiting places of interest in and around the city, lunching and dining with the famous and the powerful, and generally having a good time. The two men were received by Cornelius Vanderbilt, the tycoon whose niece would be the next Duchess of Marlborough, among many other major figures of the time. Even more important for Winston than these more public activities were the private chats with Cockran, running late into the night, when Barnes was apparently already asleep. Cockran's speaking abilities struck Churchill as extraordinary, his political views impressed the young man, and his ability to express ideas became a model for Winston. A firm friendship was struck up between them.

Among many other places and things, Churchill and Barnes visited installations of the US military, including a warship in the Hudson River, and most interestingly the US Military Academy at West Point, north of the city. There Churchill, like many other visitors accustomed to a more relaxed British military tradition shared by most Commonwealth armies, was shocked by what he thought silly and excessive discipline unconducive to producing officers for a modern army. The US Navy impressed him more and he wrote to his brother of his conviction that, while soldiers could be made out of many peoples, sailors of quality seemed to be the 'monopoly of the Anglo-Saxon race'.[14]

The junior officers extended their time in New York for a further three days as a result of the good time they were having and thus were using up more of their ten-week leave than planned. But doubtless it seemed to Winston time well spent. Certainly the friendship paid off quickly in ways the luxury-loving Winston appreciated. The Atlantic crossing in the luxurious *Etruria*, while rough at times and about which Churchill, who hated sea travel, complained to his mother, was now to be followed by the two men travelling in nothing less than a stateroom on the train. They set off southward on the morning of 17 November and they must have made quite a picture as the norm for such luxury would have been elderly people of means or successful middle-aged businessmen. The thirty-six-hour journey passed in style therefore but Winston makes no mention of his impressions of the countryside or anything else in letters home. The trip took them close to the eastern seaboard through Washington and Savannah, arriving in Tampa, the last town on the railway route, on the evening of 18 November.

The next day they took ship. This was no *Etruria* but it was a perfectly acceptable smaller steamship, the *Olivette*, which did two return trips to Havana from Tampa each month for part of the year, increasing that frequency to three return voyages a week in months when the demand was greater. The *Olivette* had been built in 1887 and was usually found, until the summer of 1895, working on the Charlottetown (Prince Edward Island) to Boston service. It was small at 1,678 gross tons but comfortable and reliable in the service provided. Churchill referred to it as a 'little steamer' but 'very clean', and the 'captain and all the officers made everything as pleasant and convenient as possible'.[15] It was already well-known in Cuban separatist circles as the ship that had brought José Martí, the national hero, from Havana to Key West in his 1891 speaking tour of Florida, when it was doing similar duties. After the 1878 peace Spain had allowed a great many former rebels to return and to travel back and forth to Cuba, and Martí had taken advantage of the offer.

It is typical of the way Churchill's life seemed to be linked to wider events that later the ship was to be used to carry injured from Havana home to the United States after the explosion of the USS *Maine* in Havana harbour in early 1898. Later that year, in the Spanish–American War, the vessel was used as a hospital ship by the American Red Cross, and Clara Barton, the famous nurse, spoke of it in her book about that organisation.[16] It is interesting to think that the same officers of the merchant vessel that were so pleasant to Churchill were probably still serving on her two and a half years later when they were in on another story linked to espionage. Captain Sigsbee of the *Maine*, after the disaster, was sent to Key West by the US Navy in order to keep a close eye on events in Cuba. He and the US consul-general in Havana kept in touch by secret messages carried by the *Olivette* between Havana and Key West over those months.[17]

The *Olivette* continued to be involved in notable events. On 3 July 1898, she acted as a hospital ship, picking up survivors from the Spanish fleet after the Battle of Santiago, where that force, hopelessly outgunned, was destroyed by the US fleet. The survivors included those of the Spanish flagship, the battleship *María Teresa*, with Admiral Pascual Cervera, the unfortunate but courageous commander of the ill-starred fleet.

CHAPTER 4

CUBA: ARRIVAL AND DEPLOYMENT

The earth is yours and the fullness thereof.

The *Olivette* had a peaceful passage to Havana, described by Churchill as 'comfortable', stopping briefly at Key West to pick up further passengers and mail, although, just before dawn on 20 November, what Churchill called a 'violent storm' broke on the vessel waking the young officer up but allowing him to be on deck when the ship approached Cuba and the glorious harbour entrance to Havana. The scene then and now is dominated by the brooding height of Morro Castle, standing to the port side at the entrance to the narrow slip of nearly 2km of water that constitutes the only means of reaching the huge inner harbour from the sea. Built in 1589–1609, the giant defence work, sometimes called Drake's Castle because it was reputedly built as a defence against Francis Drake's continuing threats to Havana, is the largest fortification in the insular Caribbean. Across from it to starboard lies Punta Castle, low-lying and menacing for any enemy daring to approach the city.

Churchill was suitably impressed. Although he termed Morro Castle only of 'formerly great strength', since modern technology had already put most of its advantages out of play, he still said that it 'commands the channel to the port', and later waxed romantic about how he felt as they reached their destination:

When first in the dim light of early morning I saw the shores of Cuba rise and define themselves from dark-blue horizons, I felt as if I sailed

with Long John Silver and first gazed on Treasure Island. Here was a scene
of vital action. Here was a place where anything might happen. Here
I might leave my bones … Cuba is a lovely island. Well have the Spanish
named it 'The Pearl of the Antilles'. The temperate yet ardent climate, the
abundant rainfall, the luxuriant vegetation, the unrivalled fertility of the
soil, the beautiful scenery – all combined to make me accuse that absent-
minded morning when our ancestors let so delectable a possession slip
through our fingers … The city and harbour of Havana … presented a
spectacle … in every respect magnificent.[1]

He refers in his lamentation here to the situation at the end of the Seven
Years War in 1763 when Cuba was returned to Spain partly in exchange
for Florida under the terms of the Treaty of Paris. In fact, only Havana and
the west of the island had been effectively taken by the British in the 1762
campaign, and the rest of the colony was still resisting British occupation.[2]
Be that as it may, Winston was immediately taken by Cuba, a country for
which he had a special regard for the rest of his life.

On arrival, his letters of introduction immediately proved their worth.
Both officers were carrying their pistols in their luggage, and such weapons
were subject to the strictest of controls, as can be imagined on an island
with a serious insurgency. Customs officials would normally have taken a
dim view of these weapons, but Churchill recounted to his mother how,
once the proffered letters from high Spanish authorities were read by the
local officials, they were let through at once with their weapons. They hired
a carriage and were driven through the peaceful streets to their hotel, the
Gran Hotel Inglaterra, a mile or so away. Though Churchill describes the
hotel as only 'fairly good', it was one of the very best in the city, if not the
best, and its location was *sans pareil*. On the main square of what was then
the 'new' city, just across the park from what is now called Old Havana (*La
Habana Vieja*), the Hotel Inglaterra played host to virtually all the main visitors to the capital.

In addition, the hotel was the prime place to stay for journalists covering
the island and most of those covering the war were lodged there or close by.
Even more importantly, the Louvre Café, on the principle street terrace of
the hotel, was the main café and meeting place of the most important government and business people in the city. Even today it is central to the city's
life but in the mid-1890s one could frequently see the Captain-General or

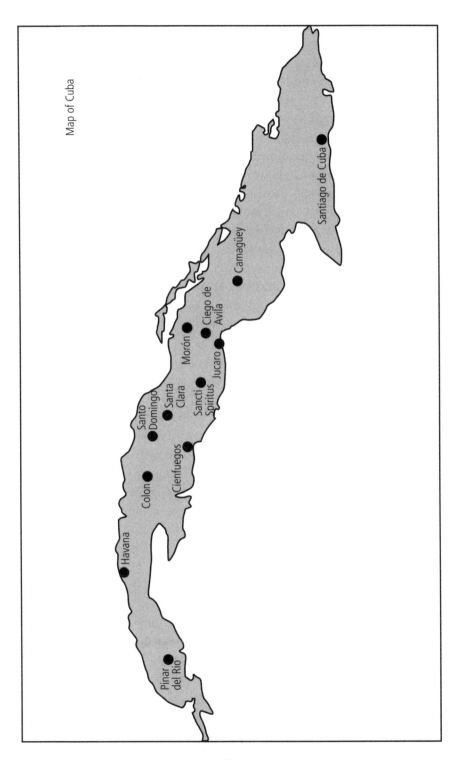

Map of Cuba

Santiago de Cuba

Camagüey

Ciego de Ávila

Morón

Jucaro

Santo Domingo

Santa Clara

Sancti Spiritus

Cienfuegos

Colon

Havana

Pinar del Río

his senior officers there, mixing with the other powerful people of Havana's vibrant life. It was close to both the main opera houses and the Prado which, like Barcelona's, was and is a main artery leading from the higher centre of the city down to the sea. Churchill was where he should be, and was expected to be, as both a journalist and a scion of a significant British aristocratic family. After the voyage and before any official duties, Barnes and Churchill sat down to eat some fresh oranges and to have a very first Havana cigar in that most valued of future Churchilliana's home town.

Alexander Gollan, the British consul-general, had been at the pier to meet them. Gollan was the classic 'old Latin America hand' in the British Foreign Service. Born in Inverness in Scotland in 1840, he was first posted as a young lad to the British vice-consulate in Pernambuco, Brazil, in 1856. By the time of his next move, in 1867, he was vice-consul in that city, and he had married a Brazilian. Posted then to Coquimbo in Chile, he subsequently moved on to Greytown in Nicaragua. Speaking by now both fluent Spanish and Portuguese, he was next sent to the important post of vice-consul for Rio Grande do Sul in southern Brazil, a place of considerable British trade and investment. In 1885, he left Latin America, but not the Spanish-speaking world, when he became consul in Manila, where he was to stay for seven years. From there he went in 1892 to Cuba as consul-general. By 1895 he was well known and well connected in Havana and, as opposed to his predecessors in the days of slavery, he had no duties as consul-general that the locals resented. British consuls before 1889 had a major responsibility for keeping an eye on the slave trade which Britain and the Royal Navy were sworn to stamp out, and Spanish and Cuban officials, as well as much of the aristocracy of the colony, did everything they could to avoid British attempts to end the trade and, in the bargain, to make the job of the British consul-general as close to impossible as it could be made. This was by now a thing of the past for most Cubans and Gollan was influential in helping many British subjects, and perhaps especially journalists, pass their time in Cuba profitably. Gollan was to be rescued by HMS *Talbot* in July 1898 when he and a number of other starving war refugees were evacuated by the Royal Navy from a Havana then under siege by the US Navy.

He had clearly heard from Drummond Wolff in Madrid of the officers' arrival, although he would in any case have had the information from the major Havana papers, which had covered Churchill and Barnes' journey from their departure from Liverpool, such was the perceived importance of this visit to the island.[3] A short note in the *Diario de la Marina*, the official government paper but also the most widely read, was followed by articles on Churchill's arrival in New York (Barnes was not in this one) and their arrival in Havana. The phrasing of the articles could easily give the impression of British, or at least Churchill and Barnes', desire to serve alongside the Spanish Army in the suppression of the revolt. On departure from Liverpool, under the title 'British Officers', appeared the following short bit of news:

> Mr Winston Churchill, officer of the British Army and son of the late Lord Randolph Churchill, embarked today in Liverpool, via New York, for the island of Cuba with another officer with the idea of adding themselves [*agregarse*] to the Spanish Army on the island.

And on arrival in New York, in an announcement dated 12 November under the title 'Mr Churchill', appeared the following: 'Mr Winston Churchill, a British Army officer, is heading to Cuba with the object of joining [*agregarse*] up with the Spanish Army.' The news of Churchill's arrival was available for anyone interested in Cuba and the way it was phrased gave a clear impression that he, both officers or even the British government were in favour of the Spanish cause and against the insurgency.

In 1895, a situation such as the one from which Gollan was later rescued seemed impossibly remote. The city was calm and there was no sign of war to be seen, although the state of war prevailing meant, as he complained to the Foreign Office in London, that Gollan had had no leave in that year.[4] The diplomat greeted the two officers warmly and told them that he had already arranged for them to see the second-in-command of the colony, the Segundo Cabo, that very afternoon. Major-General José Arderíus y García was an interesting officer. Like several others serving in Cuba, he had actually been born on the island.[5] He had likewise fought there in the Ten Years War of 1868–78 and knew the island very well. He was, in a way common in the Spanish Army of the late nineteenth century, the brother-in-law of the captain-general, Arsenio Martínez Campos, who was then in Santa Clara, some 270km from Havana, where he had moved his field headquarters on 4 November in an attempt to bar the route to the advance of rebel forces from the east towards the richer lands of western Cuba.

Arderíus is a little-known figure who deserves to be better studied. When he had had the opportunity to be acting captain-general from July to September 1893, he had used the occasion, with peace still prevailing, to bring together ex-rebels from the previous conflict and senior Spanish military officers and other officials, to talk about the future of the colony. The former rebels stated at the meeting that the situation was in fact quite clear: if there were meaningful reforms, Cuba would remain loyal; with no such reforms, renewed revolution was inevitable. Arderíus probably agreed with this view but too few in Madrid or even in Havana listened. The initiative itself, however, was both an interesting and a courageous one for an acting Captain-General in office for such a brief time.[6]

The general received the two young officers and their accompanying diplomat at his headquarters a few hundred metres from the hotel at the Plaza de Armas, the central square of the old city. The trip to his HQ would have been an eye-opener for the two newcomers as it would have reinforced their view of the city as one at peace. They did see many soldiers, although many of them would have been the *voluntarios* (volunteers) to whom Churchill makes reference in his first 'letter from the front' written for the *Daily Graphic* in Cienfuegos a couple of days later. But they were about the only sign of an on-going war they were to see in the capital. Arderíus had received some time earlier news of the arrival of the two British officers and may even have been behind the extra coverage given by the press, itself controlled to a high degree, to their coming. As Churchill himself suggested in his first dispatch, the control of the press was almost total:

> The town shows no sign of the insurrection, and business proceeds everywhere as usual ... What struck me most was the absence of any news ... London may know much of what is happening in the island – New York is certain to know more – but Havana hears nothing. All the papers are strictly edited by the Government and are filled with foreign and altogether irrelevant topics.[7]

More proof of governmental control of the press, and of Spanish interest in turning the visit to their account, were two full articles in papers with an even more pro-government line than the rest. In an article published the day after their arrival, in the section of the newspaper called 'News of the War', thus linking in the reader's mind the relationship between Churchill's arrival and the conduct of the war, and under the title 'Mr W.S. Churchill', the *Diario del Ejército* (the army newspaper) positively gushed:

> The Army Newspaper is pleased to greet and give a welcome to the young British officer who has come to share with our comrades in arms the pains of the campaign with the object of studying this, from so many angles, so special war. Our military colleague tells us that British officers are accustomed to operate in the most diverse climates, and to make war in all the countries of the world where man is found, and we do not doubt that Mr W.S. Churchill will obtain in Cuba great lessons, and will see the difficulties that are presented to a regular army when the enemy he confronts employs the tactic of fleeing a fight at the first sign of the lightest resistance, and he will observe on more than one occasion one of the virtues of the Spanish soldier: sobriety and endurance to suffering ...
>
> We wish this illustrious officer that he may be pleased living among us and that he makes for himself the same brilliant career in arms as his father did in the politics of his country.[8]

This article spent half of its space describing Churchill's father, Lord Randolph, making certain that the importance of the visit was not so much in that of an unknown second-lieutenant but in the quality of the person that second-lieutenant represented and his background. It is not known if Churchill and Barnes saw this article at this time but Winston must have been perplexed to be described as an 'illustrious officer' if he could hardly be displeased to see his father so praised.

General Arderíus welcomed the two officers, gave them advice on the trip to Santa Clara, and assured them that he would advise General Martínez Campos immediately of their coming. He treated them, Churchill wrote later, as 'an unofficial, but nonetheless important, mission sent at a time of stress by a mighty Power and old ally'. The two officers tried hard to dispel any such notion but their protestations had the opposite effect. The Spanish would not, if they could help it, take this visit as anything but a chance to suggest that Britain was, or at least these two British officers were, very sympathetic to Spain's plight.[9] They were then dismissed back to their hotel, from whence they saw a little of Havana and Churchill wrote his first letter home to his mother as well as another to Bourke Cockran.

The First of Many Armoured Trains

During the Boer War, half a decade after the Cuba visit, Winston Churchill, the still-young war correspondent, reached pan-imperial hero status with his well-known adventure with a British Army armoured train, his capture by the Boers, and his spectacular escape from their prisoner-of-war camp and return to British territory through neighbouring Portuguese East Africa. His own account of those events still makes stimulating reading: *London to Ladysmith: Via Pretoria* was published immediately after his return to London in 1900. What is much less known is that his first contact with the phenomenon was not in South Africa but in Cuba five years earlier. The Spanish Army was in general quite capable of holding onto the main and even the secondary towns of Cuba but, as so often in counter-insurgency campaigns, it had no such control over large parts of the countryside. The level of support of the Cuban people for the idea of independence, as Winston himself quickly noted and wrote about in his letters, had grown to a level nearly universal. Continued misgovernment and the failure to honour the promises of reform made to islanders in the government's bid to win the first war for independence meant that the continuation of rule by Madrid had received near general rejection by Cuban-born people. And, whereas in the first war most Cubans, especially in the west, not only remained loyal but frequently fought for Spain against the rebels, this was not the case in the final struggle.[10]

This meant that the Spanish Army had to provide logistical support for its far-flung army garrisons with a system of trains and mule- or oxen-based convoys that brought them all the needs that were difficult for them to obtain in a hostile and often barren countryside. The extensive rail system that western Cuba enjoyed helped with this and, because of the great wealth engendered by the sugar industry, and the need for that product to be transported by rail, Cuba could boast one of the best in Latin America by 1895. Cuba in fact had its first railway as early as 1837, when a line was opened between the capital and the rich sugar town of Güines, years before metropolitan Spain had one. The *mambises* were not stupid, however, and realised that not only were the Spanish dependent on the railway but that trains were vulnerable to insurgent attack at many points and were often the source of the rich booty that the rebels needed to survive and continue the war.

Churchill and Barnes were to see right away the advantages and disadvantages of railway dependence for an army when they headed off to Santa Clara the day after their arrival on the island. The first point to remember here is that Spanish strategy was stymied by a perceived need to not only field an army to engage the main rebel forces but also to garrison the many towns and villages of Cuba while also putting very small garrisons of regular troops and/or *voluntarios* onto the rich but vulnerable sugar plantations of the island. This sapping of the regular army, and the reduction in its capacity to field sufficiently significant forces for operations other than static ones of local defence, was a highly detrimental effect of the policy of showing local landlords that they would be defended in case of rebel raids. Since, for reasons we will later discuss at length, the *mambí* army was mobile and rapidly moving, neither objective was truly achieved. The army's small detachments often proved entirely unable to deter or defeat enemy raids because the rebels did not attack unless they enjoyed the element of surprise added to superior numbers. But, despite the huge army Madrid deployed, the deployment of such small garrisons meant that there were never enough soldiers to field an army of operations that could best the rebels in sustained combat.

On the morning of 21 November the two British officers boarded a largely unarmoured civilian train in Havana bound for Santa Clara, normally a twelve-hour trip. As Churchill remarked in his first 'letter' for publication in *The Daily Graphic*, at first the train moved along normally as there was little fear of rebel attack for some time after leaving Havana. But after Colón, a big farming town in the province of Matanzas, little more than 100km from the destination, the danger of attacks on the train increased. The rebels would attack with rifle fire or dynamite or just prepare a trap of some kind causing the train to derail. Thus a pilot engine and armoured car were added to trains as they went through Santo Domingo, still over 70km from Santa Clara, and an escort of soldiers now travelled in the last carriage. At this stage of his career Winston appears to have been quite pleased with the idea of an armoured train. In the South African War, five years later, he criticised them heavily:

Nothing looks more formidable than an armoured train; but nothing is in fact more vulnerable and helpless. It was only necessary to blow up a bridge or culvert to leave the monster stranded, far from home and help, at the mercy of the enemy.[11]

This assessment applied in Cuba as well, although the rebel enemy had no artillery or machine guns, as did the Boers, to take advantage of the train's vulnerability to the maximum. By the end of his time in Cuba Winston was already having doubts.

The trip eventually took more than nine hours because, shortly after passing through Santo Domingo, the young officers learned that the line had been cut. They were therefore obliged to take a more roundabout route via the village of Cruces, some 30km to the south, causing greater delay. But worse news was to come. The train in front of theirs, carrying the very officer with whom they were to spend time in a couple of days, Major-General Álvaro Suárez Valdés, had been derailed by enemy action in what the Spanish newspapers immediately began to call a rebel attempt to assassinate the general. A number of Spanish soldiers had been wounded. This was getting close to the real thing. Danger lurked around every corner and Winston was clearly loving the experience.

With the train creaking into Santa Clara well behind schedule, though not all that late in the day, Churchill and Barnes were met by a staff officer who took them across the square to a large and handsome military building housing the field headquarters of the captain-general. General Arsenio Martínez Campos y Antón was in fact a field marshal and a very senior officer indeed. His background was legendary in both Cuba and Spain.

Born in Segovia in 1831, he had joined the army as soon as he could. He served in the African War with Morocco in 1859–60 and in Mexico in the intervention of 1861–62, where he distinguished himself on the staff of the expedition commander, Lieutenant-General Conde de Reus. He was made brigadier in 1869 at only 38 years of age in the peculiar conditions of that year when the Bourbon monarchy fell and a short-lived republic was ushered in. He was involved in suppressing a rebellion at home in 1873, and gave his own decisive push conducting a *pronunciamiento*, known as the Conspiracy of Sagunto, which brought the Bourbon dynasty back to the throne.[12]

In 1876, he was named Captain-General of Cuba at a decisive moment in the Ten Years War, and conducted an exceptionally humane 'carrot and stick' campaign which ended in less than two years in the total defeat of the rebels under the same Máximo Gómez and Antonio Maceo he was trying to tackle when Churchill and Barnes arrived at his HQ in Santa Clara. In the famous Pact of Zanjón in 1878 the key remaining rebel leaders surrendered in return for promises of reform in the colony and a degree of democratisation as well as autonomy for Cuba. Though desultory fighting still persisted for some months under recalcitrant leader Maceo, that 'war', termed the *Guerra Chiquita* in Cuban history ('small war', to distinguish it from the *grande* or Ten Years War), ended in a fizzle. Martínez Campos became a hero to Spaniards and Cubans alike as peace was restored, prosperity slowly returned and reforms were begun. Soon, however, as we have seen, Madrid backed down on the reforms and no real progress was made, despite Martínez Campos' attempts to use his influence to ensure his promises to the Cuban rebels were honoured; even his time as a minister in a short-lived government in 1879 could do nothing to make progress with colonial reform. Only his commitment to the abolition of slavery was to eventually prosper.

In 1893 Martínez Campos was given command of Spanish forces in North Africa, where Spain had few possessions but ambitions to increase their number. Here too he did a good job and his reputation grew. He was therefore first given the captaincy-generalship of Castilla la Nueva, a quiet post, and then the captaincy-generalship of Cataluña, the troubled province of great industrial wealth on the north-west border with France and a hotbed of separatism, republicanism, trade unionism and anarchist terrorism. While there, a short sharp war broke out with the Carlists, a right-wing monarchist grouping backing another pretender to the Spanish throne, and once again his humanitarian handling of the conflict increased his prestige. The same heightened reputation continued when he was then sent to command the Spanish troops in the Melilla War of 1895, another short conflict concerning a Spanish outpost on the northern coast of Morocco.

His return to Cuba after the outbreak of the new revolution reassured those who wished for a quick suppression of the rebellion and a rapid return to a state of peace. Here was the victor of 1878 and the humanitarian reformer all could trust. It was this man, now a 64-year-old marshal, both fatter and older than in his heyday seventeen years earlier, who received the two subalterns in his office, in the middle of a war that was not going at all well despite his taking charge, that late November day in 1895.[13] If he was troubled by the way things were going, he did not show it to his visitors. His arrival, which had done so much to raise both civilian and military morale among royalists, did little to change the situation on the ground. The marshal was first bested in the eastern province of Oriente, moving his headquarters to central Camagüey province. After further reverses he moved it further west, to Santa Clara, where Winston and Reggie caught up with him. Worse, Máximo Gómez had crossed the great Trocha with ease at the beginning of October with a fairly large force and was now in Las Villas province marauding and tying down large numbers of Spanish troops who could not pin him down to open battle.[14] The insurgent strategy was to use this force to keep the Spanish busy while Antonio Maceo was preparing an even larger expedition whose crossing of the Trocha would be assisted by the fact that Gómez's troops were masking their movements and keeping royalist troops busy and unable to reinforce the trench line effectively. The idea was thus to effect a juncture of the two forces west of that line and proceed to the dream of all rebel leaders since the days of the Ten Years War, to take the war to the rich west and wrest the area from Spain, making it impossible for the mother country to continue to wage war.

It was the west that Churchill characterised as so wealthy in his description of why the stakes in the war were so high. Obviously impressed by what he saw in the western lands through which he had just travelled, not to mention in the prosperous capital of Havana, he wrote:

> Very few people in England realise the importance of the struggle out here, or the value of the prize for which it is being fought. It is only when one travels through the island that one understands its wealth, its size, or its beauty. Four crops a year can be raised from the Cuban soil; Cuban sugar enters the market at a price which defies competition; she practically monopolises the entire manufacture of cigars; ebony and mahogany are of no account in the land, and enormous wealth lies undeveloped in the hills. If one appreciates these facts, guided by the light of current events, one cannot fail to be struck by the irony of a fate which offers so bounteously with the one hand and prohibits so harshly with the other.[15]

In the previous war, this dream of an invasion of the west had always proven illusory. In 1874, forces under Gómez had indeed crossed the Trocha and made it into the territory of the west-central province of Las Villas. But in the first battle in which they engaged, the hard-fought action at Las Guásimas, despite a tactical victory when the insurgents were left holding the field at the end of the day, the result was actually a strategic defeat for the rebels. The exhaustion of their precious ammunition supplies meant that they could no longer carry on with the planned 'invasion' of the west and were obliged to turn back.[16]

In 1895, however, things looked very different as the days of late November moved on. As mentioned, Cuban frustration with Spain and the lack of prospects of real reform had grown in the previous seventeen years along with the US economic connection to the detriment of the Spanish. In addition, the smoothness with which the abolition of slavery had been implemented, along with massive white immigration, was rapidly reducing white Cubans' fears of racial strife in case of independence. Finally, the image of a great cause, expounded brilliantly by José Martí and, after May, symbolised by his martyrdom, made the former dream of independence now a goal of almost mystical value to many. Militarily, the situation was even more favourable for the insurgents. The rebellion, once its main leaders had reached the island in April, spread rapidly across Oriente and deep into the centre of the colony in ways unknown in the first war. Poor white, black and multiracial people flocked to the red, white and blue colours of a free Cuba. Equally important for the revolution's prospects, white leaders began to appear in larger numbers than in the past. And several 'expeditions', those ships arriving from abroad with men and weapons, were getting through the controls the Spanish Navy was attempting to establish over Cuba's coasts and coastal waters.

What was needed was the *invasión*, the centrepiece of any insurgent strategy since the beginning of the independence movement. Spain conducted both its counter-insurgency wars and also its international wars in the region with Cuban colonial treasury funds, as we have seen. Cuba was suffering from a system of taxation that sometimes beggared description, Churchill himself quickly seeing the results in what he called 'an island which has been overtaxed in a monstrous manner for a considerable period', adding that this meant that 'so much money is drawn from the country ever year that industries are paralysed and development is impossible'.[17] This money came essentially from the rich provinces of the west and the centre of the island, especially Havana and Matanzas. Without that revenue the Spanish war effort would suffer greatly. And without the prosperity of Cuba's sugar industry the movement for independence would be much stronger than it was.

It was vital to do two things. First, the rebels had to take the war to the west in order to take those resources away from the imperial treasury. Second, if the great landholders who owned the sugar estates did not voluntarily agree to stop the milling of the sugar cane on which the whole economy was based, the insurrection would be obliged to apply a policy of scorched earth imply-ing crop burning on a vast scale in the richest sugar zones to reduce further any possibility of resources coming into the Crown's hands. This strategy, termed the *tea* (literally 'the torch'), had been applied to a lesser degree in parts of the colony during the first independence war. Now Gómez was not joking. He issued a series of decrees warning the sugar mill owners that any attempt to mill would mean the destruction not only of their crops but of the buildings and machinery used to process the cane. And almost everywhere his forces went the policy was applied ruthlessly leading to vast damage to the economy and the likely ruin of *hacendado* and rural labourers alike. Since the western provinces produced the vast majority of Cuba's sugar crop, with Havana and Matanzas provinces accounting for 57.5 per cent in 1894, and Las Villas a further 32.1 per cent, the threat posed was real.[18]

This invasion was greatly feared by the Spanish who understood very well what the rebel strategy was and that it was based on a sound analysis of the strategic situation of the day. Spanish commanders were urged to have as a priority the disruption of any moves by the rebels that would bring forward the date of the invasion, considered as the moment in which a truly major rebel force crossed the Trocha with the intention of staying on its western side. Now, as late October gave way to the first days of November, the strategic context seemed grim. Gómez was already west of the trench line with a large force of mostly cavalry tying down the Spanish. His horse-borne mobility allowed him to move at will while the cumbersome Spanish columns, almost exclusively based on infantry, plodded along attempting to catch up with him and especially to finally bring him to battle. He was having nothing of major combat which he would almost certainly not only lose but also in which he would expend his most valuable asset: his ammu-nition. And, as Churchill said of the Cubans in general, the combination of mobility and good intelligence, the latter available because of the essen-tially 'unanimous' support for the revolution on the part of the population, meant that 'As long as the insurgents chose to adhere to the tactics they have adopted – and there is every reason to believe they will do so – they can neither be caught nor defeated.'[19]

The view of white western Cubans of the prospect of invasion is well summed up by Louis Pérez, the pre-eminent American historian of Cuba:

The Júcaro–Morón trocha represented something more than a fortified line of Spanish military defenses. In fact it gave palpable form to a
boundary demarcating the eastern provinces from the rest of Cuba, fixing
militarily a long standing political-cultural division between east and
west. The very construct of the separatist offensive in the west, designated
as the 'invasion' – one region of Cuba 'invading' another – offered dramatic expression of the deep regional distinctions existing in the minds
of nineteenth-century Cubans. The west viewed the approach of eastern
insurgents as nothing less than an onslaught of barbarians, threatening the
very foundations of civilization in Cuba.[20]

It is interesting to note that this lack of friendly feelings for easterners on
the part of those in the west was reciprocated by easterners, with deleteri-
ous military effects. Perez writes again that, 'Orientales, for their part, had
an equally low esteem of the west, a region they perceived as the bulwark of
metropolitan authority, estranged from the historic traditions of the island
over which orientales felt a peculiar custodial responsibility.' In fact, there
was considerable opposition from eastern senior officers and troops to the
idea of the invasion and desertions on the way west were so frequent that
Maceo had to threaten the firing squad for those who left his ranks without permission.[21] In this context it was simply essential to actually conduct
the invasion because only by that means could they show a dubious west
that there were many whites in the Liberation Army, that its officers were
mostly white, and that its troops were by no means the undisciplined hordes
of black ex-slaves, hungry for vengeance against their former overlords
and owners, but rather a proper army bringing with it the real prospect of
national independence.

Into this situation came our two young officers, who knew precious little
about Cuba, Spain, the politics behind the war or indeed the actual war
into which they were thrusting themselves. For example, when Churchill
wrote to his mother first laying out the plan, he mentioned his idea of arriving in Havana, 'where all the Government troops are collecting to go up
country and suppress the revolt that is still simmering on'.[22] In fact, Spanish
forces tended to arrive close to or directly in the zone of operations, when
they came from the metropolis, often via Spain's other Caribbean colony of
Puerto Rico, to join the fight. Thus Santiago, Cienfuegos, Gibara, Nuevitas,
Baracoa and any of a number of Cuban ports directly received Spanish

reinforcements; in no way was Havana a collection point for them before they were to move 'up country'. It is also of course wildly inaccurate in the second half of October to speak of the revolt as merely 'simmering on'. It was on a fierce boil and had been for at least five months by then.

Here was Churchill, for the first time in his life, at a critical point in the history of a nation, Cuba, an empire, the Spanish, and, it can be argued, Latin America. It is scarcely credible that a coincidence of this kind could mark his young life. For at that moment exactly, as he came into the war zone, the Cuban invasion contingents, one under Gómez to the west of the Trocha and one under Maceo still to the east, were converging to effect the attack and finally invade the western provinces with the intention of decisively defeating the colonial forces and giving Cuba its independence. And two young British subalterns, one of whom would deeply affect the history of the next century and of the whole world, were there to see it and indeed to participate in the moment.

The meeting with Martínez Campos went off very well and Churchill described him as receiving them 'affably'. The general, to say the least very busy with the long-awaited enemy invasion clearly on its way and virtually upon the Spanish, gave them what time he could. He then detailed a long-standing young member of his staff to help guide the British officers in the next stage of their journey. In another coincidence, that new Spanish officer was the eldest son of the Duke of Tetuán, the Spanish Foreign Minister from whom Drummond Wolff had obtained permission for Churchill and Barnes to go to Cuba.

Captain Juan O'Donnell y Vargas was in 1895 a 31-year-old cavalry officer, a one-time hussar, with his regiment being the Húsares de Pavia although, like Churchill, he was not to spend his whole military career in one regiment but also served for a time with a dragoon regiment, the Dragones de Lusitania. But he would certainly have felt a kinship with his fellow hussars, whichever army they came from. He was the first Spanish junior officer with whom the British officers would have had some time. A future general, third Duke of Tetuán, Grandee of Spain and minister of war in the Primo de Rivera dictatorship of the 1920s, Captain O'Donnell was at that time something of an aide-de-camp (ADC) on the staff of Martínez Campos.[23]

He had only been promoted to captain's rank that March, for *méritos de guerra* rather than seniority, so it was through combat that he came to the notice of senior officers, who ensured a more rapid promotion than would have normally been the case. O'Donnell had served in the Army of Africa in the recent Melilla campaign, doing the job of ADC for General Martínez Campos in that war as well. But he had just arrived in Cuba from the Philippines via Spain on 7 November after combat experience in which he distinguished himself in Mindanao. The later Philippine rebellion to win independence, like the Cuban, was a second attempt, the previous one also having failed in the 1870s. But when O'Donnell was there it had not yet begun, although there was desultory fighting in the southern island much earlier than the formal outbreak of the rebellion in 1897. He had thus only been on the staff in Santa Clara for a couple of weeks when Winston and Reggie arrived but he already knew Martínez Campos very well.[24]

Tasked with advising the two Britons and, not surprisingly given his family background, speaking English very well, Captain O'Donnell spent some time with them and told them that the column commanded by Divisional General Suárez Valdés, the one that Martínez Campos had arranged for them to join, had left earlier that day and that they would have to meet up with it later. They asked if it would not be possible for them to ride to catch up with the general but were told by one of the other Spanish subalterns as he shook his head, 'You would not get five miles.' To Churchill and Barnes' question, if this were the case, as to where the enemy were, he replied, 'They are everywhere and nowhere. Fifty horsemen can go where they please – two cannot go anywhere.'[25] This remark has been taken up by various Cuban authors to show a short but sharp description of insurgency as it was fought in Cuba in the War of Independence. O'Donnell explained that they would now have to meet up with the column in the town of Sancti Spiritus, only some 80km away but in current conditions much further because it was more complicated to get to.

Winston and Reggie would have to take a train from Santa Clara to Cienfuegos, some 80km, take ship from there to Tunas de Zaza, a sea journey of 120km, and board another train from that coastal town inland again for the 50km trip to Sancti Spiritus. As Churchill put it in already characteristically original fashion in his next letter to *The Daily Graphic*, 'Though this route forms two sides of a triangle, it is – Euclid notwithstanding – shorter than the other'.[26] They set off at once so Martínez Campos was not troubled further by them as he attempted to make dispositions to stop the rebel advance. He would only meet them again two weeks later on the train back to Havana and by then in an entirely transformed strategic context.

Fortunately there was a train to the beautiful port city of Cienfuegos still available that day and they boarded it with alacrity. The trip went without incident. Churchill does not say if they were met by any military officers at the train station, whose bright colours still greet visitors to the city just as they did when Churchill and Barnes arrived that evening. Cienfuegos was a safe city for the travellers, with a large garrison, a naval base of importance and a significant force of locally recruited *voluntarios*. Winston sat down to write his first newspaper 'letter' that night.

They boarded a coastal vessel the next day, the kind that plied Cuban waters constantly and were vitally necessary for the island's communications because of the dismal state of the roads, especially outside the richer provinces of Havana and Matanzas. This trip was again without incident and they could see the dark and brooding hills of the central Escambray Mountains chain, scene of much more guerrilla warfare in the twentieth century when both Castroist and later anti-Castro insurgents fought there, to the portside as they travelled along. They stopped briefly at the sixteenth-century town of Trinidad, now a stunning United Nations World Heritage Site, and continued on to Tunas de Zaza, which Churchill continually referred to incorrectly as 'Tuna'. This was pretty much the true back of beyond. The sugar industry to its north ensured that the town, really a village, had a pier and some facilities but, when the officers arrived there that afternoon, they wanted only to move on by train inland just as quickly as possible. Although Churchill writes later that they were assured that military trains were getting through to Sancti Spiritus from Tunas de Zaza regularly, and the route there was strongly guarded by troops and blockhouses, this was to prove an optimistic assessment. Instead they found that the daily scheduled train had already gone but was soon to return to the port as it found en route that the line had been cut, so there was now no communication between Tunas de Zaza and Sancti Spiritus. They were thus obliged to stay the day and night in 'the local hotel', termed by Churchill, doubtless accurately, 'an establishment more homely than pretentious'.[27]

The story gets chronologically a bit murky from this stage of the trip. It is not entirely clear when the two young men left Tunas de Zaza, and whether they stayed one night or two there. It seems from Churchill's account that things improved the next day, 23 November, with the Spanish military and local civilian engineers repairing the damaged line and trains able to move again. This meant that the two officers were on the first one out, and moved along what was the eastern end of the Escambray Mountains, 'which the insurgents occupy in great force'. Churchill writes that 'the line runs close to the mountains' and suggests 'These thirty miles of railway are the most dangerous and disturbed in the whole island'. Yet the train got through without incident and the travellers were able to get into Sancti Spiritus station, again, according to Churchill, just before the column commanded by General Suárez Valdés marched into town after his three-day march from Santa Clara. This seems all right but contrasts with the reports to Martínez Campos made by General Suárez Valdés of his column's progress towards Sancti Spiritus. He repeatedly referred in messages both up and down his chain of command to his arrival in that city on 24 November. This would suggest that Churchill and Barnes had two nights in Tunas de Zaza and successfully got through on that same day.[28]

The two Britons were not impressed with Sancti Spiritus. The pleasant colonial town of today, with its cobbled streets and lovely homes, was then nothing of the sort. It was not a small place, having at the time, according to today's city historian, a total of about 168 *cuadras* or blocks and with some 1,200 stone or other solid non-wood material houses.[29] But disease was everywhere. Churchill wrote of the town as 'a forsaken place, and in a most unhealthy state. Smallpox and yellow fever are rife.' The garrison town it had become during the war was greatly affected by its use in the campaigning close to the enormous Ciénaga de Zapata swamp, well to the south-west. Mosquitoes did their worst and the local military hospital had consequently a great many cases of yellow fever and malaria.

The officers found a hotel which Churchill described thirty-five years later as 'a filthy, noisy, crowded tavern' and speaks of waiting there until Suárez Valdés arrived the next evening, but in fact they stayed in the town's best accommodation, the Fonda El Correo, on the relatively posh San Rafael Street right in the centre of town. In his second 'letter' to *The Daily Graphic*, written that night in Sancti Spiritus, he mentions that the column arrived shortly after they arrived and on the same evening.

Despite the tension he must have been feeling given the strategic situation, and with a long day's march that day, General Suárez Valdés saw the two officers that very night. As Commander of the Sancti Spiritus District of the Spanish Army on the island, he had not just been marching at the head of his own column but had also been busy trying to get the various units, formations and columns in his district into deployments with a view to intercepting both the Máximo Gómez force already his side of the

Trocha and the rebels coming rapidly westwards and even then approaching that fortified line. Communications were especially poor that week because of heavy rains, which curiously Churchill does not mention at any time.[30] The most important signals link in this zone was via the heliograph stations dotted here and there around the highest hills and the most vital military posts the Spanish had. They allowed almost instant communication all the way from the Trocha itself, where the heliograph functioned from the central pivot of the line, the city of Ciego de Ávila, right back to Martínez Campos' field headquarters in Santa Clara. However, dependent on the sun for its functioning, rain or cloud could mean the severing of this unique link and then commanders were unsure what was happening in a war without fronts where, to say the least, everything was fluid. When this happened, the only, and much less satisfactory, method to keep in touch was via the warships that dotted the coast in active support of the ground forces. These were usually small gunboats, *cañoneros*, built in Great Britain or the United States, and recently delivered to the Spanish Navy in Cuba. These had been the general's main method to try to bring his various bodies of troops under effective command and coordination.

There had been no major incidents on the march from Santa Clara although some twenty rebels had briefly fired on the column on 23 November and then, following the usual insurgent pattern, dispersed. He had at least four columns out trying to find the enemy or on other duties while he marched eastwards but was obliged to ask the commander at the post at Placetas, between Santa Clara and Sancti Spiritus, to try to find out where they actually were. He also advised the Commander-in-Chief at headquarters that reports were of 2,000 insurgents operating locally.[31]

It was this harassed general who met the two young British officers that evening in his headquarters. Suárez Valdés was one of the most respected commanders the Spanish had on the island and it was for this reason that he was given command in Sancti Spiritus, not only a hotbed of insurgent support but also a key zone in any possible march by the rebels westward because of its location just behind the Trocha.[32] The Spanish would have wished to ensure that, if the rebels were successful in getting across that line, they would be engaged immediately and pushed back across it. This would have been the general's principal aim in such an event and the reason why he was so keen to be in touch with all the elements of his command while the strategic picture darkened for the Spanish. The propaganda effect of a successful rebel crossing

would have been immense and it would have been vital to follow such possible news with others saying how it had been decisively beaten and driven
back into more eastern Camagüey. The general would have been anxious to
hide as much as possible of this negative context from the British officers
although doubtless he also was in the dark about the fact that one of these
young officers was writing for a major British newspaper and was not there as
merely a visiting British Army observer.

General Álvaro Suárez Valdés y Rodríguez San Pedro was at this time a
division general, usually translated as major-general. He was born in 1831 in
Grado, Gijón, and considered himself an Asturian, from that northern province, home to generations of important generals and countless soldiers of
the Spanish Army. He was 64 years of age at the time Churchill and Barnes
visited his forces.

He had a highly distinguished career behind him although he had joined
the infantry in 1857 when he was 25, rather later than was usually the case.
He made up for lost time, however, and served abroad first in a then peaceful Cuba in 1860 in both Havana and Santiago, but followed this with active
service in the Mexican intervention of 1861, from which he returned to the
island the following year only to be posted to the Santo Domingo conflict
in 1863. From there he returned sick to Havana but upon recovery was sent
back into the fray on the neighbouring island. He did well and was promoted captain for *méritos de guerra*. In 1866 he was back in Cuba and served
with the famous San Quintín regiment but before the rebellion broke out
at Yara in 1868. He fought in the Carlist War of 1872 and was then posted
to Puerto Rico, having been yet again promoted to the rank of *comandante*
(major) for wartime merit. He was promoted again the very next year, to
lieutenant-colonel, again for his wartime service. He was quite clearly an
officer to be watched.

He was eventually called upon to go to fight in the Cuban War in 1876
when things were finally going well for the royalists. He saw much fighting as a full colonel in the Ciego de Ávila area and actually took part in a
combat at La Reforma, site of the fighting wherein Churchill and Barnes
were soon to experience their first action. He was to get to know most of
Las Villas province at that time. The *Guerra Chiquita* found him still in Cuba
and he took part in operations in Oriente as well over those months, returning to command jobs in the re-established peaceful island until 1886 when
he finally returned to Spain for command and professorial tasks including at

the War College (Escuela Superior de Guerra). Briefly during these years he was also the Governor of Santiago de Cuba.

When war broke out again in February 1895, the army sent this Cuba veteran immediately back to the island, where he arrived in the eastern port of Gibara on 17 April. Thus he had been on campaign for more than seven months when our young officers met him in Sancti Spiritus. But first he fought in the east, was decorated for his actions there, and on 25 August was called to Havana, from whence he was sent immediately to command the 5th District of Las Villas.[33] He had thus been on the ground in an area he already knew well for three months when the interview with the British subalterns took place.

Churchill gives his own account of how that interview went. Once again, the Churchill sense of humour breaks through:

> [Suárez Valdés] explained, through an interpreter, what an honour it was for him to have two distinguished representatives of a great and friendly Power attached to his column, and how highly he valued the moral support which this gesture of Great Britain implied. We said, back through the interpreter, that is was awfully kind of him, and that we were sure it would be awfully jolly. The interpreter worked this up into something quite good, and the General looked most pleased.[34]

While humorous when written a third of a century later, this was hardly a joking matter, either for British foreign policy at the time or especially for the young officers' future careers. The general then said he was going to march on the very next day, Churchill suggesting that this was because the town was so full of disease. Much more likely, however, is that the general was not about to take the two foreign officers into his full confidence and describe to them the real strategic context the Spanish, and his columns in particular, faced at that moment, and tell them of the vital need to get moving in preparations for the rebel movements then taking place. Conversation at dinner, to which Suárez Valdés then invited them, must have been vibrant if circumscribed by the context of the moment for all three. Thus while Maceo prepared to cross the Trocha a few leagues east of Churchill and Barnes, and Gómez, while moving east to join up with him, was still harassing Spanish forces nearby, the two British officers finally found themselves in a fighting force moving to meet the enemy, for the first time in their lives.

CHAPTER 5

OH BLISS! COMING OF AGE AND COMING UNDER FIRE

There is nothing so exhilarating as being shot at without result.

Horses and orderlies were found for them from the column and they joined the Spanish troops early the next day. If Churchill's account is accurate, that would have been the morning of 25 November. But Suárez Valdés makes it clear that it was the morning of the following day, 26 November. Churchill and Barnes were now 'at war', moving deep into a war zone, in an area with a disaffected population almost entirely given over to the rebel cause, and where the enemy was numerous, if not as numerous as Churchill seemed to believe, and active. Churchill wrote of that morning in his later book of reflections and memories of his youth:

Behold next morning a distinct sensation in the life of a young officer! It is still dark but the sky is paling ... We are on horses, in uniform; our revolvers are loaded. In the dusk and half-light, long files of armed and laden men are shuffling off towards the enemy. He may be very near; perhaps he is waiting for us a mile away. We cannot tell; we know nothing of the qualities of either our friends or foes. We have nothing to do with their quarrels. Except in personal defence we can take no part in their combats. But we feel it is a great moment in our lives – in fact, one of the best we have experienced. We think that something is going to happen; we hope devoutly that something will happen: yet at the same time we do not want to be hurt or killed. What is it that we do want? It is that lure of youth – adventure, and adventure for adventure's sake. You might call it tomfoolery.

To travel thousands of miles with money we could ill afford, and get up at four o'clock in the morning in the hope of getting into a scrape in the company of perfect strangers, is certainly hardly a rational proceeding. Yet we knew that there were very few subalterns in the British Army who would not have given a month's pay to sit in our saddles.[1]

The column's objective was now to escort a rations convoy, organised also by Suárez Valdés, to the garrison at the village or large ranch (*hato*) of Iguará, well to the east of Sancti Spiritus and to various other smaller posts on the way and near there, finishing off at the fortified village of Arroyo Blanco. There the nearly 4,000 men would split up with one column convoying supplies to other posts and the main fighting force heading off, in the general's words when reporting to Martínez Campos, to '*operar sobre enemigo*' (go after the enemy). The general was meanwhile very anxious to have news of his other forces, scattered widely in the Spanish manner in this war, and of course of the enemy about whom there were rumours galore but little firm intelligence. He sent orders to all the units he could reach telling one column (General Luque, thought to be in Iguará) to march to Santa Clara immediately to reinforce the troops there collecting whatever other troops he could, another (General Aldave, commanding in the Trocha) to send whatever information he had on enemy movements, and in general ordering a '*reconcentración ocasionada por presencia Maceo y Gómez*' (concentration brought on by the presence of Maceo and Gómez).[2] Advising his commander in Santa Clara of his plans, he then received from Aldave on the Trocha intelligence of a clearer kind: Maceo and Gómez were indeed both approaching the Trocha, from their respective sides, apparently to effect a juncture, suggesting that his forces on that line were deployed to intercept them but that, if they did get through, he would be available for joint operations with Suárez Valdés to then stop the rebels.[3]

Churchill and Barnes, without knowing it, were closer to action of an important kind than they would know either then or even later in life. Meanwhile, they were marching to war for the first time and getting to know the way the Spanish Army worked, at least in conditions such as those of this war. Their column marched steadily that first morning toward Iguará, stopping very early, by British Army standards, after about 8 miles of marching and at about nine o'clock. By that hour the sun was high and the heat was great. The troops had breakfast and a siesta, the junior officers and men stretching out on the ground and the staff officers in hammocks slung between trees. Churchill was thoroughly impressed. The men had done this distance at a rate of about 3 miles an hour, considered by European armies of the day to be a good marching speed, and they had done so across country that was difficult, undulating, with roads that hardly deserved the name and tracks that were usually so narrow that the cavalry could not reconnoitre ahead, and the infantry was required to march in single file, leaving the enemy the initiative to choose where he would carry out an ambush or other acts of harassment. They would continue this for the rest of the day once the siesta was over and Churchill would note that virtually no one fell out of the column and the marching was good by any standards. The two officers had been told that the Spanish infantry was made up of young conscripts, unbearded and undisciplined, and found this not to be the case, at least in their column. But it is worth remembering that the Spanish were unlikely to place foreign observers, especially these two foreign observers, with a column of troops that were not the best available. There were plenty of regiments that were made up, partially or almost completely, of half-trained youths, 'conscripts recruited against their will and formed of unbearded soldiers', ill suited for the job of suppressing an enemy as active and determined as the Cuban insurgents, but the British officers were to see few of these during their stay.[4]

His favourable impression was greatly assisted by his observation of the siesta and its highly positive effect on the troops. He wrote later at some length on his reaction:

> The prolonged midday halt was like a second night's rest … The rest and spell of sleep in the middle of the day refresh the human frame far more than a long night. We were not made by Nature to work, or even to play, from eight o'clock in the morning til midnight. We throw a strain on our system which is unfair and improvident. For every purpose of business or pleasure, mental or physical, we ought to break our days and our marches into two. When I was at the Admiralty in the [First World] War, I found I could add nearly two hours to my working effort by going to bed for an hour after luncheon.[5]

Given its importance to Churchill later on in life, it is perhaps worth saying something more on the siesta at this time. He became deeply dependent on his afternoon nap to carry on his work at times of peril such as, during the First World War, as First Lord of the Admiralty, or the Second World War, as prime minister of the United Kingdom and effective leader of the British Commonwealth of Nations. His arguments for this pause in the middle of the day are convincing, but, while he found it essential for his work, it could be, to say the least, annoying to many of his wartime staff who had to sit up for meetings late into the night with a still fresh Churchill when they had, of course, in the British way, not had any such break at midday. Carlo D'Este quotes one senior government official during the Second World War as saying that Churchill, 'by sleeping half the afternoon himself and then flogging tired men to work half through the night, is killing more of his own countrymen than Germans'.[6] While of course not meant to be entirely serious, and needless to say, inaccurate in a variety of ways especially in terms of the amount of time Churchill actually spent napping daily, it is still true that Churchill did have the advantage on most other men at anything like a late night meeting.

To return to the column, it continued for two days making good time and without incident and 'without a sign or sound or sight of war', until it reached Iguará, the first garrison to be resupplied. While consisting of only a few houses and barns, it provided an occasion for the officers to sleep comfortably before heading off once again early the next morning for the less than one-day's march to Arroyo Blanco where the column would split and the preparations for further operations be made. The marching of the Spanish infantry continued to impress Churchill and the troops proved hardened and strong. They 'march splendidly. Yesterday they went twenty-six English miles between sunset and sunrise, carrying 150 rounds of ball ammunition a man and all their kit – blankets, cooking-pots, and the like.' The tactical situation of the column concerned Winston, who reported home that the:

> intricate nature of the ground prevents anything like a thorough recon-
> naissance, and much has to be left to chance. Numerous undulations,
> nullahs, and large tracts of forest afford every kind of facility for an active
> enemy to surprise the troops

He obviously found unfortunate the fact that these conditions caused:

the column to straggle over a couple of miles. The cavalry reconnoitre all they can, and whenever the country opens out the flanking parties are detached at once. As a rule, however, it is impossible to do more than go straight ahead, and often it is difficult to do that.

All these matters made ambush easier for the enemy and Churchill began to understand better what the Spanish were up against in this war. Given his interest in military history, it was not surprising that he later linked what the Spanish faced in Cuba to what the French faced in Spain during their occupation of the peninsula some nine decades earlier. 'Here were the Spaniards out-guerrilla-ed in their turn. They moved like Napoleon's columns in the Peninsula, league after league, day after day, through a world of palpable hostility, slashed here and there by fierce onslaught.' It was also during this march that Churchill saw his first 'traces of the insurrection. Burned houses and broken-down fences mark the rebels' lines of march and places of bivouac', and first heard, on 27 November, the ominous news that 'Máximo Gómez is encamped with 4,000 men a couple of leagues to the east and early to-morrow we start after him'.[7]

Arroyo Blanco was 'a temporary halt' for the column but, compared with what they had seen so far, it must have seemed like a town and not the 'village' Churchill calls it in the third letter, written there, according to the date he gives, on 27 November. It should be noted that Suárez Valdés reports to his headquarters that they arrive in the village on 28 November. By Cuban standards it was blessed with proper houses, perhaps a score of them, but single-storied and bereft of floors for the most part as a Briton would have known them. The place was a fortified camp and almost all of the civilian population had moved or been removed because of the wartime conditions for a village used by the Spanish in a central role in regional defence. Around the town a 'tent city' had grown up to house the large number of extra troops and of course the new column's arrival greatly increased the size of these extensions. The Spanish, as mentioned, had a heliograph station here, the closest one to the Trocha and thus essential for relaying messages to divisional headquarters in Sancti Spiritus and from there on to Martínez Campos' army headquarters in Santa Clara. It sat atop a nearby hill, of which there were several, all sporting small blockhouse forts which provided the outlying security to the garrison. There was also a military hospital and a church complete with Spanish-born priest. This was in itself not unusual for Cuba because the island, for a variety of reasons and much different from the experience of other Spanish colonies in the Americas, produced a tiny percentage of the priests the Church needed for the colony. The majority of priests would therefore come out from the peninsula or occasionally from other parts of Latin America. This situation persisted after independence and to some extent even to this day.

Into this relative comfort Churchill and Barnes were to settle for either one and a half or two and a half days, the first period being what is given by Suárez Valdés and the second by Churchill. Here the splitting of the column was effected, the garrison was properly resupplied with rations, as no one knew what the next few days would hold, and Churchill wrote his 'letter' home describing issues as they stood. He wrote of several matters including Spanish optimism about a 'speedy end to the war', and the officers' 'hope to crush the rebellion before the spring'. He opined that he did 'not see how this is to be done' for reasons we have already seen. And he spoke for the first time of rebel advantages and disadvantages. Their principal asset, in addition to access to superb intelligence and popular support, seemed to be in their wonderful 'short, heavy, broad-bladed sword or machete' (see pp. 208–9 for a fuller discussion of the machete). And he noted that:

> every peasant carries one, and uses it to cut the sugar cane and to per-
> form every kind of chopping or cutting work. Accustomed by long use,
> they attain a marvellous proficiency, and can sever with a single blow, and
> without apparent effort, branches that would need several strokes from
> most men. In fact, instances have been known, both in this war and in the
> last, of rifles having been cut clean in two at one blow.

This is just as well, he says, because they are 'very bad shots, and it is only at close range that their fire is effective'. That is not their only disadvantage, the chief of which, is 'the scarcity of ammunition'. As we will see later, this is a very accurate assessment of what is doubtless their major challenge.[8]

The Fighting Column

The division of the original column into two, one to convoy the remaining rations to the other posts that required them, and the other to form a new fighting column to find and engage the enemy, allows us to now look more closely at this group of soldiers with whom the two Britons are going to march and whom they will observe in action on several occasions. Even more important for Barnes and Churchill, the adventure was now going to become much more dangerous and provide what they were most looking forward to, that moment which is the subject of so much thought, worry and dreaming: the dreaded but much sought after baptism of fire. We are not certain about Barnes' thoughts on this matter, although if he were not interested in facing that test he surely would not have come. But we know a great deal about Winston's thoughts which he put on paper more than once.

Churchill's private rehearsal was about to take place in the company of these men. How many subalterns would not prefer to test their mettle in a context where their own troops were not watching and dependent on the outcome, that is, dependent on their officer passing this basic test for any soldier – coming under fire for the first time, experiencing the immediacy of death or maiming, knowing that people not far away are determined to kill you, and having all the sensations of excitement, fear and confusion that usually attend this moment in most soldiers' lives. Indeed, in many ways this is what training is all about, so conveying to the soldier what action will be like, and how he must behave in it, that his reaction will be something akin to second nature and he will pass the test despite all the fears and challenges involved. In words that many young subalterns and soldiers generally could easily share, Churchill spoke of his case later on in life and with reference to the very background of his decision to come to Cuba in the first place:

> From very early youth I had brooded about soldiers and war, and often I had imagined in dreams and daydreams the sensations attendant upon being for the first time under fire. It seemed to my youthful mind that it must be a thrilling and immense experience to hear the whistle of bullets all round and to play at hazard from moment to moment with death and wounds. Moreover, now that I have assumed professional obligations in the matter, I thought that it might be as well to have a private rehearsal, a secluded trial trip, in order to make sure that the ordeal was one not unsuited to my temperament.[9]

In fact, the first brushes with danger, in one case serious, had already occurred before the column moved off on 30 November, Churchill's

21st birthday and hence, by tradition, his 'coming of age'. On the march from Iguará some solitary horsemen occasionally showed themselves, shadowing the column in order to report its movements to the rebel command. And at one stage at least a 'small body' of rebels showed up and 'let off their rifles', and on one such occasion a 'chance bullet killed an infantry soldier'. But Churchill insists that, up to Arroyo Blanco, they had 'met nothing that could be called resistance' and he had clearly had no sense of being 'under fire' himself.

A closer call awaited Barnes and Churchill at Arroyo Blanco. The chief of staff of the division was Lieutenant-Colonel Antonio Díaz Benzo, another highly experienced officer with the Spanish Army. Díaz Benzo had just turned 40 and had just completed twenty-two years of service with the colours. He had previously served in Cuba at the end of the Ten Years War but had soon fallen ill and was sent home by the then captain-general Martínez Campos. Dogged by ill health his promotions were consistently held up. He therefore found himself in a series of posts working on military history and geography projects for the army and served under Martínez Campos again on a tactics project while teaching that subject as a professor at the War College. While there he had written a book on tactics and strategy, *Las Grandes Maniobras de España* (The Great Manoeuvres of Spain). On tactical issues he was known for his '*inteligencia, celo y actividad*' (intelligence, commitment and activity).[10]

With the renewed outbreak of rebellion in Cuba, he was in March posted back to Cuba, arriving in mid-April and attached to Suárez Valdés' staff at that time still in Santiago. By late April he was on operations with his new commander and was in action on several occasions in the east before both he and his commanding general were ordered to Las Villas. Arriving with Suárez Valdés in very late August he had had only three months on the ground, and most of that dashing about the province, to get to know the lay of the land. Thus he had not yet been able to visit the outposts of the garrison and to go up to the heliograph station during the column's stay in Arroyo Blanco and invited the two British officers to accompany him. Díaz Benzo did not actually know where the heliograph was and it turned out to be further away than he had thought. They were riding with only a small escort of half a dozen Guardia Civil mounted police and in the event left the Arroyo Blanco base rather late in the day with the result that, as Churchill put it:

as we turned back the sun sank, and five minutes later it was dark. We had a very exciting ride back – a mile and a half through woods infested by the rebels. They did not, however, for some unexplained reason, fire at us … Night in Cuba comes on with startling rapidity, and one has to be very careful not to be caught by it. The sun gets low on the horizon, and without any intermediate period of twilight darkness sets in. The woods then become nearly impassable, and even the surefooted little ponies are unable to avoid the numerous pitfalls.[11]

These were mere tastes of danger, but they were the first. Now they were to march into danger, with people they still hardly knew and in territory they knew not at all. Suárez Valdés' column, now freed from the encumbrance of the ration waggons, was ready to move out at 5 a.m. that 30 November and advance on the rebel camp at La Reforma, on the modern border between the provinces of Sancti Spiritus and Ciego de Ávila, and at least harass the movements of the now joined-up forces of Gómez and Maceo, let them know that the Spanish were ready for them, and that they did not have, entirely at least, the initiative as the campaign wore on.

But the insurgents had already seized that initiative in the months and weeks preceding the crossing of the Trocha by the reinforced, largely cavalry force of Maceo. For the long-held dream of an invasion of the west was now becoming a concrete reality before the horrified eyes of the Spanish high command. And nothing, seemingly, could be done to stop it. It had all gone according to Gómez's overall strategic plan. He would have crossed the Trocha first, as previously mentioned, on 30 October, weeks before Maceo's forces, which were then marching all the way from Oriente hundreds of kilometres to the east, to actively harass the Spanish forces in Las Villas in order to tie them down, wear them out and make it impossible for them to assist their comrades in more eastern Camagüey in holding up or defeating outright the column of Maceo.

In the event, Maceo moved steadily westward, picking up more troops, especially cavalry, and reached the area some days before he actually crossed the Trocha on the now historic night of 28/29 November, his movements masked by the activity of Gómez on the other side. On the way, they had crossed the battlefield of Las Guásimas, scene of the 1874 tactical victory but strategic defeat of the previous attempt at invasion when the Cuban rebels had exhausted their ammunition and were thus obliged to call off the whole scheme. There would be no such examples of early full open battles with the Spanish this time. Instead the followers of Cuba Libre would avoid combat as much as possible, except where the enemy was weak, until the invading forces were deep into western Cuba and had found ways of organising resupply of that precious commodity. Maceo's forces crossed the Trocha in the full knowledge of the historical importance of their march and did so with bands playing and colours waving. Gómez's message to Maceo from across the line on 29 November could not have been more indicative of the absolute failure of the Spanish to cause the rebel Commander-in-Chief's forces any serious trouble: 'I have four to five thousand Spaniards on operations on top of me, but I have them entertained without doing me any damage, and without tiring me, until your arrival.'[12]

With both crossings now complete, the two generals quickly met at a secluded spot and their forces then joined up at Lázaro López, well to the west of the Trocha, in what became the most famous *abrazo* (hug) in Cuban history. The general commanding harangued the troops with a powerful speech, and the president, Salvador Cisneros Betancourt, and government of the self-styled 'Republic of Cuba in Arms', also present for the occasion, shared the general jubilation before their return to safer zones. Gómez's biographer, Bernabé Boza, also an officer of the Liberation Army, described the scene which clearly shows to what extent Spain's generals would have to work hard to regain the initiative now so clearly lost to the rebels:

> Emotional was the hug between Gómez and the most brilliant of his lieutenants, in front of the two assembled columns, with colours flying, and to the chords of 'La Bayamesa', so evocative of the past. Gómez, trotting about on his white and frisky native horse, did not hide his joy, his confidence in victory. At last, the so longed for desire, the dream so often sought, had been converted into reality.[13]

While Spanish tactical intelligence tended to be not as good as its strategic counterpart, the news Churchill had been given a couple of days before was essentially correct. The new invading column was composed of some 4,000 men, the largest force ever to cross the Trocha or indeed be fielded on the rebel side, in either war. Crucially, however, it was not known on the Spanish side if this force comprised mostly cavalry or of infantry. If the latter it could be expected to be strong but to move rather slowly. If cavalry the Spanish would be up against an entirely different problem of a quick-moving, powerfully striking and very large force entirely outclassing the Spanish in that arm of war so vital in the Cuban countryside.

Suárez Valdés' original column was made up, as usual in this war, of something of a hodgepodge of forces amounting to something under 4,000 men. Spain's chronic lack of cavalry throughout this conflict made it vital to shift those resources about the place on many occasions so that often that force was not made up of full squadrons from the same regiment but rather of small groups of cavalrymen from a variety of units. But even the infantry, often detached in penny-packets hither and yon, found it difficult to conduct operations without full individual battalions with the same unit loyalties, traditions and recent practice of working together, commanders known to all the men, and the usual advantages of formed units rather than patched-together ones in conducting warfare. Columns were often simply thrown together with what units, or portions of units, were available for a commander and a mission. This could also pose serious logistics problems because, though the majority of the troops certainly by late 1895 had been issued the new Mauser rifle, many still had the Remington, which used an entirely different cartridge.[14]

After sending off about half of his original column, Suárez Valdés organised the other half into the fighting column briefly discussed above. This was based on the previously existing column of Brigadier-General José García Navarro, with which Churchill had marched so far, and additional elements of mounted troops.

General García Navarro was a well-known officer much appreciated by the pro-Spanish elements of the population and by the army. He was born in 1846 so when Churchill and Barnes got to know him, he was 49 years of age. He had joined the infantry in 1862 when only 16 and was almost always thereafter promoted for *méritos de guerra*. His promotions to lieutenant-colonel in 1874 and to colonel in 1879 were particularly rapid and were a result of effective soldiering in Cuba. By 1893 he was made brigadier-general, again in recognition of war service.

Like others we have seen, he was with the Army of Africa until 1894 and was serving as a brigade commander in the Melilla campaign in early 1895. He was almost immediately posted to Cuba when the rebellion broke out and stayed on the island from May 1895 to March 1896. Like many other officers he had been to Cuba a number of times before. He was on the general staff in 1872, and moved back and forth between Spain, Cuba and Puerto Rico throughout the first rebellion and fought in Puerto Príncipe (now Camagüey) and further east. In fact, in the first war, from 1875, he had the post of chief of staff in Sancti Spiritus that Lieutenant-Colonel Díaz Benzo had in this. In that job García Navarro saw action throughout Sancti Spiritus, Santa Clara, at the Trocha and even in relatively peaceful Trinidad.

Poor health caused him to be sent home in 1876 but with a promotion and many kudos from commanders. He also went to serve as a professor at the War College. In 1878, with the war winding down, he was yet again posted to eastern Cuba and was in action against the valorous but controversial rebel general Vicente García.[15] He was present at the peace talks between rebel leaders and Martínez Campos in May 1878 which led to the end of the war. By 1895, he therefore knew Las Villas especially well not only because of previous wartime service there but because he had become chief of staff for the province after the peace agreements mentioned. He was in that job when the *Guerra Chiquita* broke out and he fought the other great rebel commander Calixto García, with such positive results that García gave up shortly afterwards and that short and last insurgent stand ended. From then on until 1881 García Navarro served in Trinidad.[16] He was a Cuba veteran of the first rank and it is hardly surprising that his services were much sought after later when things were going badly.

They were certainly going badly in early November 1895. On 2 November, Martínez Campos, under increasing pressure to provide positive news to calm a worried public opinion, had asked for daily reports from all commanders of columns about their activities, not so much so as to be able to keep up to date in headquarters as to be able to show the public, and the government, that the army was actively engaging the rebels and not letting up in its pressure on them.[17] At the beginning of that month, General García Navarro was in Oriente, commanding a brigade out of the town of Alto Songo, north of Santiago. He had been decorated in August with the Gran Cruz del Mérito Militar (Grand Cross of Military Merit) for 'his special qualities of tact and energy which are a guarantee of his accomplishment with skill of such commands and commissions as are confided to him'. Headquarters records of his command describe 'a zone of a limitless extension of land, the island's most broken, with its centre in Alto Songo'. In constant operations throughout this territory he fought in several important actions. On the defensive as well, he had apparently done well, being responsible for the construction of some forty-eight small fortifications over a seven-week period, while constantly under rebel harassment.[18]

He was called on with urgency on 7 November to cobble together rapidly a column of two battalions of his own infantry in Alto Songo and the area around it, pick up a section of two mountain guns and their crews, head for the coast and board transport to the centre of the island to help counter the likely crossing of Maceo's troops into western Cuba.[19] The researcher is fortunate in that the Spanish military archives in Madrid have considerable detail on the make-up of the troops sent with García Navarro, units which he chose himself and hence those with whom Churchill and Barnes served in this column. States of the units involved were prepared to simplify their transport so great detail can be found. In fact the battalions under his command were spread about as were so many Spanish units among local defence duties, garrisons and the mobile force in Alto Songo. In addition, heavy rains were not just a problem in Las Villas: the same problem plagued the Spanish command in Santiago as it tried to get the reinforcements asked for into shape to leave.

Nonetheless, the effort bore fruit. Colonel José Izquierdo, commanding officer of the 1st Battalion, Regimiento de Cuba No. 65, whom Churchill and Barnes were to see a great deal of, reported on 9 November with the numerical state of his battalion saying that he would be taking with him his full unit made up of 2 field officers, 22 junior officers, 570 soldiers, 21 horses and 18 pack animals, but would have to detach the Agüero Company with its 4 officers and 140 men who were required for other duties. This regiment of Cuba's 1st Battalion, it is important to note, was merely another line battalion of the Spanish Army with the historic title 'Cuba' but it had no other connection with the island, did not recruit there and was not normally stationed there.

The commanding officer of the other chosen battalion, the Cazadores de Valladolid, No. 21, Lieutenant-Colonel C. Francés, who would also get to know the British officers over several days, sent in his report saying that he had under command 1 major, 4 captains, 1 medical officer, 7 full lieutenants, 2 second-lieutenants, 16 sergeants, 30 corporals, 11 buglers and 543 other ranks, along with 18 horses and 28 mules, to be shipped west. This battalion was to all intents and purposes just another line battalion as well. A *cazadores* unit was the equivalent of what in the British Army would have been a rifles regiment, or one of light infantry, similar to the one Churchill's father and the Duke of Cambridge had been so anxious for him to join. Previously a rifle regiment would have had duties quite different from a line regiment, scouting, ambushing and harassing the enemy and often broken up into small packets for such duties far away from the bulk of the army. To do this job they had more modern and expensive rifles (muskets with rifled barrels for greater accuracy), not smooth-bore muskets, received special training in such operations, and were expected to be skilled at field craft and camouflage. They wore green or earthy colours in order to blend into the countryside instead of the bright colours of field regiments. And most importantly individual initiative and action were highly called for in such units as opposed to the mechanical movements of the line infantry soldier ranged in battle to exchange volleys with his enemy counterpart.

By the end of the nineteenth century, this romantic past was irrelevant. There were few tasks given *cazadores* regiments, or their *schützen, chasseur* or other cousins in similarly organised European armies, which could not be given to any other line regiment. Training was little different either and all soldiers had rifled muskets well before 1895, not just the *cazadores* or their equivalents. Nonetheless, to some extent the traditions lived on and still do in such regiments to this day and in 1895 at least some historical elements of specialist training reserved for this unit would have survived. Specialists or not, this battalion was one with which Suárez Valdés had himself served in the Ten Years War and for which he would doubtless have had a soft spot, even after such a long time.

To these two regular battalions was added a mountain artillery section, that is two artillery pieces often under the command of a lieutenant of that corps but in this case a captain. These troops would be made known to the world through a splendid sketch by Churchill, published in his letter from Tampa Bay of 14 December in the *Daily Graphic* of 13 January 1896. They were from 1st Section, 6th Battery, of the Spanish artillery force in eastern Cuba. The commander was Captain Antonio Planas, and he had one other officer, one sergeant, four corporals and fifty-one gunners under him, and the more or less normal animal support of twenty-four mules. His two guns were Krupp 75mm cannons, weighing some 388kg each, so they were normally relatively easily transported by their four assigned mules, though this was hardly always the case in Cuban campaigns where the heavy and sudden rain storms could produce a nightmare of mud and bog down guns and caissons. They fired at a rate of 6–10 rounds a minute and could be employed firing high explosive, canister or shrapnel rounds. Their ammunition used, like the Mauser rifle, smokeless powder.[20] It was generally considered an excellent artillery piece and the Spanish were well pleased with it.

The urgency with which the Spanish treated the constitution and movement of this force is evident from the series of pressing messages from headquarters in Santa Clara and the relevant authorities in Oriente. General Arderíus in Havana cabled on 9 November that Martínez Campos 'wishes to know urgently [*desea saber con urgencia*] when General Navarro embarks with two battalions'. Two *vapores* (steam ships) leased to the Spanish Army, the *José García* and the *Villaverde*, were hastily put at the disposal of the eastern command, and sent to the nearby port of Firmeza near Santiago to pick up the troops. In total, the commander in Santiago reported, 2 lieutenant-colonels, 27 officers and 872 men sailed with General Navarro for the west to support the Commander-in-Chief and eventually to join Suárez Valdés in his operations. They left later than that general hoped, sailing only on the night of 8/9 November 'as a result of difficult roads which were a consequence of the rains', and they were not 'organic', that is formed, standard, fully up to strength battalions because of the dispersal of the units around the Alto Songo region. Otherwise, of course, the strength of the two battalions would have been much larger.

The speed of the embarkation at Firmeza also spoke to the urgency with which the Spanish were pulling together this rather ad hoc formation. While the *José García*, closer by, was able to take some time to embark its assigned troops, mostly of the 2nd Battalion of the Cuba Regiment, the *Villaverde* only arrived in port at 3 a.m. and was already sailing off, with most of the Cazadores de Valladolid and the other part of the 2nd Battalion Cuba Regiment on board, an hour later. García Navarro arrived in Cienfuegos the next day, marching from there to Santa Clara, arriving on 11 November.[21] His column came under fire on that march while skirting the Escambray Mountains where, as we have seen, the rebels were strongly established, but otherwise arrived in fighting trim at Martínez Campos' headquarters. So while Churchill was enjoying his time in New York, and getting to know the US Army through his visit to West Point, the force that he was to join and which he was to admire so much was urgently assembling at his final destination.

The Spanish reasoning was obvious enough. Arderíus told General Moreno, commander in Santiago, why there was such speed required in a cable of 7 November: 'The General Commander in Chief advises your excellency that the departure of forces from Oriente for Las Villas at the moment when ... the destruction of crops [is so great] obliges ... [him to order] that General Navarro come to Cienfuegos with the greatest speed with two battalions and two guns.'[22]

This column, known by its commander's surname as was the custom at the time, and sent from hundreds of kilometres away, was the base around which the new Suárez Valdés column was formed. The general was able to obtain another detached company of the Chiclana Regiment, also of line infantry, for the new formation, yet another sign of how split up units of the army were at that time. Added to this infantry and artillery was a small group of regular Spanish cavalry and another small *guerrilla*.

The regular cavalry consisted of the pitifully small couple of troops of horsemen from the Pizarro Regiment that were with the original column out of Santa Clara. But they were professional soldiers all. The Spanish cavalry in Cuba were detached from their central regimental headquarters to posts and towns across the island. Thus major cities might have one or two squadrons of one of these regiments and towns even less. In fact, even major garrisons might have less than half a squadron of cavalry. Later on we will discuss the strategic and tactical significance of this but here it is important to note that a vital column, given the task of closing with the largest rebel force ever to take the field, and certainly containing at least 1,000 cavalry and probably more, even by the most optimistic Spanish calculations, had forty regular cavalry from the Pizarro Regiment, together with thirty members of the Yero Guerrilla. The Yero small sub-unit was not from Las Villas but had been ordered in late September to that area by the captain-general himself, and specifically to Sancti Spiritus, presumably because Martínez Campos knew very well the tiny size of the cavalry force available in that military district. It was commanded by the officer who founded it and gave it its name, a Captain Yero, an experienced commander of horse, and apparently a devoted royalist.[23] But its addition to the column still meant that Suárez Valdés had for his total mounted force no more than seventy men. This would mean his reconnaissance would be minimal, his ability to cover any withdrawal the same, but most importantly it would mean that, if the enemy continued to apply the tactic of moving away at speed from any engagement, he would not be able to force them to battle. Since his intention was to seize the initiative from the invaders, this inability to make them fight him, and thus tie them down at least to some extent, was a crucial flaw in the plan. And without greater cavalry strength his lack of mobility would limit his ability to act in vital ways in the days to come.

The *guerrilla* troops would help to some extent, of course. *Guerrillas* were of two kinds in this war. Since infantry units and columns moved about often unknown and difficult to reconnoitre countryside, from early on in the previous war, those units had been authorised to raise their own *guer-rillas*, which would bear their names, and were made up of small groups of local Cubans or members of the regiment itself, who were good horse-men, knew more of the country than most non–islanders, and had skills and aptitudes likely to make them do a good job as mounted soldiers and reconnaissance specialists.

The other type of *guerrilla* was one normally organised in Cuban cities, or in other smaller localities, mostly out of native-born Cubans prepared to fight for the mother country, or the occasional Spaniard who knew the country well. They were a type of *voluntario* but not of the largely infantry units which Churchill remarked upon so soon after his arrival in Havana. These soldiers were often on their own, far from the discipline of senior commands and membership of larger formations, and often did maraud-ing of their own at the expense of their fellow Cubans who supported the *mambí* cause. Stories of their cruelty abounded, although these were doubt-less often exaggerated for rebel propaganda purposes. One especially critical Cuban rebel source described their raising:

> The Spanish Government took special care in forming guerrillas not to admit into them honest men: murderers, thieves … degraded beings out of the cesspools of prison, and others especially taken from those places … those having been condemned for crimes, who wear on their fore-heads the stigma of rapist, murderer, arsonist, counterfeiter, etc. etc.; these were the badges of honour, the credentials of the *guerrillero*.[24]

Cuban-born troops, regulars or *voluntarios*, fighting for Spain were custom-arily shot as traitors by the rebels if they surrendered to them. But as can be imagined, the fate of captured *guerrillas* could be worse than mere death. Spain still managed to recruit thousands of them, however, even in this war and they often served hard and well, even if their discipline and military administration left much to be desired. And thus the army in Cuba had at its disposal bodies of horsemen, too few to be sure, who worked well on the flanks of columns, and in scouting and reporting on the enemy, as well as with communications and more general tasks.

They were not full-blown cavalry though, as were the men from the Pizarro Regiment. They would know little of formal charges, defensive measures of size or other European cavalry matters. Suárez Valdés had in them and in the regulars a tiny mounted force useful for reconnaissance and flank duties but utterly incapable of major or even minor offensive operations against a significant enemy, especially a mounted one.

The total strength of the column was 1,290 men, according to the general in his reports to the Captain-General, and of these about 1,150 would have been infantry, seventy mounted *guerrillas* or proper cavalry, and just under sixty gunners, with his small command staff in addition. With this force under command, one can easily imagine the challenges he had to consider. Gómez had 4,000 men and, despite consistent reports that the majority of these were infantry, Suárez Valdés would have had a good idea that such reports were overly optimistic.[25] He would therefore have to plan on the basis of his going out to meet a force vastly superior in mounted men and strong in infantry as well.

How to wrest the initiative from such an opponent, especially when his morale would never have been higher, was not easy to conceive, and with such an opponent as Máximo Gómez, with exceptional skills as commander, strategist and tactician, the means for the completion of the objective was even less obvious. While the Spanish government, the government-controlled press and the army rarely gave Gómez his due, Suárez Valdés knew very well that he was up against an agile, experienced, determined and brilliant commander, and one who had under command a force which, while lacking no doubt the formal discipline of a European army, knew how to conduct its own particular way of war very well.[26]

Spanish morale cannot have been high at all, at least among the senior commanders who knew the truth of the situation. The fact was that Martínez Campos' chief objective to date, the stopping of the two main rebel leaders joining forces for the invasion, had not been met, in spite of orders he had given to his commanders in Las Villas and Camagüey to at all costs obey to the letter, and the rebels, now very strong indeed, were across the Trocha and into the central provinces, rapidly moving towards the west. Thus the orders were necessarily now for those same generals, and Suárez

Valdés in particular as the commander with the force closest to Gómez, to bring the enemy to battle and 'pull another Las Guásimas', by forcing him to deploy, engage and use up his supplies, especially ammunition, thus ending the threat of further progress by the invaders.

This was infinitely easier said than done. And the relatively small size of the Spanish column, and especially its lack of cavalry and thus of mobility, made the realisation of the objective virtually impossible. It must surely be for this reason that Suárez Valdés considered it his duty to at least find and fight the enemy, however briefly and inconclusively, in Suárez Valdés' own words to the commander of royalist forces on the Trocha, 'to find him as soon as possible and avoid that his movements answer [only to] his own thinking'.[27] The Spanish had to find and engage Gómez to at least show him that this would not merely be a question of riding westward with the full initiative in his own hands, as it had been in his parading around Las Villas over the previous month, but rather a campaign in which the Spanish would always be right after him and constantly trying to bring him to battle. The column commander was doing just this as he rode to engage the rebel invading force, while at the same time, by cable, rider and heliograph, he was organising the other columns close at hand to be ready to receive orders to move to the fight.

Churchill in all probability knew little of any of this. There is no hint in his letters to the *Daily Graphic* of the Spanish being near panic in terms of their strategic failure to halt the rebels short of Las Villas. While he spoke of Spanish military challenges, and even of the rumour of a major defeat in the centre of the island, he did not elaborate upon the matter or even come close to suggesting that momentous change in the strategic context of the war had just taken place and might only be the forerunner of even more startling changes soon afterwards. It is almost certain that he and Barnes were kept carefully in the dark on these matters until, hopefully, there would be a more positive assessment of the military scene to unfold to them. Even the question of the relative size of the forces, as Churchill believed he knew them, with probably 4,000 on the rebel side and what Churchill himself gives, inaccurately, as his own column being of 1,700 men, does not come up. After all, he would certainly not be unaware that there was, to say the least, very little likelihood of an even fight between the two forces in an engagement. And, although he had not come to have a high regard for the fighting prowess of the Cubans, having a regular's disdain for both hit and run tactics and a strategic avoidance of battle, and having commented unfavourably on the shooting capabilities of the insurgents, he would have known not to discount such a huge disparity in force.[28]

He was not, however, informed of much and heard the Spanish officers around him, cavalrymen of the Pizarro Regiment, infantrymen of the Cuba and Valladolid regiments, Cuban *guerrillas* of the Yero Guerrilla, and gunners of the artillery, speak of the speed with which they hoped to win a decisive victory and end the war, and how they were fighting for their country's national unity. Doubtless the two officers were, as Winston suggests, especially impressed when their new friend Colonel Díaz Benzo, with whom they had just shared significant exposure to danger for the first time, spoke emotionally about what Cuba meant to him and to all Spaniards and how for them the war 'which we are fighting [is] to preserve the integrity of our country'.[29] Churchill and Barnes, as Churchill relates, ate with these troops, slept alongside them, joked with them, marched with them to front and rear, spoke with them at halts and during the evenings of the march, and generally came to know them and, it is clear, to like them.

While language divided them, as Churchill says, French, the lingua franca of the day, compulsory at the cadet colleges of both countries' armies, and the cultural language of the whole of Europe, united them, if only partially. French had been the dominant language of not only culture but especially military affairs since the end of the seventeenth century. Most military manuals, including those on tactics, were written in French and while most military thinkers, such as Clausewitz, would write in their own languages, they knew very well that breaking into an international market meant the key role of an edition in French. Antoine Henri de Jomini, a French-speaking Swiss, Clausewitz's contemporary and himself a great strategic thinker, naturally wrote in French. The heroes and great strategists and tacticians of the recent past, such as Frederick the Great, Eugene, Napoleon, Turenne and De Saxe, also wrote in French and knew that thereby they could reach the very largest foreign market. Gentlemen of the age tended simply to speak some French as a matter of course, whether they were military or civilians but especially in the former case. The young Winston had taken French from early on at school, like other upper-class children and, although he did not always like studying it, he accepted it as a matter of course for a young gentleman of his time. Churchill suggested nonetheless that the French he spoke with his hosts, on both sides, was terrible. This is extremely unlikely. It may not have been that good but it was probably not all that bad. The Spanish school system took French in the second half of the nineteenth century almost as seriously as the British and the military education system in particular did so.

Churchill probably spoke French at least tolerably well at this time. After school he had to continue with it, as did all cadets, at Sandhurst. There is no reason to believe that his French was all that bad, although doubtless he had not used it extensively for some time and it might have got quite rusty. He had not only studied it most of his life but he had been on extended holidays in France and la Suisse romande on the only international visits he had made prior to 1895. In 1883, at the age of 8, he had gone to France, unusually with his father. In 1891, at 17, he had travelled there again, this time with his French master from Harrow, from where, only four years before the Cuba trip, he had written home, 'I have already made great progress in French. I already begin to think in it.' And only two years earlier he had gone on a walking tour of French-speaking Switzerland during which his tutor described his French as positively 'voluble'. Moreover, as he said himself, he liked French and, for him, that was vital: only subjects he liked could really attract his attention. It is probable that his French was actually more than passable at the time of the Cuba visit and that, while the Spanish junior officers may have had some trouble making themselves understood, Churchill had much less.[30]

The conversations had their impact, and it was to complicate Churchill's ability to be balanced in his reporting for some time. As he wrote:

> Hitherto I had secretly sympathised with the rebels or at least with the rebellion: but now I began to see how unhappy the Spanish were at the idea of having their beautiful 'Pearl of the Antilles' torn away from them, and I began to feel sorry for them.[31]

But that sympathy did not extend to thinking the Spanish could win.

> Imagine the cost per hour of a column of nearly 4,000 meandering round and round this endless humid jungle, and there were perhaps a dozen such columns, and many smaller ones, continuously on the move. Then there were 200,000 men in all the posts and garrisons, or in the block-houses on the railway lines. We knew that Spain was not a rich country as things went then. We knew by what immense efforts and sacrifices it maintained

more than a quarter of a million men across 5,000 miles of salt water – a dumb-bell held at arm's length.[32]

Churchill and Barnes were now truly marching to war. Around them were nervous but strong-willed men, marching with determination towards the enemy, and the soldiers, at least, were doing so with high morale. Winston was more and more impressed by these men.

Birthday and Baptism: The Most Probable Story

Winston Churchill's 21st birthday, traditionally considered a young person's 'coming of age', was 30 November 1895, St Andrew's Day. He was still at this stage more or less merely the eldest son of a 'maverick politician', as many people on both sides of the House of Commons would have had no difficulty in accepting as a description of Lord Randolph. While they would have credited his great skills without a murmur of dissent, most would also have agreed on the difficulty of working with him as a partner in anything. After all, William Gladstone himself, the enemy of all good Conservatives, had called Lord Randolph the 'greatest conservative since Pitt', a reference to William Pitt, the revered prime minister of the great wars with France. But working with him had proved too much for more than one prime minister of the later nineteenth century.

Cuba was to bring Winston to the public limelight in his own right, if not as dramatically as he was to know later on, still in a fashion that got him talked about in the press and among the educated public. And one of the features of that arrival in the public's gaze is the well-trumpeted story of his baptism of fire on his 21st birthday. This romantic and remarkable version of the story came to light only in 1930, when he wrote it up in *My Early Life*:

> The 30th November was my 21st birthday, and on that day for the first time I heard shots fired in anger, and heard bullets strike flesh or whistle through the air ... The firing seemed about a furlong away and sounded very noisy and startling. As, however, no bullets seemed to come near me, I was easily reassured ... [later] close at hand, almost in our faces it seemed, a ragged volley rang out from the forest. The horse immediately behind me – not my horse – gave a bound ... The bullet had struck between his

ribs, the blood dripped on the ground, and there was a circle of dark red on his bright chestnut coat. He hung his head but did not fall. Evidently, however, he was going to die, for his saddle and bridle were soon taken off him. As I watched these proceedings I could not help reflecting that the bullet which had struck the chestnut had certainly passed within a foot of my head. So at any rate I had been 'under fire'. That was something.[33]

If, however, we contrast this version with his report of that day, made only five days later in his letter to the *Daily Graphic* of 4 December 1895, written fresh from the event, we see a deeply different rendering. After the column set out from Arroyo Blanco at 5 a.m., the convoy of rations with two battalions and a squadron of cavalry headed off to the north-west while the fighting column moved east to find the rebels. He wrote at the time:

No sooner had we got clear of the town than we heard the sound of firing, showing that the convoy, which had started earlier, was already engaged. For about two miles we retraced our steps in the direction of Iguará [westward], in order to deceive the enemy's scouts, and then struck off to the left and marched due east ... Of the enemy nothing was to be seen. [later] ... the cavalry were just dismounting, when a party of about twenty-five insurgents ... was seen making off across the fields ... The cavalry remounted and pursued those fellows with the greatest promptitude, but they were unable to catch them before they reached the edge of the forest into the depths of which it was impossible to follow. It was evident that the enemy was very close ... The next morning ...[34]

This alone would give grave doubts about the accuracy of the much later version of the story written entirely from memory and a few notes. But this is not all. For the very next day, Churchill gave an account much more similar to his later story of events in the same letter to *The Daily Graphic*. For 1 December, he writes:

The next morning [1 December] at a quarter-past five we marched out of our bivouac. The sun had not yet risen, and a mist hung over all the low-lying ground. We had not gone half a mile when a sharp fire opened on the column from the edge of a wood about 200 yards to the left. As nothing could be seen, the troops did not reply, and after firing for about ten minutes the enemy retired ... At eleven o'clock we came into a small clearing about two hundred yards wide. Here we lunched – or rather proposed to lunch, for no sooner had the column halted than we were fired at from the edge of a clearing. The Staff [with whom Churchill was posted] was, of course, selected as a target, and the guide had his horse shot under him. [35]

While one cannot be entirely certain of any of this, it seems even from these two elements that it is likely that Churchill later confused the events and dates and gave what was essentially a new account of his baptism of fire, a much more dramatic one because it included not only the death of the horse nearby, giving rise to all sorts of mythological accounts locally in Cuba and abroad, but also the bullet passing so near his head, and of course the romantic question of coming of age on the same day one first came under fire.

Even this, however, is not all that should give us pause in accepting the later version of what happened. Martínez Campos, as we have seen, was keen to know what his columns were doing, both for the information's intrinsic value and also because it allowed him to give press releases as to how busy the army under his command was in its fight with the rebels. Under increasing pressure politically to win the war and end the insurgency with the same efficiency with which he had terminated the previous conflict, and increasingly criticised in the press for not achieving those objectives, he was vitally concerned to be seen as working hard to win back the initiative and at least begin to best the rebels.

As a result of this personal and military situation, reporting from columns, especially if it involved any type of combat, improved greatly, and fighting or just coming under fire, even of the most innocuous kind, was scrupulously written up and sent to higher headquarters. For 30 November, army records include no action and nothing about the column having been fired upon although the shooting at the now far-off convoy is documented. For the next day, 1 December, there is clear mention of the incident at lunch with firing occurring against the column, including presumably that from the flanks which killed the scout's horse. [36] For all of these reasons it is extremely difficult to accept the accuracy of Churchill's later version of these events. There simply seems to have been a quite normal lapse of memory here as there is at many points in his later recounting of events in his by then distant youth. It is regrettable to have to question what is, after all, a great yarn, but, in the interests of historical accuracy, it appears to be necessary here to at least invite the reader to think more on this matter before accepting a much-loved but probably inaccurate story from Winston's youth.

The Column Does Enter Action

After this brief period under fire, Churchill did not have to wait more than a few more hours to properly come under fire and have that baptism of the fierce experience that he so longed for. In an entirely verifiable story that is both true and out of a story book, Churchill and Barnes had a close call much more dramatic even than their previous night-time ride back from the heliograph station a couple of days previously. Churchill's own words record the story best:

> The day was hot, and my companion and I persuaded a couple of officers on the Staff to come with us and bathe in the river. The water was delight-ful, being warm and clear, and the spot very beautiful. We were dressing on the bank when, suddenly, we heard a shot fired. Another and another followed; then came a volley. The bullets whistled over our heads. It was evident that an attack of some sort was in progress. A sentry, sitting on a tree about fifty yards higher up stream, popped over it, and kneeling down behind, began to fire at the advancing enemy, who were now about 200 yards away. We pulled on our clothes anyhow, and one of the officers, in a half-dressed state, ran and collected about fifty men who were building shelters for the night close by. Of course they had their rifles – in this war no soldier ever goes a yard without his weapon – and these men doubled up in high delight and gave the rebels a volley from their Mausers which checked the enemy's advance. We retired along the river as gracefully as might be, and returned to the general's quarters. When we arrived there was a regular skirmish going on half a mile away and the bullets were fall-ing over the camp … After about half an hour the insurgents had enough, and went off carrying their wounded and dead with them.[37]

This was more like it. This was what they had come for – real adventure. And there was much more to come. That night, the enemy applied its traditional tactic of trying to wear down the Spanish by constant harassment during many of the dark hours. This, the rebels always hoped, would tire their opponents and make them less effective the next day. And, while Churchill's account of the fine infantry soldiers with whom he was marching would show that no such effect was had on them, doubtless with less seasoned troops there would have been. In any case, the rebels did return that night, at about 11 p.m., and harassed the column's tents for about an hour, though in his much later account he refers to it as 'through the night' and showed his keen but subtle sense of humour:

> I was soon awakened by firing. Not only shots but volleys resounded through the night. A bullet ripped through the thatch of our hut, another wounded an orderly just outside. I should have been glad to have got out of my hammock and lie on the ground. However, as no one else made a move, I thought it more becoming to stay where I was. I fortified myself by dwelling on the fact that the Spanish officer whose hammock was slung next between me and the enemy's fire was a man of substantial physique, indeed, one might almost have called him fat. I have never been prejudiced against fat men. At any rate I did not grudge this one his meals. Gradually I dropped asleep.[38]

The next morning, 2 December, the column began its advance early once more. Again there was a mist from which the rebels soon began their harassing fire, this time 'well directed', according to Churchill. Falling back from one position to the next, the enemy steadily gave ground and about 8 a.m. the enemy's main camp became visible to the Spanish column. But, before that, once again with what was soon to be known as his characteristic slightly impish sense of humour, Churchill wrote:

> There was a sort of block, caused by the battalion of infantry having to go in front instead of the cavalry, and during this halt the enemy's bullets whizzed over our heads or cut the ground underfoot. The soldiers grinned and mimicked the sound of the passing projectiles, and generally behaved very well. General Navarro, who commanded the advance guard, discovered the whereabouts of the insurgents. As soon as this was known, the magazine rifles of the regulars crushed their fire and the column moved off. From six to eight o'clock we marched continually opposed and under constant fire. The enemy falling back took advantage of every position, and

though not very men were hit all the bullets traversed the entire length of the column, making the march very lively for everybody.[39]

It is important now to return to the insurgent side of the story so that Winston's account can be understood within a more logical framework for analysis. The column was approaching the base camp for the combined force of Gómez and Maceo, which had joined together three days earlier. The campsite, the site of two other engagements in these wars, was called La Reforma and the action that day variously styled as the 'battle' or 'the action' at or of La Reforma. The force under Gómez's overall command would now have been in the neighbourhood of 4,000 men and while it is uncertain to what extent Suárez Valdés knew the details of that enemy body, it was broken down into no less than 3,000 cavalry and 1,000 infantry. Thus, whatever the details were, the Spanish were vastly outnumbered and relatively immobile as well.

They may also have been out-generalled. As we have seen, Suárez Valdés was a respected and competent general, with enormous military and command experience of a largely successful kind, despite recent reverses on the island. It is no slight to suggest that he was perhaps not up to the likes of Gómez and Maceo on their own turf. Now that Churchill is going to be in action only a few hundred metres from Maceo, and only marginally more from Gómez, it is important to provide a few more details about these two giants of Cuban history, and particularly of its military past.[40] Indeed, such was their importance to the cause of independence that the Spanish President, Antonio Cánovas del Castillo, once said that, to win the war in Cuba, one only needed two bullets: one for Gómez and one for Maceo.[41]

Máximo Gómez Báez was born a Dominican, in 1836. At 19 years of age, in the face of a Haitian invasion of his country, he joined the army as a cadet but was soon promoted to lieutenant for his wartime service. As a captain of cavalry he was incorporated into the Spanish Army when Madrid reintegrated the Dominican Republic into the empire in 1861. When resistance to that move among some Dominicans meant that an anti-Spanish rebellion was spawned, Gómez was promoted to major and fought for Spain. And when the rebellion triumphed in 1865, he, like many other loyalist officers and men, was posted to Cuba but soon requested his release from the military and in short order, like several other Dominican veterans then living in eastern Cuba, began to conspire against Madrid's continuing rule over Cuba.

While at first only named a sergeant in the rebel ranks when the Ten Years War broke out in October 1868, his fighting and command skills were recognised within days and he was appointed major-general in the insurgent forces. He is particularly known in Cuba for his conducting of what is thought to be the first '*carga al machete*' (machete charge) of the independence wars. We have already heard of Churchill's respect for this singular national weapon but its use in cavalry charges is part of the most deeply ingrained lore of the Cuban nation to this day. Although Gómez himself, and modern scholars, have reminded Cubans that it was only useful in the last resort and caused very few casualties in the Spanish ranks, it was certainly held in respect by Spanish soldiers and continues to have a near mystic value in Cuban historiography.[42]

Gómez fought throughout the first war for independence and was for most of that conflict the generalissimo of the rebel forces. Martí desperately sought his acceptance of the same post for the final war. Despite problems on several occasions with civilian political figures of importance, usually about the perceived dangers of militarism, he survived as Commander-in-Chief until the United States intervention in the war in 1898. As a Dominican, Gómez gave the US military authorities the excuse to not consult the rebels about very much to do with Cuba's future when US victory was quickly achieved in its war with Spain. The deaths of Martí, Maceo and a host of other Cuban-born commanders made for very few senior officers of the rebel army whom the US would have to recognise as having anything to say. He has gone down in history as the architect of the strategy of invasion of the west as central to any hope of victory against Spain, as a master of the use of cavalry in insurgencies, and as a master of guerrilla warfare *tout court*.

Antonio Maceo Grajales is always considered his lieutenant and his best general although, in the history of the first independence war, the figure of Camagüey's simply brilliant cavalry commander Ignacio Agramonte shines as bright as Maceo. Maceo was multiracial, born in Santiago in 1845. He won his sergeant's stripes the first day of his military service when he joined the 1868 rebellion only two days after it began. And within eight days, such was his obvious military talent, he was commissioned a lieutenant in the rebel army. He fought throughout the first war and indeed his rejection of the Peace of Zanjón, proffered to the defeated insurgency by Martínez Campos in 1878, was the inspiration of the *Guerra Chiquita*. Known then and now as the Bronze Titan, his importance in the insurgent forces permitted the

Spanish to make much of him as a commander of what they termed the 'black hordes' that the rebel army was supposed to be. By tradition when he finally fell in battle in December 1896, his body had some twenty-seven wounds on it, twenty-one from the first war alone.

These two generals, the most important in all Cuban history even by Fidel Castro's account, were now just across the field from Churchill and Barnes, at the culminating moment of Cuba's military and thus political history. Even by the exceptional standards of Churchill's life of coincidences, this must be among the most extraordinary. That he could just happen to have planned to go to this war, at this time, to have been attached to this column, the first Spanish force to engage an enemy which had just accomplished the long sought after invasion of the west and which would eventually, by twists and turns, lead to Cuba's independence, is remarkable on so many points as to almost defy recounting.

To return to the column, however, as it arrived at this point, in front of the insurgent base, the rebels had been involved for some hours in breaking camp and beginning their long march westwards deep into Las Villas province. They wanted to avoid a major action, and to break out from the area of the Trocha into the rich country beyond, specifically for a day's march which should end in the small hamlet of Trilladeras to the west and south. But Gómez had not yet been able to move his impedimenta into the column he had formed for the march west. The ground was such that they were closest to the nearby river, and it took some time to gather all the animals and waggons together and get up the neighbouring hill to join the fighting soldiers on the march. These impedimenta deserved richly the term. They were, to say the least, typical of the rebel army, varied and often rather stuck in the mud of the river bank: waggons, livestock, unarmed or unmounted men, and even camp followers. While they were engaged in getting organised and moving up the slope, the Spanish column burst upon them.

Maceo was in command of the rear guard at this time and engaged in the process of pulling in the advanced posts of the camp, getting the impedimenta on their way, and generally completing the invasion column. He of course could hear the sounds of the enemy's advance and had reports of it from the steadily retiring troops he had sent out to slow the Spanish march. Now, seeing that he would need more time to get the impedimenta into order with the rest of his rear guard, he called for the sixty or so riflemen from the nearby Prado Infantry Regiment that Gómez had detached to the rear guard to take up posts on the ridge overlooking the river and the field into which the Spanish were moving, and engage them with as heavy a fire as they could manage, hopefully slowing even more their advance while the rebels made good their withdrawal with impedimenta attached and complete. These men were under the command of yet another famous Cuban rebel senior officer, Brigadier-General Serafín Sánchez, who rapidly responded to his commander's orders and deployed the men in question.

Serafín Sánchez was an infantry commander of great experience and had fought in both major wars and the *Guerra Chiquita*. He was also a native of nearby Sancti Spiritus and one of its most famous sons, exemplifying for many Cubans then and now the spirit of rebellion of that province. He was an energetic 49-year-old at the time of the action at La Reforma and had just been formally named the commander of the 4th Las Villas Army Corps (essentially the column's infantry) with the newly founded invasion force the day before. He would be killed in action late the next year not very far from La Reforma battlefield.[43]

Sánchez stood by to respond to further orders from Maceo, who might have needed still more infantry support if the situation turned ugly for the *mambises*. This was just as well because that need presented itself quickly as the Spanish continued to advance quickly upon the rebel camp. More infantry were brought into action by Maceo to hold up the Spaniards and some cavalry also joined in the fight as they withdrew from posts they had occupied further north from the retiring rebel column.

The various accounts of the main action differ considerably, as is usual in such combat, and almost generalised in the case of the Cuban rebellions. Churchill, almost certainly without a full and frank briefing from his Spanish hosts, gave his account both in a letter of the time to the *Daily Graphic* and later on in *My Early Life*. The other two main accounts are those of General Suárez Valdés in his formal report to Martínez Campos and the rebel recounting which is done by several different authors but which in the main follows the same lines of analysis and description.

In Winston's report, two days later, he described what happened and spoke of his column being able to see 'the main position' of the enemy as of 8 a.m. The idea of a position may, however, be misleading. There were no prepared trenches or other elements of a defensive 'position' at La Reforma. Gómez never intended the temporary camp to be anything but very temporary indeed for the invasion column. The 'position' was then merely where the infantry had been directed by Maceo and Sánchez to go to ground and from which to begin fire. Winston then wrote that he was not going to give a detailed description of the battle because no one reads such things in sufficient earnest to actually understand the context. He therefore gave a brief overview of the ground saying that a barbed-wire lined 'ride' runs down from where the Spanish were debouching into the open area overlooking the river, where the Cuban impedimenta were attempting to get started up the slope, and in front of the higher ground on which the Cuban riflemen were arrayed. Behind this enemy force was a dense wood. Suárez Valdés decided to attack this enemy immediately.

The lead battalion of the column, the 1st Battalion of the Cuba Regiment No. 65, under Lieutenant-Colonel José Izquierdo, marched out on to the broken ground, and threw two companies forward and to each flank. The cavalry meanwhile deployed to the right of the track and the guns moved up the centre. The general and his staff, including Churchill and Barnes, moved forward about 50yd behind the advancing infantry firing line. The second battalion of the column, the Cazadores de Valladolid, then deployed behind the Cuba Regiment troops, still in column but by companies. For the first 300yd of the column's advance across the open area, the troops did not come under fire. Then from the distant crest the fire of many rifles began to be seen by the puffs of smoke the Remington's still produced as they were using old smoke-emitting rounds. The sound of that firing was heard immediately afterwards and it extended shortly along the whole length of the enemy's line.

The Spanish infantry, continuously advancing, began to respond to the enemy fire and the level of firing became heavy. The general and his staff advanced within 500yd of the enemy line where it stopped and endured the enemy fire for some ten minutes. Churchill wrote to his mother:

> The General, a very brave man – in a white and gold uniform on a grey horse – drew a great deal of fire onto us and I heard enough bullets whistle and hum past to satisfy me for some time to come. He rode right up to within 500 yards of the enemy and there we waited till the fire of the Spanish infantry drove them from their position. We had great luck in not losing more than we did – but as a rule the rebels shot very high. We stayed by the general all the time so were in the most dangerous place in the field.[44]

And in his account for *The Daily Graphic*, he wrote:

> Here we halted, and the infantry fire fight raged for about ten minutes
> evenly. The general, in his white uniform and gold lace, mounted on
> a grey horse, was a mark for every sharpshooter, and consequently the
> number of casualties on the Staff was out of all proportion to those of
> the rest of the force. Presently the sound of the Mauser volleys began to
> predominate and the rebel fire to slacken, till finally it ceased altogether.
> For a moment I could see figures scurrying to the shelter of the woods,
> and then came silence. The infantry advanced and occupied the enemy's
> position. Pursuit was impossible owing to the impenetrable nature of the
> woods to the rear.[45]

The Spanish official account of the action differs little from Churchill's,
except of course it is in the form of an official report and has the usual
features of such a document. It was prepared by Suárez Valdés in at least two
drafts, both of which are extant in the Spanish military archives:

> Upon setting up camp on the 1st in Grullas, a league and half from
> Reforma, enemy groups opened fire on the camp, continuing all that
> night. On the 2nd from 5 in the morning when I raised camp until 11
> I sustained combat with the combined forces of Máximo Gómez and
> Maceo who were grouped three kilometres from my camp towards the
> higher part of the pasture of Reforma in the direction of Guayos. Their
> positions and camps were taken pursuing them to Trilladeras. My column
> was made up of the Cuba and Valladolid battalions, 30 horsemen of the
> Yero Guerrilla, 40 from Pizarro, and section of artillery and a company of
> Chiclana, total 1290 men. According to remains left in captured camps and
> traces left 4000 men of infantry and cavalry. I have had seven wounded.
> The enemy left no casualties on the ground, some horses were captured
> and in his camp some 12 dead horses were found. Behaviour of the troops
> worthy of note for their discipline under fire.
>
> I have great satisfaction with my force who, with serenity and real
> enthusiasm, and after painful marches, threw Máximo Gómez and Maceo
> from all their positions, in the first immediate action after the joining
> up of the two chiefs in La Reforma. The enemy come out of this very
> punished as is shown in the first place by the evident signs of his losses

that he has left at the scene of the action, and secondly [by the fact] that during my return from Monte Guayos to Jicotea, my column crossing La Reforma and Río Grande, not one shot was fired.[46]

Cuban insurgent accounts of the lead-up to the main action and that action itself read rather differently (and carry much more propaganda in them) from those of Churchill and Suárez Valdés and contrast dramatically with Churchill's version on several points. It may be useful to show one giving the general picture as seen by the rebels and another with a more detailed look at events unfolding, from a distinctly insurgent and critical perspective. Boza, poetical even by his standards, wrote of the context overall:

During the whole night [1/2 December] groups of infantry and cavalry prepared for this task harassed him [Suárez Valdés] continuously. This system is the result of a magnificent practice and a great advantage we have over the Spanish, who cannot use it against us.

The next morning this [the Spanish] column, slowed down by its wounded and sick, occasioned by the shock of that fire which constantly surprises them, of fatigue and tiredness, of the dreams interrupted by those volleys that succeed one another at short intervals, and launch projectiles that carry death in their black wings, and cross in all directions the [Spanish] camp, that is surrounded on all sides by an enemy they do not know, of whose numbers they are ignorant, and that danger and imagination exaggerate, making all the more terrible the silent and mysterious night.

Those soldiers who we don't let sleep, for all the courageous, long-suffering, and sacrificing that they are, when comes the dawn, and their commanders force them to begin the march again, continuing the pursuit of an enemy who, if he does not wish to, does not even let himself be seen, and who for the next night is again preparing for them the same terrible fire …

From La Reforma, the invaders moved the next morning [2 December] towards Trilladeritas where they camped, except for 100 infantrymen who remained in ambush position to fall on the troops of Suárez Valdés. At nightfall 99 men – for one had fallen in combat – rejoined the rest of their companions after having fought with valour.[47]

In his more detailed if still highly propagandistic account, Miró Argenter wrote:

On 1 December Suárez Valdés raised his camp at Trilladeritas to get closer to the Rio Grande, in full knowledge that Gómez was there and with some hints that Maceo was as well; but he did not attack that day although he had the time to do so; he set up camp at four in the afternoon, under fire from the Sancti Spiritus cavalry which had been around the enemy camp since the day before. All troops were told to stand to at five in the morning.

The attack that was expected at dawn, began about eight, when most of our forces were already en route, via a swampy track, and only the rearguard, to which the advanced posts still had to join, had not begun its march. To send forces back to engage in a formal action, especially with the difficulties produced by the track for the order and speed of such a manoeuvre, was not something expected but was done on the fly. It was urgent to defend the baggage which could be threatened by the enemy ... Our rearguard remained formed up awaiting the return of the advanced posts in order to start their march. From them Maceo took 60 men on foot to place them on a low-lying height, but covered with bushes, and ordered two sections of cavalry to go to the aid of those troops. Our caudillo [commander] was so skilful in positioning the infantry, with that so clear coup d'oeil and with his usual speed and sagacity ...

The centre of the Spanish division remained in the first positions occupied by its vanguard but this force, shortening the distance through a transversal movement, was obviously moving towards the place where the 60 infantrymen with the order not to fire unless the target was assured. Thus the volley, brusque and sure, shattered the most advanced guerrilla formation, who were obliged to make a retrograde movement as the volleys were repeated, the second file finding themselves obliged to fire at will, one knee on the ground the horsemen in dispersed order. The centre of the column then deployed its battalions to the right and left with an excessive military show to take a position that hardly appeared invulnerable, but such a grand show allowed Maceo to take the measure of the offensive capacity of his competitor, and he reinforced with 40 riflemen that position in order to give time for the impedimenta to cross the swamp and join the cavalry. The fire flowed and the cannon of the Spanish column sounded: it was now a real battle for the enemy general! There remained to General Maceo 200 more infantrymen under Brigadier Bandera, but given the alarm the cannon blasts were causing in our impedimenta, he ordered these men [elsewhere].[48]

A last memoir from the rebel side gives us an even better idea of where Maceo was vis-à-vis Churchill and Barnes and the usual errors on both sides where enemy casualties were concerned:

> General Maceo stayed with the rearguard with some 80 infantrymen of the 'Prado' Regiment and some groups of cavalry, engaged in sharp combat for the space of an hour ... The Gral, with the highest of skill, held the enemy, being the last to retire from the fight after looking over the scene of the action. Our losses were 7: one killed and six wounded. Those of the enemy must be considerable given the accurate fire of our infantry that fought with calm and valour.[49]

It is difficult to agree that this is a real 'battle' in any very real European sense. On the other hand it is clearly not a skirmish either. Several hours of fighting, culminating in a significant firefight and deployment, is a military action of note at least in the context of the relatively small *combates* which were the norm in this war, as in so many others in the Americas. Even though both sides exaggerated the importance of the action and their own success, Churchill and Barnes had had their baptism of fire, their private rehearsal, and not in any minor way. If it is true that the actions of later years, including those of the North-West Frontier of India, were not only vastly more lengthy, more bloody and involved Churchill in the actual conduct of the fighting, this does not mean that this was any less a real baptism of fire with death, bullets, wounds and sustained exposure to danger over a considerable period.[50]

Certainly Suárez Valdés seemed impressed. There is no reason to suspect that it was only for reasons of policy that he wrote favourably of the two officers in his report on the column's operations over these days to Martínez Campos. They had shown courage and calm in the action and the preceding days and had done so under repeated fire. He wrote of them to the captain-general:

I underscore to Your Excellency with the greatest of pleasure the serenity and interest with which the officers of the British Army Mister Spencer Churchill and Reginald Barnes have followed all the incidents of these operations and of the action in which they were at my side.[51]

The Captain-General would have been able to understand the full meaning of those words. If the two officers were 'at his side' throughout the combat, that meant they had been in the thick of the action and had shown calm and interest throughout, despite being, as Churchill wrote to his mother, in the most dangerous part of the field that day.[52]

CHAPTER 6

THE SEQUEL: IMMEDIATE AND LONG TERM

> History is written by the victors.

The Immediate Sequel, on the Ground

In traditional nineteenth-century military terms, the battlefield was in Spanish hands at the end of the day and that, under normal circumstances, would have meant a victory could be claimed by the colonialists for their action that day. But things were rarely normal in Cuba or in its wars.

In the first place, the enemy was attempting to leave the ground on which the action took place as the Spanish arrived and did make good his departure despite their arrival. In addition, as research in both archives shows, the Cubans did not lose many men. While Churchill gave later a suggested casualty figure, somewhat flippantly to be sure, of thirty to forty dead among the rebels, in fact the *mambises* appear to have suffered only one fatality at La Reforma.[1] Certainly there were dead horses on the field, as Suárez Valdés reports, probably the result of the cannonading of the impedimenta, but there is no record of any fatalities among the troops except for the rifleman to whom reference has already been made. There were six wounded as well but no further dead. The Spanish likewise seem to have had only one dead and that was before the actual main action of 2 December. The complete list of casualties in Suárez Valdés' report to higher headquarters showed there was a total of seven wounded. As Churchill remarked repeatedly at the time, one of the biggest surprises of the war is how few soldiers on either side were actually killed in action with the enemy.

It did not matter, however, that La Reforma was not a major victory for the Spanish, or indeed not a victory at all. What mattered was that Spain needed it to be a victory. It had not been possible for even the strict controls of Spanish censorship of the press in Cuba to silence the rumour that both Máximo Gómez and Antonio Maceo had successfully crossed the Trocha and were in the centre of the island with the strongest forces the rebels had raised in any war. All the reports on the industry and drive with which Spanish commanders, especially Martínez Campos himself, and his troops were attempting to keep the rebels away from that success, first in Oriente and then in Camagüey, could not hide the fact that they had failed. The result was consternation in Madrid and real fear in Havana.

Thus it was highly important for both commander and government to show that, although the rebels were across, their first action with loyalist forces was not only a defeat for them but a major one. That this was not true was, as in so many wars, really neither here nor there: it had to be touted as a victory and a significant one. This was immediately clear in Martínez Campos' reply to Suárez Valdés' report on the fighting. Valdés had written at the end of his message:

> General Navarro, in command of the vanguard cavalry and infantry force, has demonstrated once more his bravery and intelligence. I recommend [for recognition] to Y.E. that general, major Izquierdo, captain Guerrero and second-lieutenant Palacios of the Cuba Battalion, who went at the front of the first vanguard companies, Staff Captain García Caveda and cavalry lieutenant Navarro for having seconded the order General Navarro needed to give to the vanguard in the first moments of the action.[2]

The Captain-General was having none of this. He would press for even more recognition of the actions of the troops in order to ensure that the supposed great victory was recognised as such. He quickly wrote back that 'the action at Reforma seems to me very well done. I propose to Y.E. the "writing up" of two major judgements and four more officers plus ninety individuals ... and I charge you in all eastern combats by columns ... [more of the same be done]'. Martínez Campos was clearly trying to show that the troops were fighting well, that success was at hand, and that he and the other commanders were actively engaging the enemy. Little wonder the reaction of British consul-general Gollan expressed in his message to Lord Salisbury of 13 December, 'Meanwhile, if the Spanish forces are not covering themselves with glory they are at least getting covered with honours and rewards. The most trivial action is magnified into a deed of heroism, and medals, and crosses, and promotions are the order of the day.' Clearly few people, and certainly not the British diplomats on the ground in Cuba, were being fooled by the propaganda of the day.[3]

This was the context for the rest of the visit by Churchill and Barnes. The Spanish could no longer claim the rebellion was under control nor that there was not a highly serious threat to colonial rule on the island. Martínez Campos would soon head back to Havana, not only because the threat was rapidly moving past his headquarters in Santa Clara but also because moves to unseat him as Captain-General were afoot in both Havana and Madrid. More and more the name of a much fiercer general, Valeriano Weyler, was being mentioned as the man of the hour and the only person who could save the situation. His reputation for cruelty and a heavy hand dated back to the Ten Years War and made his appointment much feared by many, who felt such methods would only precipitate US intervention in the war. But others felt that only this approach would finally work to bring an end to the conflict and keep Cuba Spanish. Even Martínez Campos, embattled as he was, admitted that such methods might be the only way to win the war, at least temporarily, but that his moral principles did not allow him to conduct war in that manner and that if that was the only way forward, he would prefer to go.[4]

The huge rebel force, under Gómez and Maceo had, the day after the fighting at La Reforma on 2 December, engaged in a major fight of much greater intensity. At Iguará, the Spanish column commanded by Colonel Enrique Segura, with only sixty cavalry and 450 infantry, more or less stumbled into the major rebel force and in a fierce fight proved that, if the Spanish were not being very efficient at bringing the rebel invasion force to a halt, it was not because they were not prepared to try hard to do so. This battle, where Segura had eighteen killed and the rebels counted some fifty-four casualties dead and wounded, is often called the first of the post-Trocha crossing battles because of the small size of the La Reforma fight.[5] This is probably unfair, but the Iguará action was certainly much more of a 'battle'.

After this the rebel cavalry forces, mobile and powerful, struck off along a northern route westward, while the infantry moved more slowly down towards the area of Trinidad where, with the support of rebel elements in the Escambray Mountains, they did not have to be as mobile as when they worked with the cavalry. The main cavalry column moved with maximum speed to the west and north arriving as far as the small northern town of Yaguagay, almost at the north coast, only two days after the La Reforma fighting and the day after the Battle of Iguará. At this rate Spanish efforts in the zone of Las Villas would be very much too little and too late.

Suárez Valdés, however, remained busy with both orders to his commanders and suggestions to his boss. He had little choice but to attempt to organise the defence as best he could. He knew his enemy much better now and made every effort to get his subordinate commanders to coordinate their efforts to intercept the enemy, but with sufficient force, for if Gómez and Maceo were moving together only the largest of bodies of government troops could hope to fight them successfully. He also knew the rough strength of the rebel invasion force, accurately reported to Martínez Campos in his 2 December report as about 4,000 men. This was helpful to higher command as wild rumours of all kinds were circulating that up to 8,000 enemy were in the vicinity.[6]

The columns of generals Aldecoa, Garrich, Luque, Navarro (now without the presence of Suárez Valdés, Churchill and Barnes), and Oliver were now all instructed to concentrate on two fronts as were those of Colonel Segura, who had withdrawn into Iguará with many casualties after the battle he had had with the main rebel cavalry column on 3 December.[7] Two further columns under colonels Galbis and Rubín were to attempt to intercept the infantry of Banderas while the rest of the columns would attempt to do the same with Gómez and Maceo. While it must have seemed in many ways mere wishful thinking to do the latter with the pitiful number of Spanish cavalry, the idea of intercepting Banderas and his dismounted force was a real possibility. It was something of a priority as well since his orders were to burn the cane in the very rich valley of Trinidad and then continue on to link up again with the cavalry column in Matanzas or even Havana province.[8]

The main interest of this book is in the Churchill presence in Cuba and there will be no attempt to discuss the operations of the two armies in the period after his departure on 8 December. Nonetheless, since the Spanish did not suggest, as far as is known, that the two officers should leave their columns after 3 December, it is worth mentioning at least what was going on for their last week on the island even if they had returned to what was from then on only the relative safety of Havana.

Suárez Valdés tried his best to sort out columns of sufficient size to intercept both the Quintín Banderas infantry moving south on Trinidad and the major cavalry column, under the chief rebel commanders, moving west with the intent now of carrying the war right across the breadth of the long island of Cuba. Such was the disarray in the Spanish command that no successful interception was made and, in a few days, Gollan could report to London that the rebels had not only crossed deep into Las Villas but the rebellion had spread 'even to the Province of Matanzas, which is next door to Havana'.[9]

The slow-moving infantry columns of the Spanish forces in Las Villas, eastern Matanzas and even Havana simply could not manoeuvre the rapid cavalry forces of Gómez and Maceo into a battle in which they might be able to stop them or even defeat them entirely. Spanish cavalry was so weak that often it could not even reconnoitre and thus get vital information of the enemy because it was so outnumbered by the enemy's own horsemen that it could not get close enough; in reconnaissance terms, it could not even 'fight for intelligence'. It is true that a large part of the Spanish cavalry's twenty-seven squadrons in the colony were in the central region, and complaints of this state of affairs from both east and west were common. But, even with that, the centre's actual cavalry strength was paltry at best, and would now be shown to be so. Concentrating even a major portion of this cavalry proved impossible for the Spanish at any time during the war, and the cost of this state of affairs was crucial to the war effort.[10]

Churchill and Barnes Leave the Column

As Churchill remarked in his fourth letter to the *Daily Graphic*, with the rebels having been driven from their position, the idea of pursuit made impossible by the dense and impenetrable woods, and the lack of rations, Suárez Valdés decided to call it a day and march down to the village of Jicotea to resupply and rest. In his fifth letter, which is dated ten days later (14 December), he made some telling criticism of the Spanish conduct of the war (which will be discussed in the chapter on Churchill's military analysis) and then described what had happened next:

A long march under a very hot sun brought us at about four o'clock within sight of La [sic] Jicotea. Here were regular houses, also beds, primitive, but welcome. The principal citizen, a well-to-do Spaniard, entertained us with a magnificent banquet. All the Cuban delicacies were represented on his table – 'brains', Guayaba jelly, sausages and English cider. To these we did ample justice. The battalions of Valladolid and Cuba were bivouacking outside, and after dinner was over I went out to take a last look at them. The only street of the village presented a wonderful sight. Round a score of fires were grouped fourteen or fifteen hundred cotton-clad figures, some cleaning their rifles, others cooking their dinners, but all chattering and singing merrily. These men had marched that day about 21 miles over the worst possible ground, carrying their kit and ammunition, and had in addition been fired at for the best part of four hours. They are fine infantry.[11]

The scene was so appealing to Churchill that he made one of his most attractive sketches of it, later published in *The Daily Graphic*. He does not mention it but the moon was full the night after the La Reforma action and the image of the troops relaxing after such a gruelling experience must have simply been too much to resist for a light cavalryman who now, after his training, could at least do basic sketches.

The two British officers had clearly decided to return home now. The reference in his letter to his mother, seen above, saying that he had 'heard enough bullets whistle and hum past to satisfy me for some time to come', written on 6 December, would seem to indicate this. Suárez Valdés refers to this decision being the wish of the subalterns, '*que desean regresar Habana mañana*' (who wish to return to Havana tomorrow) so it is clear that he had not said they should leave, although he may not have been unhappy to see them go, busy as he was and doubtless embarrassed by the dreadful turn of events of recent days.[12] Churchill, perhaps as a good friend of the Spaniards, made no mention of that embarrassment, although it is highly unlikely that he was entirely unaware that things were going very badly despite the supposed importance of the 'victory' of which he was a close observer. The Navarro column was carrying on in the area after the Jicotea rest and would be going after Gómez immediately. The two officers could certainly have tagged along, especially after they had surely got to know the general well during the previous few days. There was no reason they could not stay with his column. In addition, Martínez Campos' introductory letter, on Churchill and Barnes, to his subordinate column commanders mentioned the two officers' access to their columns in the plural, '*para incorporarse a las columnas en operaciones*' (to join the columns on operations) and not in the singular so it would presumably not have been impossible for them to ask to go to another column.[13]

It may have been that their leave was coming to an end by then, but it is more likely that they had done what they had come for, had seen action of a serious kind, and enough of it, and now wished to get home for Christmas. Certainly their leave would not have been over until well after the Christmas holidays and neither the regiment nor the army would have been troubled by them staying to see a bit more action before returning to England. The day of their departure from Liverpool, 2 November, was a Saturday, so presumably their ten-week full leave would have begun on Monday 4 November. Thus they would not have been due back, leaving aside the undoubted additional Christmas leave, until at the earliest 13 January 1896. It is interesting to note that as late as 20 November, in a letter written from the Hotel Inglaterra in Havana to Bourke Cockran, Churchill wrote that they intended to be on the island until 16 December, showing that it was not their original intention to return to England so soon or to have the Christmas holiday with their families since such a possibility would not have been available given the time needed to move from Havana to Tampa, on to New York and then Liverpool and London.[14]

They did not do so, however, and chose instead to travel with Suárez Valdés the next day, 3 December, to the key pivot of the Trocha, the town of Ciego de Ávila, whose entrance Churchill sketched for his newspaper, though misspelling the name. The ride was quickly accomplished, the town being only about 15 miles from Jicotea. Lunch was taken, at least by local tradition, in the still attractive and well-maintained central Spanish military headquarters of the day, and Churchill and Barnes got a look at this part of the defensive line about which they had heard so much. Given the urgency of the situation, the general had a gunboat ready in the port of Júcaro, the southernmost point of the Trocha Júcaro–Morón, to speed him to Tunas de Zaza, from whence he would return to Sancti Spiritus, despite Martínez Campos' instructions not to seek battle with the rebel main force, but rather to concentrate on coordinating the columns doing so, and to keep military movement through that city to a minimum because of the increasing problem of *vómito negro* there. The two British officers were invited to make the first leg of their trip back to Havana in his company first in a military train from Ciego de Ávila to Júcaro and then in the gunboat to Tunas de Zaza.

The train journey gave them an even better opportunity to see the defensive line and through the hot afternoon they crossed the flat plain through which it ran (and where its substantial ruins remain to this day), arriving without incident at the dismal port town of Júcaro in the late afternoon. That evening they boarded their first of two Spanish *cañoneros*, the *Cometa*, one of the Alerta class of such vessels. This very small naval ship, built in Scotland and having only just arrived in Cuba, was on transport, support and signals duty between the various ports of central-southern Cuba, Cienfuegos, Tunas de Zaza and Júcaro, which were particularly active at this time, for reasons that are obvious. It had a complement of twenty-two men and was quite well armed, having one Nordenfeld quick-firing 42mm gun and one 37mm machine gun.[15] Stood to for this duty only a few days after it entered service in Havana on 25 November, the ship set out that evening for Tunas de Zaza where it arrived at 11 p.m. The trip cannot have been all that comfortable as even the new admiral commanding the Apostadero de La Habana (naval forces in all of Cuba), Admiral Navarro, said that in this vessel, 'entering the wardroom is like one putting a letter into a letter box'.[16] Despite this, and Churchill's famous dislike of sailing, the trip could not have been that bad as it was soon over, the ship being capable of a respectable if unexceptional 11.1 knots per hour, and he does not refer to it at all in either his articles for the *Daily Graphic* or his letters home to his mother.

The officers remained in Tunas de Zaza for three hours that night embarking again in the wee hours of 4 December, 2 a.m., for Cienfuegos, with a gunboat placed at their disposal by the general. This time they were to travel in the *Ardilla*, a sister ship of the *Cometa*, also built in Britain and recently arrived and taken up duties on the south coast. The Spanish interest in making the most in propaganda terms of the British officers' visit had, if anything, increased as the situation became worse over the time of their stay. Thus it should not surprise us to see the *Diario de la Marina* picking up their traces in its edition of 7 December saying the two officers had been aboard the *Ardilla* and the *Cometa* with the general and that 'they carry with them an infinity of objects taken from the insurgents and at the same time are very satisfied with the behaviour they have been able to observe of our troops as well as their way of fighting'.[17] The implication, that the British had seen the Spanish victory and were impressed with it, cannot have been a useless one for the Spanish authorities to have visible to those they wished to have interpreted favourably what was happening in Las Villas.

Suárez Valdés in any case returned to Sancti Spiritus leaving Tunas de Zaza at noon that day, determined to find a way to outsmart Gómez and drive the rebels back east. Churchill and Barnes meanwhile continued their journey back to Havana. However, such a trip involved them automatically in train travel via Santa Clara, which they had been invited to visit by an important landowner soon after their arrival in Cuba some two weeks previously. Given the train timings, they arrived during the day on the 4 December and stayed at the relatively posh hotel named for that city and located on the main square, now Parque Vidal, at the centre of town. Local lore is very clear on this stop, although it is not mentioned by Churchill at all except in a reference to meeting the gentleman in question in a letter written to Winston's mother on the train out of Havana on 21 November.

According to a not terribly serious article written much later, Churchill and Barnes stayed at the Hotel Santa Clara and their names figure prominently in the register of names of guests therein for the night of 4/5 December. The article is so full of errors that it is tempting to not reference it, but, given the importance of the issue at hand in order to follow accurately Churchill's movements, it is useful to know of it and to work with its findings, insofar as possible. On their way to the war they had met the powerful sugar farmer Vicente González Abreu and were struck by his industry and importance. He had invited them to visit his sugar mill and establishment, which they apparently did and were duly impressed by it. At the hotel people flocked to see the young Winston, although the article does not say why he was so well known or why he might be so interesting to the locals. But the article actually names several young people who came to see him, so it is at least interesting to that extent.

Certainly the loyalist portion of the population, rarely without importance in a town of Santa Clara's size although often not numerically impressive, would have known of his being in the neighbourhood through the official media. Others not so well informed might merely have known that González Abreu felt it would be worthwhile to meet him. The prestige of England may have done the rest. The article is otherwise of little interest being short on accuracy throughout. It has Churchill sent by the Queen and her government to Cuba as 'an officer of great prestige as a war correspondent …

wise and valiant for having participated as a war correspondent in other conflicts'. Of course Churchill was not sent by his Queen or government, had
never been a war correspondent before, and was certainly not known yet as
either wise or valiant. The author of the article, Isaac Pitrulla, makes the firm
statement that the Spanish sent him to Sancti Spiritus so he would not see
the 'real fighting' around Santa Clara. He was, according to this, 'deliberately
manipulated by the Spanish so that when he returned to England he would
write a report totally unfavourable to the Cuban forces'.[18]

The author, however, does seem to have seen Churchill's signature in the
hotel register and for that alone the article is of interest. This is because it
helps answer the question as to when Churchill got to Santa Clara, whether
he spent the night of the 4/5 December there, and when he might have left
for, and thus arrived at, Havana. It is very likely that he did indeed spend the
night in question in that city and left the next day for the capital, arriving
on 5 December. It helps but it does not necessarily give the last word on
this matter.

This stay produced one more coincidence for it so happens that Martínez
Campos had chosen that same day, 5 December, to return to the capital on
the obvious business of damage control for the crisis as it was developing,
not only in Havana but in Madrid, and which was occasioning increasing
calls for his resignation and replacement. This led to another meeting with
Churchill, on the train in which they were all travelling, where he told the
young officer that Suárez Valdés and he had recommended to the Queen
Regent that he and Barnes be awarded the Red Cross of Military Merit for
their behaviour during their time with the column in the areas of Sancti
Spiritus and Ciego de Ávila.

It could not have been better news. Not only was he to have a medal, but
it was to be for meritorious conduct under fire, just the sort of thing that
he was certain would attract the kind of attention to his person that would
be useful for political purposes later in life. And, in this regard, not only was
he to have it, but it would also be announced widely as Spanish decorations
always were, and in the press. While he pretended to downplay it in his letters to his mother, he was obviously very pleased with this turn of events.

The next night he wrote to his mother from Havana's Hotel Inglaterra:

I can't tell you the pleasure it gives me to be able to write and tell you that
we have got back safely. There were moments during the last week when

I realised how rash we had been in risking our lives merely in search of adventure. However, it all turned up trumps and here we are ... the General recommended us for the Red Cross – a Spanish decoration given to officers & coming in the train yesterday – by chance I found Marshall Campos & his staff & was told that it would be sent to us in due course.

Churchill and the Press after Return from the Column

The article referred to already on the return of Churchill and Barnes from the war zone was only one of the many dealing with the fight at La Reforma and the two officers' role was a minor, although not meaningless, part of a campaign to convince the public that things were not as bad as they seemed and that victory was still somehow around the corner for the loyalist side. If the British youths could come back encumbered with booty from the victory, the press too could do its best to give the most rosy view of what was taking place, which was, in this crucial moment of Cuban history, the invasion of the rich west by insurgent forces of a size never before assembled in Cuba.

The Spanish government and the *integrista* press would now take that situation and do their best to make it seem as if the rebels were deeply weakened by Suárez Valdés' attack, that the enemy had been soundly bested in a major battle from which he had barely recovered, that the invasion had at least been blunted, that the Spanish forces still had the initiative, and that victory was still at hand if the public would merely remain calm and continue to support the forces of order. Only in a note dated 1 December, but released on 3 December, did the *Diario de la Marina* refer to the crossing of the Trocha by Maceo on 29 November and this remained unconfirmed by the paper. Even then the news was issued in an edition of the paper highlighting infinitely more the arrival of thousands more reinforcements for the army in Cuba from Spain than any possibility that Maceo had crossed the line.

The next day, with dateline Santa Clara on the headline, the *Diario* admitted indirectly that Maceo had got across by printing an article on the action at La Reforma which followed the highly favourable report sent in two days later by Suárez Valdés, which we have seen. The main headline was 'Santa Clara' and the short résumé was that Suárez Valdés, along with

General Navarro, had fought the 'bands' (*partidas*) of Gómez and Maceo on 2 December at La Reforma 'causing them heavy casualties, taking their positions and camps, and pursuing them to Trilladeritas'. Loyalist forces had had only seven wounded despite the fact that the column was composed of only 1,200 men against 4,000 rebels. The full article came under the title 'Official News: Important Actions'. It followed the Valdés text closely and even included the praise of the commanding general for Churchill and Barnes: 'General Suárez Valdés makes great praise [*grandes elogios de*] of the serenity and valour with which the officers of the British Army, Messrs Spencer Churchill and Reginald Barnes have followed the incidents of the operations and the action, at which they were at his side', carrying on to say that 'The enemy has come out very much hurt as is demonstrated in the first place, by the 12 clear indications of his losses left on the field of combat, as in the horses with their saddles that were recovered, as well as several dead who were seen.'[19]

Similar reports appeared in the *Diario del Ejército* and other official media and in the various organs of the *integrista* press. At no time was any space given over to a discussion of the strategic consequences and wider meaning of the fact that a large rebel army had for the first time ever crossed the Trocha and was advancing on the capital. Needless to say, the Battle of Iguará was treated by the media during the young officers' stay in a similarly optimistic way. With no Spanish, it is perhaps not surprising that Churchill made no mention of this state of affairs either to his mother or to his paper, although perhaps he felt he did not have to, given his comments on Spanish censorship in his first 'letter' over two weeks earlier.

The international press was, however, not to be so easily taken in. Several reporters and more than one editor, doubtless miffed, knew from Churchill's earlier stay at the Hotel Inglaterra before his joining the column, that he had been able to actually go out with the army and see operations in the field, and not just report the latest rumours from the bar of the hotel. There was also probably more than just a rumour of a 'scoop' by Churchill about to appear since his first letter had been sent to London some two weeks earlier and was about to come out in print in a week's time. In any case, something happened among the press correspondents in Havana and Churchill must have been at least in some way responsible. On 3 December, Charles Michelson, correspondent for *The Journal* of New York and *The Examiner* of San Francisco, petitioned the Captain-General for 'a pass of safe conduct that would facilitate my free transit to the theatre of war in my role as correspondent for those two newspapers'. The request appears to have been granted the very next day.

No sooner was Michelson given his permission than William Francis Manning, correspondent of the *New York Times*, asked on 4 December for a similar 'safe conduct pass' to go the theatre of war. This appears to have been approved on 5 December.[20] To what extent this fire placed under some correspondents was the result of the breaking news of the crossing of the Trocha and the first actions after that event, or was rather the only possible reaction of editors to the idea that one paper seemed to be able to get its correspondent to the front while others could not, is not known. It may be related to both factors. But it is tempting to think that Churchill was somehow behind the dash to send reporters to the front instead of having them sit in hotel bars. Whatever the context for the decision, and despite the favourable replies from Spanish headquarters to the two American correspondents, it does not appear that either of them was able to actually go with units of the army and see the fighting. Instead, it appears they merely got closer to the actual fighting as it was finally coming closer to Havana, and not needing Havana to go to it, in order to know what was happening. The only 'scoop' to be had was Churchill's alone.

The Spanish opposition press at home was likewise not convinced by the positive spin put on things. Many papers had negative reactions and even the *Correspondencia Militar*, a thoroughly pro-army journal, began to lambaste the conduct of the war.[21]

The 'Dark' Hours: What did he do in Havana on 5–8 December?

Assuming that Churchill and Barnes returned to Havana, as is highly probable, on 5 December, and that they only sailed on the return journey to Tampa on 8 December, it would be interesting to know what they got up to during that brief stay in the exciting and now excited capital of the colony. But there is simply no reference to any activity there over these two and a half days and nothing apparently produced as work either except for a sketch Churchill did of the Captain-General inspecting one of the regiments that had come as reinforcements over those days.

Conjecture is, as so often with Churchill's undocumented and unre-searched times, alluring. Two young officers, with at least some money in their pockets (although colonial Havana was not a cheap place to live or play), having just gone through a death-defying series of events, surrounded by women who in Latin America are often billed as the most beautiful in the region, and, at least in Churchill's case, away from home and home country for the first time as a free adult, must have had many temptations thrust in their way.

There would in any case have been much to observe on the military front. The arrival and settling down of some 25,000 more troops was a major event, even for a garrison city like Havana in the middle of a war. Warships dominated the harbour. Tourism, despite the war, had not entirely died since newspapers abroad constantly harped on about the way the city was spared so much of its impact. And, though this was still an era long before mass tourism, visitors, chiefly but not only from the United States, had already begun to make the short trip to the island. Correspondents from many media sources were present in many of the hotels.

Churchill may even have met Lieutenant Félix de Vidal, whose exact dates in Havana and in Cuba we do not have. Vidal was a French army lieutenant who also went out with a Spanish column to see the fighting at first hand, though little has yet been found on this officer and his stay on the island. He appears to have been in his early to mid-30s, and to have arrived also in late 1895. He was certainly authorised by the French army to be there and was officially termed an *agregado* or attached officer. Hence his status would have been more official than that of the British officers. This may reflect France's more pro-Spanish posture on the rebellion than that of Britain or most other foreign countries. There is a photograph of him in a Spanish book of the period, in a uniform doubtless very similar to that of the British subalterns, highly appropriate for the climate and conditions in which he was to work. He was attached to yet another mobile column commanded by General Suárez Valdés and was probably present at the action at Vereda Nueva in early January 1896, a small vil-lage in Havana province taken by the Liberation Army under Gómez and Maceo. This must also have been embarrassing for the Spanish as here the garrison surrendered to the insurgents and 150 rifles were captured. Fortunately for the Spanish, Lieutenant Vidal, we are certain, stayed long enough to also witness a few days later the action at Santa Cruz de los

Pinos, as a member of Suárez Valdés' staff, an action that went much better for his hosts.[22]

Even if he did not meet the only foreign officer on similar duties in Havana of whom we know anything, he would certainly not have been bored. His stories would have been in great demand at the bar of the Inglaterra and also the source of both professional and personal envy on the part of many people there, especially the correspondents. The opera season was in full swing at this time of year and his hotel was only a few metres away from the Gran Teatro, the splendid opera house built in 1837 and one of the compulsory stops for big European stars and companies on their way from New York to Buenos Aires for the two main seasons in the Americas. Opera was also given at the Teatro Payret, across the street. Without Spanish the active theatre scene of Havana would, however, probably have offered little appeal. In addition, the Cuban musical scene, though not as active as today, was still impressive and Havana was its epicentre.

The neighbourhood would also have been alive with hotels, bars, houses of ill repute and all sorts of other entertainment especially aimed at the large army, naval and merchant marine temporary presence in the city, a tradition going back at least three centuries. How he would have used his time is thus anyone's guess but it was probably not exclusively for work. There was, however, something of a ceremony on 6 December when he was presented with his medal. Though not ratified by the Queen Regent through War Minister Azcárraga until 25 January, the reward came with the citation from Her Majesty:

> I have been notified by His Excellency the Commanding General of the 5th Military District [Suárez Valdés] of the distinguished comportment observed by you in the military action held on the 2nd of this month in Guayos against the joint forces of Máximo Gómez and Maceo … [grant] Red Cross of the Order of Military Merit, First Class, of which I notify you for your knowledge and satisfaction.[23]

While the lowest rank of the order, it was handsome, of red enamel and, most importantly, it was a medal and Churchill had won it. This was what he had come for and there it was. And, though officially banned by the War Office from wearing it on military uniform, Churchill, especially as he became more senior, increasingly forgot this ban and wore it anyway.

There is also confusion as to when Churchill and Barnes actually sailed from Cuba, again on the *Olivette* to Tampa. On 7 December, Churchill gave a short informal interview to the *Diario de la Marina*:

We have had the pleasure of greeting Sir Spencer Churchill, who after a trip to the interior of the island, where he stayed for several days accompanying the column of General Suárez Valdés in its latest operations, arrived yesterday in Havana. The distinguished gentleman said that the duty of delicacy imposed on him an absolute reserve over the events which he had witnessed feeling that, as a foreigner, he was not in a position to emit any opinion on matters which, by their nature, should remain with those with an interest in them, without there being any deduction from this, in the slightest way, that he could have any other conception of the Spanish character than that which it had always been able to win. As a result, he told us, he carried away most pleasant memories of the gentlemanly way in which he had been treated by General Suárez Valdés and the attention he had received from all the officers and authorities in Cuba, and that he admires the work that such a campaign imposes on the heroic and long-suffering soldier and on the officers in a country where roads are so bad and where they are obliged to pursue without rest an enemy who knows so well the ground. Mister Churchill leaves this afternoon on the Olivette for the United States ...[24]

Neither Churchill nor Barnes left that afternoon.

The Return to a 'short but gratifying controversy'[25]

If the press were after him for interviews in Havana, this was nothing compared to what awaited him in the United States and on his return home. As mentioned, the press in both countries had a distinct pro-insurgent bias and it was known for some time that Churchill was using his leave to go to Cuba, on a basis not always understood on Fleet Street or elsewhere in the English-speaking world's then burgeoning press.

No sooner did the ship dock in Tampa on 9 December than the press was after this son of a famous British politician who had come so far to be with the Spanish in their campaign on the nearby island. Indeed, Tampa, with

Key West, were the key centres for Cuban workers in the tobacco industry who put the finishing touches on many of the famous Cuban cigars of the day and there was a special interest in Cuban affairs among the population in both towns. The first known reference to Churchill's planned activities in Cuba had appeared in the US press as early as 20 November, the day of his actual arrival in Havana. Thus the local press would have been aware of his being there from very early on even if they had missed the reports of his departure for Cuba on 9 November. In a seven-line item that day in the *New York Times* titled 'Randolph Churchill's Son in Cuba', the startlingly inaccurate phrase announced the news that Martínez Campos had accepted the young officer's services 'in the Spanish Army in Cuba'.[26]

The *New York Times* had shown its interest in Churchill's activities on the eve of his second passing through the US as well. On 6 December, an article said Churchill 'repeatedly found himself in the thick of the action' in recent fighting, and told of how both he and Barnes had deserved 'especial mention' for their 'valorous conduct' in action. It was indeed the medal for this conduct that seemed to spark most of the controversy especially as it seemed so clear that it proved the assertion of some that the two officers were actually fighting with the Spanish and not just observing the war. Some papers were even suggesting, in the light of the current Anglo-American crisis over the Venezuela–British Guiana boundary, that the two officers were on a secret mission of the British government to yet again defy the Monroe Doctrine and further contribute to improper British influence in the Americas, with even the suggestion that they were somehow helping to train the Spanish in how best to beat the insurgents.

The first skirmish with the press took place during the very short stopover in Tampa. Churchill told the press there, 'I have not even fired a revolver. I am a member of General Valdez's [sic] staff by courtesy only.'[27] A second took place after their second thirty-six-hour journey by train in America, when the two officers stopped in New York, staying in Cockran's flat again, though he had just sailed to Europe. It is not clear whether Cockran actually arranged a luxury cabin for the two officers for their return from Tampa to New York as he had been able to do on their way south the month before, and as Churchill had asked him in his letter of 20 November. But they certainly did not suffer in that city as they stayed in his flat from Wednesday to Friday of that week before taking ship on Saturday. Given who they now knew there, it is certain they were also well treated on this trip.

Arriving at the quayside just minutes before the *Etruria* sailed for their return journey to Liverpool, Winston gave an impromptu press conference on the Cunard Line pier where, as in Tampa, he denied the accusations that he had 'fought' with the Spanish, saying that he had only carried a pistol and even that with strict orders that he could only use it in self-defence, the usual practice for observer officers.

There may be more politics in this than at first meets the eye. In any case, the newspaper magnate Joseph Pulitzer, Cockran's friend and client, was the key man to influence at the *New York World*, which raced into print the very next day in defence of Cockran's guest, saying that Churchill could not possibly help train Spanish veterans, nor was he part of a sinister British plot, 'knowing only the amount of strategy necessary for the duties of a second lieutenant', and that the trip was only the result of 'youthful enthusiasm'.[28] The *New York Herald* also weighed in, on the actual day of the meeting on the pier, agreeing without equivocation with Churchill's statement that the alleged political significance of the trip was 'rot'. This paper was one of the few that had always taken Cuban political propaganda with a grain of salt.[29]

The reception at home, however, was not to be so smooth. News of the good conduct of the two officers had reached London's official circles early via Sir Henry Drummond Wolff who, clearly delighted, sent Lord Salisbury the news in a despatch in which he spoke of the Queen Regent's desire for him to see news of 'the defeat of the Insurgents in Cuba under Maceo and Máximo Gómez'. He continued:

> The reason for which Her Majesty the Queen Regent wished me to see the communication was to let me know the terms in which General Valdez [sic], who in command of the advance guard 'notes with satisfaction the coolness exhibited by the officers of the British Army Messrs Spencer Churchill and Reginald Barnes during the incidents of the operations and the battle at which they were present at his side.'[30]

We have of course already seen references to this, as well as to the original report. However, it is clear that once again the Spanish wished to make the most of the British connection here and show London that good things could come out of British support. This message from the ambassador in Madrid arrived just as the controversy over Churchill's having been in Cuba was heating up.

This is the only likeness of Churchill actually done in Cuba during his stay. It is not known if it was drawn from life during an interview or from a photograph. It is an anonymous piece of Spanish propaganda work of the time.

A well-known photograph of Churchill in 1895 in the full dress uniform of the 4th Hussars.

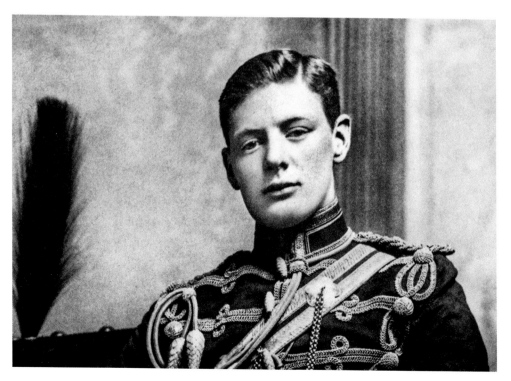

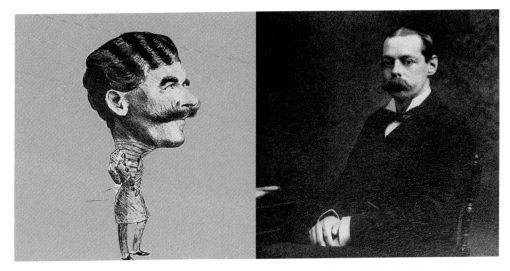

Colonel John Brabazon (left), Churchill's first commanding officer, who backed him in his bid to join his cavalry regiment; and (right) Lord Randolph Churchill, who wanted him to join the infantry.

Mrs Everest (left), perhaps the most beloved woman in Churchill's early life and whose photo hung in his office even during the Second World War. And (right) Lady Randolph Churchill, Jennie, Winston's American mother who needed convincing in order to back the Cuba project.

Lieutenant Reginald Barnes (Reggie) who was easily convinced to join in the adventure. (Photo courtesy of Queen's Royal Hussars)

Through a truly exceptional series of coincidences, any possible opposition from Lord Wolseley as commander-in-chief was avoided.

Three contemporary excerpts from Havana's pro-Spanish *Diario de la Marina*, from the editions of 3, 12, and 20 November 1895, showing, respectively, the officers' departure from Liverpool, arrival in New York and arrival in Havana.

Major-General Sir Edward Chapman, Director of Military Intelligence at the War Office, gave Churchill his first official military task beyond regimental duties.

Sir Henry Drummond Wolff, ambassador in Madrid, an old friend of the Churchill family, played a key role.

Marcelo Azcárraga Palmero

(Manila, 1832 - Madrid, 1915)

General Marcelo Azcárraga Palmero, Minister of War, accepted speedily Drummond Wolff's request.

Churchill in tropical uniform, seen here in India some months after the Cuba trip.

S. S. "Olivette," Cuba and Port Tampa Service.

The American passenger ship *Olivette* carried the two young officers from Tampa to Havana. (Author's collection)

The Morro Castle, guardian of the harbour of Havana, and first sight of Cuba for the young officers. (Glen Hartle)

The Gran Hotel Inglaterra, where Winston and Reggie stayed both before and after their experience at the front, shown with one storey more than in 1895 but in other respects looking much as it did. (Glen Hartle)

The Palace of the Captain's General of Cuba, in wartime used as their military headquarters. It is not certain if General Arderíus received the two officers here or in his own building next door. (Glen Hartle)

Major-General José Arderíus y García, second in command in Cuba, was the first Spanish officer the two Englishmen encountered. He hoped to make the most out of the propaganda opportunity presented by their visit.

After their re-routed train journey from Havana, the two officers alighted at the train station in Santa Clara, looking today much as it did then. (Glen Hartle)

Captain–General Arsenio Martínez Campos y Antón received Winston and Reggie at his headquarters across the square from the train station.

Martínez Campos' headquarters in Santa Clara. (Glen Hartle)

The famed trocha or trench line dividing eastern from western Cuba and centrepiece of the Spanish defence system. This photograph shows a typical blockhouse though slightly improved from how it would have looked in 1895. (Glen Hartle)

The train station in Cienfuegos where the two officers arrived on 21 November, and the city from which they sailed the next morning, seen today but with virtually no change from 1895. (Glen Hartle)

The Tunas de Zaza railway station virtually unchanged until today from whence the two officers finally departed for Sancti Spiritus. (Glen Hartle)

A nearly contemporary painting of the main pier at Tunas de Zaza, at which Churchill and Barnes alighted. (Photograph by Glen Hartle)

The Escambray Mountains as seen from the train between Tunas de Zaza and Sancti Spiritus, a zone judged by Churchill to be 'The most dangerous and disturbed in the whole island'. (Glen Hartle)

Again in the Spanish colonial style, the railway station at Sancti Spiritus where Winston and Reggie arrived to meet the Suárez Valdés column. (Glen Hartle)

The Fonda el Correo, where Churchill and Barnes stayed in the town Winston described as 'a forsaken place', is no longer extant. But the rest of the buildings he would have known on San Rafael Street are mostly still there. (Glen Hartle)

Divisional General Álvaro Suárez Valdés, commander of the column with which Barnes and Churchill travelled to their baptism of fire, described by Winston as 'a man of great courage'.

A scene typical of the countryside through which the column marched. (Glen Hartle)

Remains of the 'road' along which the column travelled from Sancti Spiritus to Arroyo Blanco. (Glen Hartle)

The first view of Arroyo Blanco from the road on which the column was travelling. (Glen Hartle)

The main Spanish military building in Arroyo Blanco, pictured here, was used for headquarters, logistics and command and control requirements. Father Benito's manse is to the left, just out of the picture. (Glen Hartle)

Máximo Gómez, the exceptional commander of the insurgent forces in both major wars for independence.

General José García Navarro,
commander of the advanced guard of
the column.

The troops of Navarro who so impressed Churchill are seen here in Colón some two
weeks after La Reforma battle. It is not clear whether these are from the battalion of the
Cazadores de Valladolid or the Regimiento de Cuba.

The route taken by the column upon leaving Arroyo Blanco on Churchill's 21st birthday. (Glen Hartle)

Antonio Maceo Grajales, second in command of the rebel army, commanded directly the force with which Churchill's column was engaged at La Reforma, and was only a few hundred metres from Winston during the fighting.

The river crossing point where the Spanish attack aimed to disrupt the withdrawal of the impedimenta and prevent their joining the main rebel column as it moved west. (Glen Hartle)

The Spanish column's lead battalion, the Regimiento de Cuba, deployed on this ground and came under rebel fire from the slopes in the distance. (Glen Hartle)

Churchill's own sketch, improved by A.L. Crowther at *The Daily Graphic*, depicting the deployment and firing by the Spanish guns on the rebels at La Reforma, 2 December 1895.

The centre of the insurgent 'position' is now marked by a monument to all three of the battles that took place at La Reforma. (Glen Hartle)

Only a few small houses remain of the Jicotea of Churchill's time. (Glen Hartle)

Spanish central headquarters at Ciego de Avila where almost certainly Suárez Valdés lunched with the two officers before heading out of the war zone. (Glen Hartle)

Ruins of one of the blockhouses Churchill would have passed on the rail line between Ciego de Avila and the port of Júcaro. (Glen Hartle)

An Alerta class gunboat like those on which Churchill and Barnes travelled from Júcaro to Tunas de Zaza and Cienfuegos on the journey back to Havana.

The locomotives used by the Spanish on the trains from Tunas de Zaza to Sancti Spiritus, seen here at their base the year of Churchill's visit. (Photo courtesy of Antonieta Jiménez)

The Hotel Santa Clara where it seems very likely Churchill and Barnes stayed the night of 4/5 December 1895 on the way back to the capital. (Courtesy of Arnaldo Díaz)

Lieutenant Félix de Vidal, the only other foreign attached officer serving alongside the Spanish during 1895–96. Note the similarity between his tropical uniform and that of Churchill.

The Cruz Roja por Mérito Militar, the medal awarded to both officers by the Queen Regent in recognition of their behaviour under fire.

A Second World War musical poster and song sheet with Winston's cigar in the place of honour. Winston did not get to know cigars in Cuba but he did begin a lifelong love affair with the exceptional Cuban examples. (Author's collection)

On top of the more recent 'Churchill' cigar is seen a Romeo y Julieta, one of his own favourites at the time. (Glen Hartle)

Father Benito, the village priest, lived in this manse and may well have received the two young officers during their time in Arroyo Blanco. (Glen Hartle)

Frequently termed 'the Churchill Table' by those inclined to believe in local mythology, it is nonetheless quite possible that Churchill did indeed dine with Father Benito in this room and at this table. (Glen Hartle)

Given Churchill's life-long love affair with his bath, it is also possible that local legend is right in saying that he took advantage of the priest's bathtub while in Arroyo Blanco. (Glen Hartle)

This 1895 print shows clearly an officer in the tropical uniform of the 4th Hussars of the day. This is doubtless the uniform Churchill wore in Cuba.

This stamp shows the 'jubo', the Cuban snake to which Churchill refers as a means to conduct the torching campaign of the sugar cane fields by the rebels. There is no truth to this story.

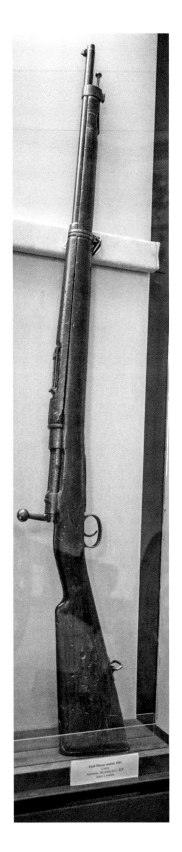

The much-respected 1893 Mauser (Argentine model). It was this rifle that fired the round Winston had in part come to check out for the War Office. British Imperial forces were to face both rifle and round four years later in the Boer War.

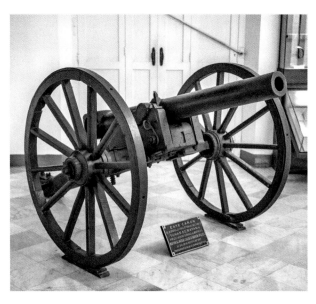

The Spanish used almost exclusively the Krupp 75mm mountain gun for their operations in Cuba. It was this gun that the artillerymen of the Suárez Valdés used at La Reforma.

Only some of the many different rifles and muskets used by the rebel army are seen here.

The railway station at Santo Domingo where a pilot engine and an armoured car were added to Churchill's train. From here on in the journey to the front insurgent action against such trains could be expected. (Glen Hartle)

The fearsome Cuban machete, respected not only by Churchill but by all ranks of the Spanish Army who at any time had to face it in battle. This one is in the museum of the Palace of the Captain's General in Havana and belonged to General Antonio Maceo. (Glen Hartle)

The bed in the Cabinet War Rooms in London in which Churchill took his famous siestas and was thus enabled to carry on working late into the night.

On 6 December, *The Star* published a short article on Churchill in Cuba. Full of inaccuracies but with some interesting points, it read:

> Mr Winston Churchill, eldest son of the late Lord Randolph Churchill, who has joined the army of Marshal Campos, and was present at a battle, is in an awkward position. If America were to recognise the Cuban rebels, as may happen, Mr Churchill would be in the position of one who has broken our Foreign Enlistment Act, and has therefore no claim on this country, while his status at international law would be that of a land pirate who fights without proper authorisation. The fact, however, is that Mr Churchill, like his father, has an anxiety to distinguish himself, but his leaning is towards romance rather than to a Parliamentary career. His mother would have preferred that he should not risk his life on such a harebrained expedition, but he has a will of his own.[31]

Harsh as *The Star* was, on the same day *The Sun* went one better, dripping with sarcasm:

> British officers are appearing in a new role – that of supporters of tyranny. We learn from the not too reliable Spanish despatches that Lieutenants Winston Churchill and Barnes of the 4th (Queen's Own) Hussars conducted themselves valorously against the Cuban insurgents. This is no doubt excellent practice in warfare, but why so far afield? The Sultan is having a lot of trouble with his Armenian subjects just now and Messrs. Churchill and Barnes might be able to render him valuable assistance.[32]

That same day the *Glasgow Daily Record* showed that a much more positive spin could be put on events, even if Churchill had actually taken part in fighting. In a short article entitled 'Lord Churchill's Son in Cuba', it read:

> A pleasing flutter has been excited in military and political circles alike, by the report that Mr Winston Churchill, son of the late Lord Randolph Churchill, took a part on behalf of the Spanish forces against the insurgents in Cuba. I saw Mr Churchill … he looked a young man, barely of age, of medium height and somewhat dark complexion. His expression was strong and determined, though not remarkably intellectual. He looked, indeed, a youth of whom one might fairly predict a successful

military career. If the report as to his presence in Cuba should be confirmed, he will be acknowledged to have given remarkable proofs of
having inherited the spirits of independence and dash of his father.[33]

With this sort of thing being written about him, the 21-year-old second-
lieutenant had little reason to complain of the controversies spilling out. As
Carlo D'Este suggests, the press, on both sides of the Atlantic, had found 'a
talkative and quotable Englishman who thrived in the limelight of public
attention'.[34] The next day the negative side appeared again when, clearly
with little knowledge of the case, the *Eastern Morning News* editorialised:

> Mr Churchill's presence in Cuba was notified by me a week or two ago,
> and the papers are just beginning to realise the fact and the curious inter-
> national problems it may create. The young man has gone to the West
> Indies on a summer tour, and though he holds a commission in the British
> Army, he has been anxious to see a little fighting. Apparently, his wish has
> been gratified, but difficulties are sure to arise, and Lord Wolseley will
> probably order [him] to return at once and report himself. A Churchill is
> sure to do something erratic.[35]

The *Newcastle Leader*, not to be outdone, did more of the same:

> If it be true that Mr Winston Churchill, the eldest son of the late Lord
> Randolph Churchill, has been gratifying his desire for military glory by
> interfering in the struggle between Spain and Cuba, we shall probably hear
> a good deal more about it before long. Mr Churchill holds Her Majesty's
> commission in the army, and all sorts of embarrassing complications may
> result for his characteristically reckless action. Sensible people will wonder
> what motive could possibly impel a British officer to mix himself up in
> a dispute with the merits of which he has absolutely nothing to do.
> Mr Churchill was supposed to have gone to the West Indies for a holi-
> day, he having obtained leave of absence from his regimental duties at the
> beginning of October for that purpose. Spending a holiday fighting other
> people's battles is rather an extraordinary proceeding, even for a Churchill.[36]

Too many papers chimed in to quote but most were wrong on one point or
another. Obviously Churchill had the approval of his commanding officer

and the army commander before he left, if not for his press reporting, at least for his visit and his stay with the army in the field. And it is clear that he did not fight for the Spanish, although he might have been tempted to do so. There was also doubtless some professional envy in some of the attacks, since the *Daily Graphic* had obviously stolen a march on many of the British newspapers by having a war correspondent on the spot, and this increased when, from 13 December, Churchill's 'letters from the front' began to appear in print.

He did not wait to begin fighting back. *The Morning Post* published an article entitled 'The Cuban Revolt: An Englishman's Experiences', date-lined New York, Sunday, 8 December, which included Churchill's reply in a cable of the day before to the accusations:

> The idea of trouble resulting from my visit here, as suggested by a London paper, is absurd. I came to witness the war. There is no truth in the statement that I have taken part in the fighting against the Cubans … When I arrived in Cuba I proceeded to the front immediately. Marshal Campos gave me letters for General Valdez [sic]. I took a leaky steamer bound for Sancti Spiritus, where, on arrival, I met General Valdez, who soon started for the front … Many Spaniards and horses were killed …. This skirmish is called the battle of La Reforma.

The newspaper added:

> He [Churchill] has been following the war simply to gain experience, as an ambitious and energetic young soldier should; he has taken no part in the fighting … we are all grateful to the young officer … at length the outside world learns something authentic about the struggle – an opinion not only honest but probably judicious.[37]

On 19 December *The Glasgow Times* joined the controversy with a short supportive note (and drawing) on Churchill, saying, 'He is a bright young fellow with a pleasant face. His career will be watched with interest as that of the first of the generation growing up which is the result of the Anglo-American marriages of the last twenty years'.[38] That career would of course in the end be watched by many others with no such interest.

The pro-Spanish press in Cuba was not without its controversies regarding Churchill's visit either. There are continued references to his presence well after he had gone, most of them not entirely favourable. This reflected what was happening in Madrid and with Drummond Wolff. The army which had been his host felt sharply the comments of a critical kind made by Churchill and apparently its command elements were especially miffed that he had suggested the Spanish were not killing many of the enemy and were expending too many resources for the results they were getting. They also followed and commented upon the debate in the United States press about what Churchill and Barnes had been doing in the colony and were particularly pleased when there were favourable references by 'Teniente Churchill' to Spanish military virtues like valour and constancy and unfavourable ones to the insurgents such as their tendency to run away from a fight.[39]

The *Diario del Ejército*, for example, the paper which had made the biggest fuss over the two officers' arrival, seemed particularly hurt by his comments to the foreign press on the seeming use of 200,000 rounds to kill an enemy soldier instead of the traditional idea of 200 even though it was more than pleased when Churchill appeared to suggest that rebel casualties were also low because of their ability to flee. In an article entitled 'Lord Churchil' (sic) it suggested firstly that it did not believe the reports had really come from this fine officer, and then argued that Churchill should have understood that this is no ordinary war and that such judgements should take the whole context into consideration.[40]

For Churchill, anyway, the experience with the press must have been good and it was to prove especially valuable practice for the many such negative moments in his future public life. The old saying, 'there is no such thing as bad publicity', must have rung in his head more than once and there was little doubt now that he was infinitely better known in the public arena than he had been a few short weeks before. In addition, whereas he had previously always been known as the son of his father, with Cuba behind him this was no longer the case.

The ship docked in Liverpool on 21 December, in time for a train to London. Churchill's letter to his mother of 6 December asked her to be there when he got home and to organise a little dinner, just for her, brother Jack, Barnes and himself. This was to be at the new house at 35a Great Cumberland Place, off Marble Arch, which she had only occupied in November and then lavishly furnished, taking there some seven servants.

Winston was quite excited by the new house, even before his trip, and now was doubly keen to see it in its completed state. His request for a '*parti carré*' was apparently granted by his mother, who now had her son home safely and for Christmas.[41]

He was still to be dogged, however, by some of what he did and wrote. One matter nearly caused difficulties with the man to whom he owed the whole success of his tremendously successful trip to the island: Sir Henry Drummond Wolff. Churchill's articles began to appear in the *Daily Graphic* on 13 December. At the same time he was asked by *The Saturday Review* to write some more on the Cuban situation. This was a step up from the level of analysis required for a daily newspaper, especially an illustrated one, and Churchill accepted with alacrity the offer. *The Saturday Review of Politics, Literature, Science and Art*, the formal name of the journal, was founded as a Liberal Conservative paper in 1855, as an unabashed attempt to combat the political influence of *The Times*.

Its editor from 1894 to 1898 was Frank Harris and it was with him that Churchill dealt over the articles he was to write. His invitation was an exceptional one especially for one just turned 21 and with little analytical experience to speak of. The journal was accustomed to ask only the most influential people to write for it and thus we see among its contributors the names of men such as H.G. Wells, George Bernard Shaw, Max Beerbohm, Oscar Wilde and even Lord Salisbury himself. The emerging if still implicit respect for Churchill was clear. Cuba here again had marked Churchill's prospects for life.

Churchill wrote his series of articles for publication in January–May 1896. They were read, as that journal's material tended to be, by many influential people. News soon got to the Spanish of what was in them, and, while Churchill was proving to be more sympathetic to the mother country than he had been before, he was still trying to tell the true story and that annoyed Madrid on many scores. Drummond Wolff felt obliged to write to Winston on 17 February, referring to one of his articles, with a mild admonishment:

> My dear Winston,
> Please read the enclosed which is attributed to you. I should be very glad if you could avoid saying things unpalatable to the Spaniards as having obtained the letters on your behalf which assured your good treatment I am reproached for the unfavourable commentaries you make. I am

sure you will be careful as this kind of thing places me here in a painful dilemma.

(signed) H. Drummond Wolff

Churchill moved quickly to make amends but he need not have done so, for his article of late February in *The Saturday Review* changed the scene entirely. Drummond Wolff wrote to him in quite another tone on 24 February, after the next article of Winston's in this series was published:

My dear Winston,
Many thanks for your letter and telegram. I have shown them in the proper quarters but they were no longer required as your article in the Saturday Review has been translated in all the papers and has created much enthusiasm. I am told in has been praised in [the Parisian] Le Temps and other French papers. Macte tui virtute puer.

(signed) H. Drummond Wolff[42]

In any case, Churchill was seen by almost all observers as pro-Spanish, and in that he was a rare phenomenon at the time, especially among English-speaking journalists. But within a year of the trip he realised he might have gone too far in the direction of politeness to his hosts and insufficiently far in following his own instinct to understand the justice of the rebels' cause. He consequently wrote in a concerned way to his mother from India. He was at that time deeply immersed in reading history, philosophy and the classics, and what he said is interesting when we attempt to find out what he took away from his Cuban experience:

I reproach myself somewhat for having written a little uncandidly and for having perhaps done injustice to the insurgents. I rather tried to make out, and in some measure succeeded in making, a case for Spain. It was politic and did not expose me to the charge of being ungrateful to my hosts, but I am not quite clear whether it was right.

He then went on to quote Polonius' wonderful advice to his son Laertes in *Hamlet*, 'This above all – to thy own self be true, and it must follow as night the day, thou canst not then be false to any man.' He concluded, 'I am sure that what I wrote did not shake thrones or upheave empires – but the importance of principles do not depend on the importance of what involves them.'[43]

The sequels to the trip seemed to have been entirely favourable, at least from Churchill's perspective. And no known admonishment came from regimental commander, the Commander-in-Chief, editors or even his mother. This may have been in large part related to the fact that it was in the interests of none of these people to prolong the controversy, or be seen to be overreacting to it.

Churchill maintained an affection for Cuba for the rest of his life.

CHAPTER 7

MYTHS AND REALITIES: '*SE NON È VERO È BEN TROVATO*'

There are a terrible lot of lies going around the world,
and the worst of it is that half of them are true.

Churchill was to become a man of such importance that there grew up
around the trip, to some extent in Great Britain and the United States, but,
unsurprisingly, mostly in Cuba, a series of stories about his presence on the
island that are still recounted but are far from always true. It is worth thinking about some of them, especially those that are likely to have some truth
to them and can therefore tell us something of value about the story, and
finally jettisoning others that are clearly untrue.

The Cigar

The most firmly anchored and most widespread of these myths is that
Churchill began to smoke Havana cigars during his trip to Cuba in 1895.
Doubtless because of how it figures in his mysticism and image, this myth is
powerful and generalised as fact to an amazing degree. That cigar, constantly
in his hand or his mouth, even in the most dangerous moments, taken with
him when he visited troops at the front or discussed the future of the planet
with the great, became closely linked to the image of eventual victory in
the Second World War, of continuity when things looked their bleakest.
Barry Singer argues convincingly that, by then, 'He had long understood
the image it could project, the sense of authority and of calm, the sense of

confidence. He employed it as a tool.'[1] If Britain had to face the U-boat challenge, then all very well, but Churchill had his cigars, a statement of the most obvious kind that Britain still ruled the waves and that imports would get through. And it all started, so the myth has it, with that trip to Cuba when he was 20.

The reality, however, is much more mundane. Many young and not so young gentlemen had by the 1890s in a prosperous Great Britain, and in many other countries, begun to smoke Cuban cigars. Their cost, and their distant and rather mysterious source of origin, contributed to a sense that they were what an aristocrat should smoke. The expression used by the hostess at the end of the seated portion of a proper dinner, to the effect that it was time to have a chat among the ladies and another, quite different one, among the men, made this clear. It was of course the celebrated 'Shall we leave the gentlemen to their cigars?' The gentlemen would then remain at the dinner table talking politics, economics and other subjects of the day, and the ladies would retire to the drawing room to talk about other things. This tradition was well in fashion long before 1895.

Most young officers, and especially aristocratic cavalry officers, would have known this tradition from a quite youthful age. Cigarette smoking was of course also de rigueur among them but cigars almost as much. At a regimental dinner, as continued to be the practice until the very recent anti-smoking days, after 'The Queen', that is, the moment when officers drink the 'Loyal Toast' to the sovereign, cigars (and/or snuff) were passed and normally a good number of officers would smoke them. Indeed, for some, the quality of the cigars was part of the reputation for hospitality of a regiment and, as we have seen in Churchill's own words, that quality, in order to be high, meant Cuban cigars, the famed 'Havanas', would have to be on offer.

Certainly, Churchill smoked cigarettes heavily at Sandhurst and even towards the end of his time at Harrow, and continued to do so in the 4th Hussars. He most certainly already knew and appreciated cigars long before he saw the shores of Cuba or a cigar factory in Havana. Such was his pleasure obtained from smoking them that his father opened an account for him at J.J. Fox Cigar Shop in St James's, still a neighbourhood associated with fine cigars and where Lord Randolph already had an account. This did not mean that Lord Randolph approved. He and Winston's mother tried to get him to stop smoking or at least cut down his consumption of cigars and cigarettes.[2] But his father still accepted that it was Winston's choice and so opened the account. Since Lord Randolph died in January 1895, and had been inactive for some time before his death, this must have occurred at the latest the previous year. According to the best study of Churchill at dinner tables, Churchill 'fell in love with cigars in 1895', and it is likely that the love affair blossomed in Cuba, although he never says so, but he had already come to like them before his trip. Larry Arnn suggests that it all began at Sandhurst. In any case, he was smitten by them and the affection was life-long. Manchester states:

> His chief playthings were his seven-inch cigars, of the Romeo y Julieta and La Aroma de Cuba brands. Most of the time they were unlit; he liked to chew and suck them anyway, and when an end grew soggy, he would fash-ion mouthpieces – 'bellybandos' he called them – from paper and glue.[3]

In any case he knew Cuban cigars well before his visit to Cuba in 1895 and while doubtless he smoked some of the best there, and at much more interesting prices than in London, the habit of smoking them was already in place. He could have certainly visited some cigar factories during his time in Cuba, but essentially only in Havana where the time was his, and perhaps he did so in those last two days in the city before the start of his trip home. The famous Partagas cigar, whose factory was only a couple of hundred metres from the hotel, may well have received a visit from him, enjoying as it did immense prestige among the cognoscenti of the cigar world, even though it did not become his favourite. Thus the myth of the young Churchill in some sense discovering cigars on the island must be discarded, although the role of the trip in the development of his affection for them is virtually certain.

But the place of the cigar in Churchill mythology most certainly may not. He started his time in Cuba on that first morning of the stay, 20 November 1895, smoking cigars with Barnes at the Hotel Inglaterra. And he finished his stay carting off plenty of cigars for the new home at 35a. Cigars were part of his time in Cuba, though far from the most important one. Yet who could deny that Cuban cigars became afterwards part of his trademark, his image, his public persona.

Especially in wartime, and perhaps mostly as prime minister, his face, almost always portrayed with a Havana cigar, expressed both zeal and determination. Perhaps it was just the originality of the stance and posture he adopted. For whatever reason, the Cuban cigar was and has remained part and parcel of the public image of Winston Churchill throughout the world, and Cuba, capitalist or otherwise, has always revelled in taking a prominent part in that image of a great man.[4]

The Lunch with Máximo Gómez

Among the most far-fetched of myths about Churchill's activities on the island in 1895 is that he had lunch with Máximo Gómez, the Cuban insurgent generalissimo, during his time with the Suárez Valdés column in late November and early December 1895. In its various versions the myth is irresistible to some. The greatest commander in Cuban history only a few hundred metres or a couple of kilometres away from the greatest man of the twentieth century, over several days in that period. Why indeed would they not have met?

The assertion is so preposterous that it is stupefying to see how the myth continues to have any credence at all. A virtually unknown second-lieutenant, in a foreign army but accompanying the Spanish Army only by courtesy and because it is in Spanish national interests that he do so, would not have been much of a priority for a commander of a Cuban invasion force finally breaking through to the rich western provinces, and concerned that his forces be able to continue their movements towards Havana.

Churchill, on the other hand, while doubtless he would have been interested, if only as a budding war correspondent, to speak to the commander of the insurgency, could not have known how to begin to bring such an encounter about. He was with a Spanish Army column whose job was to intercept and if possible throw back the invasion force, not to arrange conversations for its accompanying journalist with the enemy commander. There was no possible way the two men could have corresponded. And there is no evidence at all that Gómez knew Churchill was with the column or even, had he known, that he would have understood who he was and what significance his being there had at the moment or would have later on.

The story goes that General Gómez visited the village of Arroyo Blanco, and while there had lunch with the young Churchill and was even interviewed by him for his newspaper. The place where this amazing event took place is sometimes said to have been the manse of the local priest, which, as it happens, abuts onto the main building of the Spanish garrison. The latter structure is today certainly the most impressive one in the village, while the former manse currently houses the village museum. The priest, a Catalan who had taken holy orders in Havana in 1853, was Father Benito Juan Mariano Viladevall y Vilaseca, always referred to as 'Father Benito' in Arroyo Blanco. He had never had a parish other than that of Arroyo Blanco, a situation probably assisted by his having fathered children in the village for well over half a century. It should be said that the clergyman did act as a go-between for pro-insurgents and government forces on more than one occasion, but not on this one; it was simply an impossibility.

There is not the slightest evidence of any kind that any such meeting ever took place or that anyone would have been mad enough to try to bring it off. But other, almost as wild, rumours were flying at the time including that Churchill had in fact decided to go over to the rebels, who now had his sympathies, and that, when he tried to do so, Suárez Valdés caught him and prevented it. *Laborantes*, people living in Spanish-controlled towns and cities but pro-independence in attitude, and working quietly for that end in supply and information collecting roles, were apparently spreading such word around in order to suggest that the Spanish were manipulating what Churchill was seeing, feeling and writing. As a friend he had met in Havana wrote to him on 10 December from that city:

> The Cuban propaganda promptly started the story that you had cut your visit short on account of a row with Suarez Valdes. They gave out that your sympathies went over to the rebels – that you wished to leave the Spanish Army and join Gomez, that Valdes would not allow you to do so, and, in consequence, you returned to England. When it was known that you had received the Rioja Cruz [sic], and that in your interviews the rebels received no aid or comfort, great was the wrath of the laborantes.[5]

There could be some link between this equally far-fetched story and that of the meeting with Gómez. In any case, as we have seen, Churchill remained if anything rather pro-Spanish throughout although he nuanced this a year later. It is also true that, given the origin and nature of the priest in question, the central place of the manse in village life and its location right next to headquarters, Churchill may well have crossed its threshold during the nearly two days, according to his column commander that, from the afternoon of 28 November until the early morning of 30 November, he spent in the village. The Spanish would certainly not have wanted him or Barnes about the place all the time, especially when they were analysing the rapidly deteriorating strategic situation, or when they were giving orders in an attempt to salvage things. The priest would have known very well that the British officers were there and, as a relatively cultured individual in a backwater town, he may have thought of meeting and befriending this aristocrat and his interesting companion while they were there. Such company was not common in Arroyo Blanco although there were of course Spanish figures of note, given the village's important role in the colony's defence as a result of its heliograph and being the main base closest to the Trocha on the western side.

Churchill, like Drummond Wolff, retained a soft spot for Spain for the rest of his life. He was particularly fond of King Alfonso XIII, the king who would be deposed when the monarchy fell in 1921. He had many occasions to play polo with the King over the years and indeed was in Madrid to do just that in 1914, the spring before war broke out, when he was awarded his second medal for his Cuban experience, some nineteen years after the event, receiving the Cuba campaign medal 1895–98 directly from the hands of the King.

Churchill included the King in his book *Great Contemporaries*, written in 1929 but not published until 1937, and thought the monarch had been shabbily treated not only by his country but by observers of Spanish events elsewhere. An interesting footnote is that when Suárez Valdés, still in the fight in Cuba, was wounded in June 1896, Churchill wrote with his best wishes and complimenting him for his soldierly qualities. There is no record of a reply but it is telling that, even at that late date, Suárez Valdés promptly handed over the letter to the government-controlled press in Havana who published a front-page article on it, implying strongly the support Churchill felt due to Spain in the Cuban war.[6]

This brings other myths to mind, and perhaps these are easier to imagine. One is the suggestion, dear to some villagers, that Churchill might have dined, stayed the night or bathed in the manse during his stay, and even perhaps on the eve of his birthday. There is a move afoot to name the museum after the village's most famous visitor and a recent book launch there has focused village attention on the Churchill visit more than has been usual.[7]

The Uniform

Cuban weather, topography and vegetation have always had an impact on military uniforms. The country can be dry, rainy, hot, dusty and humid and it can change from one state to another with surprising speed. Rain showers come up in very little time for much of the year and winds can pick up quickly from calm to near hurricane force. In addition, those fierce tropical storms dominate thinking about the weather for almost six months a year.

In addition to the climate, but related to it, is the vegetation. The infamous *marabú* and other cutting weeds abound and make transiting open country a much more complicated process than meets the eye on many occasions.[8] Dense woods are common and in Churchill's time, before much of the huge clearing of woods was done to make way for the great sugar estates, they were much more common still. Winston constantly makes reference to these forests and copses in his account of his travels.

These are not conditions where formal uniforms thrive. Spain, in common with most European countries, had placed its army in relatively bright uniforms since the institution of modern armies at the end of the seventeenth and beginning of the eighteenth centuries. In general, as is well known, the Austrians were dressed in white, the French in white or later in blue, the Prussians in another shade of blue and the Russians in green. Known everywhere were the British regulars, dressed in their own famous scarlet tunics. But this is a simplification. Artillery in the Austrian Army, for example, wore brown, its cavalry wore any of a number of colours, rifle regiments wore green, and so on. The armies of Europe therefore went to war with a bewildering mix of coloured uniforms often leading to considerable confusion on the battlefield.

While Madrid initially put its regulars in full dress uniforms for duty in the Americas, it allowed many changes to slip into dress regulations over the years and especially as the nineteenth century drew on. In the Caribbean Basin in particular, there was a need to find sensible clothing for fighting and campaigning, and even just for garrisoning posts in the conditions prevailing in the area. By the mid-nineteenth century, the Spanish had come up with a *rayadillo* combination of cotton and drill which dressed the army from then on in its many conflicts locally. While working in combination with the French in Mexico, the Spanish retained European dress overall, but this was not the case in Cuba or Santo Domingo.

Full dress uniforms did exist for some units called upon to do public duties in the big cities, and for senior officers at headquarters. But in general the uniform in which Spanish troops garrisoned, campaigned, fought, paraded, and lived was light blue with white stripes, though it appeared to be a light grey of the *rayadillo* (a variant was developed for the *mambí* troops who fought them). Headdress, though it varied in some cavalry and artillery regiments, was in general a wide-brimmed floppy hat with the essential purpose of keeping off the sun's ferocious rays. Mostly the rebels were dressed in whatever they could find, and often in very little more than to cover themselves with decency, and, as Churchill noted soon after arrival, used only a removable badge as a designation in lieu of a proper uniform.[9]

Thus the Cuban scene was not linked to a tradition of grand uniforms. There was a general knowledge, however, of the fact that when the British took Havana in 1762, and occupied it for some eleven months, they had been splendidly dressed in scarlet. In Cuba, even to this day, one can refer to the British occupation as '*el tiempo del mamey*' (the time of the *mamey*), after the fruit that is bright red inside and so characteristic of the island. In a way similar to the rebellion of the thirteen American colonies of 1775, where the British troops were called 'lobster-backs', so in Cuba they were called '*mameyes*'. The British Army was then and now associated with this bright scarlet tunic even though formal uniforms other than the line infantry can be of a wide variety of colours.

It is perhaps not surprising then that many accounts of Churchill in Cuba have him dressed in the grand uniform of a nineteenth-century hussar, which would have included plumes, *sabretache*, *pelouse* and all the rest.[10] The fact is that units of the British Army of the late nineteenth century posted to tropical zones were already issued an appropriate uniform based on the khaki colour that served so well in the field in India. The heat and harsh conditions of that colony made such a uniform essential even though the British, and the French and Portuguese, had been there in less practical wear for many years before. The infantry and the cavalry were all in khaki, though units could have very small regimental 'quiffs' without posing any difficulties over all. For example, hussar regiments carried on with the tradition of wearing chain mail on their shoulders, a practice dating back centuries protecting that part of the body from sword cuts.

With the 4th Hussars having been told off for India in August 1895, they would have been in the process of acquiring uniforms for some three months before sailing; Churchill indeed had bought all his uniforms by the time of his Cuban adventure. He was no fool and would have had good advice on conditions of soldiering in hot climates. He may have carried full dress uniform with him in case he had to make any formal calls, or had to take part in a parade at some time. In fact, in the drawing of him done in Cuba for the publication *Crónicas de la Guerra* he is in formal uniform. That may be because he was posing in such dress or the drawing may have been done from a photo of him. But he most certainly would not have planned to go on campaign in such uncomfortable, impractical and hot garb. He would have given a very different description of his travails on the road if he had been dressed in a uniform designed for war in northern Europe. The heavy cloth, relatively high fur busby headdress, entirely impractical dolman and furred pelisse worn over the left shoulder and the rest of the hussar uniform would have ended his opportunities for mobility and comfort and surely attracted even more *mambí* fire.[11]

The officer's uniform depicted in the centre of the 1895 print of an officer and other ranks of the 4th Hussars is certainly the one he would have worn in Cuba. It was designed for such conditions of weather and terrain, and was the one Churchill would in any case have had for service in India. And, despite its distinctive pith helmet, it was not likely to attract enemy fire in anything like the way his own European full dress would have done. But the reality does not make for as romantic a story as having him riding around the Cuban countryside in the full dress of a British hussar. That is, however, what happened and the more striking version of the story remains again, alas, only attractive myth.

The Incendiary Snake

At least one of the myths coming out of the visit, it must be said, came from the young Winston's own pen. Even before he arrived in the war zone, he wrote in one of the most curious passages of his journalistic writing home about the *tea* or attacks by incendiaries on the sugar cane fields in order to make the harvest and milling of the cane virtually impossible:

> The cane is ripe, fit for cutting, and very combustible. It was explained to me that a piece of phosphorus, coated with wax, would be the probable

instrument of the incendiaries. This little pill is fastened to the tail of the Cuban grass snake, a common and inoffensive creature, which is then set loose. The sun melts the wax and ignites the phosphorus, and the result is conflagration, without any possible clue to its authorship. No amount of military protection or patrolling can guard against this form of outrage, and the general impression is that the planters will not grind.[12]

There is simply no basis at all for such a yarn. The snake in question, the inoffensive and common small serpent, as Churchill says, is doubtless the *jubo*, a grass snake, sometimes called the *jubito*, in the diminutive form, because it is so innocuous. It is easily frightened, although it has shaken more than one city dweller with its viper-like expanded head when alarmed. There are many studies of the incendiary campaign in both major wars, and an enormous amount on the guerrilla war and the ways in which it was conducted. And there is simply no mention, in even the most detailed account, of any such means of waging war, or even of consideration being given to such an option.

The obstacles to such a weapon being used are so numerous, and the lack of the slightest evidence of this idea ever being put forward much less employed, that we can simply discount entirely the story.[13] Churchill was still in Cienfuegos, after a relatively easy trip by rail down from Havana to that safe and secure base of Spain on the south coast of the island. It seems highly likely that some Cuban, perhaps an old Cuban hand at the Hotel Inglaterra or in one of the trains, was having Churchill on. Winston was of course very young and inexperienced on such matters and had seen nothing really yet of the war. The temptation for someone to spin him a yarn, rather in the playful way of locals to any visitor, may have been too strong to resist. Cubans in particular were and are prone to inventing stories as a joke to tease one another and especially newly arrived foreigners. In any case, there was no such use made of the snake in question and he could not have been further from the mark. The *tea* was conducted overwhelmingly by horsemen, mounted or temporarily dismounted, carrying the *tea* (torch) that gave this tactic its name. It was not conducted by anyone else nor need it have been, for the rebels only attacked when their numbers and the element of surprise made sure that defence was impossible by the small garrisons left about the place to deter them.

His wider analysis of the impact of the torching campaign was of course bang on. He was right in assessing it as the main weapon the rebels had and one against which the Spanish were almost entirely powerless. And this plays strongly into this story. The measures which the Spanish military authorities were obliged to take, in particular the dispersal of their forces in penny packets around the whole of the rich areas at risk, improved the chances for insurgent successes.

CHAPTER 8

THE YOUNG CHURCHILL AS POLITICAL ANALYST

It would be a great reform in politics if wisdom could
be made to spread as easily and rapidly as folly.

Winston Churchill showed an interest in politics from an early age. This
may have just been normal for an upper-class youngster of the time, at the
centre of a great empire, and the son of a prominent man in politics. And of
course with Winston's remarkable admiration of his father, it was only natural that he would follow what Lord Randolph was doing closely. Indeed, it
seems likely that he felt that if he showed an interest in politics, and even in
helping his father in his career, that distant figure might begin to show more
of an interest in his son.

Whatever his reasons, the junior Churchill was deeply interested in
public affairs from childhood.[1] He always loved books and read voraciously
and, though military history tended to be his main passion, political history
was also a favourite. With his trip to Cuba, he was able for the first time to
devote time and energy to writing political analysis, an activity in which he
would steep himself for the rest of his life. The demands of his job as war
correspondent would require this but soon also there were new demands
which came in from both England and America for further articles on the
situation in Cuba. These came in the form of a request for a 400-word
article for the US press and Reuters and for *The Saturday Review* series of
articles already discussed. Thus Churchill was asked by no less than three
major publications for his analysis of major political events, when he had
just turned 21.

The Letters

Churchill did not disappoint. His first 'letter' to *The Daily Graphic*, while full of other things, immediately spoke to the political situation in Cuba, despite the fact that, not only had he just arrived, but also he was woefully unaware of the island's history, political context, economic conditions, geography, demography, or really anything else at all. The Spanish control of the press, and the consequent lack of knowledge in Havana of what was occurring on the island, and especially in the war, struck him especially. The strict control of passports also impressed him, but nothing did more than this lack of news and the fact that, as we have seen, there was no sign of the insurrection and business took place as usual.

This perception was of course perfectly accurate. The capital was strongly garrisoned by the Spanish Army and the Guardia Civil, as well as by a system of *sirenos*, or local police, and the powerful and usually fanatical *voluntarios*, loyalist to the core and unwilling to stand for the slightest suggestion of radical change to the status quo. It was truly dangerous to express any thought that seemed to be pro-insurgent. Indeed, even the legal option of autonomy for the island, which had a great many supporters in the city as well as its own newspapers and political party, was spoken of only with care.

Havana was then in many ways a Spanish city as much as it was a Cuban. The 16 per cent of the colony's white population that had been born in Spain were centred on the capital, and the government, almost totally excluding Cuban-born subjects, and thus dominated by Spaniards, was of course here.[2] Cultural life reflected the tastes of the mother country, with zarzuela, flamenco and *sevillano* dancing, long, late and Spanish wine-accompanied meals, and even bull fights part and parcel of metropolitan life. Even today the city has a Spanish air to it, and with at the time a Prado heading from the central square to the harbour entrance, a Plaza de Armas, a cathedral square, castles and fortresses galore, and the latest fashions from Madrid visible everywhere, you could be forgiven for thinking in Havana that you were in the 'old country' and not the new.

By the time the first letter was written, though, Churchill was in Cienfuegos, another colonial city of great beauty, but on the south coast. It was also very Spanish, although first settled by the French, quite loyalist, with a large *voluntario* presence, and a naval base and garrison town. But Churchill was clearly even at this young age quick to distil the facts.

In less than two days on the ground, he had come close to getting behind this façade. He wrote, 'The insurrection shows no signs of abating, and the insurgents gain adherents continually. There is no doubt that they possess the sympathy of the entire population …' It is exceptional that he was able, in two of the most loyalist cities in the country, and in trains moving between them, to come to a conclusion of this force and accuracy. For the fact was that the loyalism, so strong in the previous war, had largely evaporated in the ensuing seventeen-year peace marked by continuing bad government and a sustained lack of attention to necessary Cuban reform.

He also had seized equally quickly the importance not only of the sugar industry to the country but its vulnerability to rebel attack and the firing of its fields. Such action 'means the paralysing of the staple industry of the country and the ruin of the entire island. It means bankruptcy to the planter and starvation to the labourer.'

Churchill was perhaps not quite so good here on his analysis of international factors. He believed the aim of the burning of the fields and the stopping of the milling of the cane had two purposes:

> The twofold object of the rebels in taking this momentous step is to make plain to the entire world the power they have – and so obtain recognition as belligerents from the United States – and by plunging their country into indescribable woe to procure the intervention of some European Power. Looked at from any standpoint, it is a dreadful and desperate remedy, and one which neither restriction of liberty nor persistent bad government can fully justify. It is, nevertheless, a course open to the dangerous and determined men who are in revolt, and one which there is every reason to believe they will adopt.[3]

Churchill had captured the rebellious leaders well and the general internal context. But the rebel objective was not the intervention of a European power through bringing about their recognition by the United States: US recognition was an objective in its own right, going back to the first war, and was not a stepping stone to another such as a European great power's intervention in the struggle. The main obstacle to victory from the insurgent perspective was the difficulty in getting access to arms and ammunition abroad. US recognition of them as belligerents could enormously reduce this challenge.[4]

The second letter, dated 23 November, when he had only been on the island for three or four days, continued with this extraordinary quality of analysis, although less time is spent on political matters than on military. He reinforces here what he had already said about popular support for the rebellion:

> The more I see of Cuba the more I feel sure that the demand for independence is national and unanimous. The insurgent forces contain the best blood in the island, and can by no possible perversion of the truth be classed as banditti. In fact, it is a war, not a rebellion.[5]

The Spanish insisted that the rebels were bandits, of course, throughout this and former wars, an accusation which often stuck when joined to racial slurs about the majority of rebel troops. The fact that the insurgents had to live off the country, raiding especially small towns in order to obtain food and other goods, meant that their being made to appear as bandits was only so difficult for the Spanish to achieve.

If anything Churchill went too far. There was still a significant degree of support within the Cuban population for the 'Canadian solution' of autonomy, not full independence, but it was nothing like what it had been during the recent years of peace. In essence, though, his analysis is striking in its accuracy. In the third and fourth letters, written deep in the war zone while he was with the column and often in action, the writing dealt almost entirely with what was going on around him, with military matters rather than political.

He was able, however, to return to the political scene in his fifth letter, when he re-emerges from the war zone and goes back to Havana, and thence to Tampa Bay.[6] We have seen some of this already, especially with the island's status as 'overtaxed in a monstrous manner for a considerable period', and of industries being 'paralysed' and development 'impossible'. But he goes on to deal with the vital issue of Cubans taking part in their own government or even having access to jobs with the state, a state of affairs that had a massive role in the revolutions against Spain in the rest of its American empire earlier in the century:

> The entire Administration is corrupt. All offices under the Government are reserved for Spaniards, who come to Cuba with the avowed intention of

making their fortunes. Bribery and peculation pervade the board of works, the post-offices, the Customs, and the courts on a scale almost Chinese. A national and justifiable revolt is the only possible result of such a system.[7]

He went on, however, to make the statement and analysis of the Cuban rebels which can irk Cubans to this day:

> But I sympathise with the rebellion – not with the rebels. One would have thought that a state of affairs such as I have described would have brought into the field every able-bodied man. It has not. The towns and villages are full and overflowing with patriots, who, though they weary the visitor with tales of their valour, would not hazard a brass farthing – far less life or limb – to promote the cause they profess to hold so high. The same spirit of histrionic brag is shown, though to a less extent, by their friends actually in the field.

As unpleasant as it is to say, this conclusion was often reached by Cuban patriotic leaders and commanders themselves. Martí and Gómez repeatedly spoke of the vast numbers of Cubans who merely talked of independence, as some sort of dream, while they went about their business within the Spanish colonial system without a thought for the cause or for the men in the field fighting for them.[8] As so often is the case, the war was carried on by a small percentage of the national population and, while the *voluntarios* and *guerrillas* who were fighting for the monarchy were often Spaniards living in Cuba, there were large numbers who were Cuban-born as well. Most Cubans tended to be more convinced than ever that independence was the only real option for the island but that did not necessarily mean they were willing to make significant sacrifices to bring that state of affairs about.

Churchill doubtless did not fully appreciate how often this sort of situation prevailed in wars for independence. And his own independence of thought, desire for action and determination on things which mattered to him would hardly have made these indifferent but loud 'patriots' appeal to him. A negative reaction was bound to be the result. His conclusion as to their methods of making war was even more dubious: 'These are perfectly legitimate in war, no doubt, but they are not acts on which States are founded.' In fact, of course, one hardly had to await the age of modern terrorism to discover that such acts are very often exactly the sorts of things on which states are built.

He went further still to hold up precious little hope for a stable, prosperous Cuba:

> All impartial people who have lived long in the island hold that Cuban autonomy is impossible. They consider that to exchange Gomez for Campos would be to leap from the frying pan into the fire. The rebel victory offers at the best a bankrupt government, torn by race animosities and recurring revolutions, and a State, like Hayti or Venezuela, a curse to itself and a nuisance to the world. It is a sombre outlook. Cuba is between Scylla and Charybdis.

This of course was not strictly true. Although when he used the word 'autonomy' here, he was not using something like Dominion status as his model. He meant what would now be called 'independence'. There were plenty of people on and off the island, including Bourke Cockran who had spoken to Winston on that theme before and would do so again later, who thought independence a real possibility and did not fear it. While Churchill was right in some of his main predictions, he was not to be in all. When Cuba became nominally independent after US intervention and military occupation from 1898 to 1902, it was not quite bankrupt but that was because of US actions not Cuban. More importantly the new republic was indeed torn by racial strife culminating in the ghastly repression of the blacks in the 1912 'rebellion', when they properly felt that, despite their crucial role in the wars for independence, they were excluded from the bulk of the fruits of victory. In fact, more blacks lost their lives to that repression than in any event under Spanish rule over some three centuries.[9]

Cuba, however, did not become another Haiti or Venezuela in the years of what Cubans call the 'pseudo-republic' (1902–58). When the US did leave the island after its military occupation, it had become totally dominant in Cuba's economy; Cuba's army, too, had been built on US lines and was dependent on the great power to the north. The US also retained the right to intervene, at its discretion, through the infamous Platt Amendment.[10]

Churchill did hold out one hope, however:

A middle course is, however, possible, and events seem to daily make it more probable. Spain cannot indefinitely maintain so large a military establishment but when unable to hold the country she will cling tenaciously to the ports and towns. These the Cubans can never take. A compromise alone is possible.

Here the young journalist was bang on.

The Spanish government did weary of the war and financing the struggle did become a massive problem for Spain, which was far from rich. The Weyler government and strategy, put in place by Madrid in early 1896, could not be sustained in the face of a long and brutal war likely to force US intervention at any moment and in any case certain to leave the colony a ruin. By the end of the following year, Weyler was recalled and, on 1 January 1898, an Autonomist government was established. Cubans from the Autonomist Party held almost all ministerial posts, elections to a colonial assembly were organised, and Cubans' control of their own island massively increased. Many rebels did accept the call for peace and gave up violent means to bring about change. But it was all to prove too little, too late.

The bulk of the rebellion's leadership held firm in the course towards full independence. And, with US–Spanish relations worsening, opposition to the new government among *integrista* intransigents breaking out in violence, and so much blood spilt already, the Autonomists never really had a chance to solidify their hold. But Churchill's compromise solution had seen the light of day, however briefly, and had offered some hope of success, however dim.

The Saturday Review

Churchill was asked by this highly prestigious weekly magazine to write a series of articles on the Cuban situation for publication in early 1896. We will not attempt a detailed look at these articles but will merely focus on political analysis done by the young journalist. He is once again damning about Cuban independence in his 17 February 1896 article:

Whatever feelings the Cuban revolt may or may not arouse, it affords little room for sentiment. Let us approach the question, therefore, guided alone by the steady light of common sense, and check the results of a scrutiny by a cool calculation of the profit and the loss. The rebel victory offers little good either to the world in general or to Cuba in particular. With Cuba as a Spanish colony, Spain is responsible for its good behavior toward foreign States and its respect of international law; but with 'Cuba Libra' [sic] instead of dealing with a traditionally friendly Power, we should have to prepare ourselves for another irresponsible firebrand republic of the South American type. That is not an inviting prospect for the outside world, nor does independence offer much to the islanders themselves. All impartial residents in the island are agreed that, though the Spanish Administration is bad, a Cuban government would be worse – equally corrupt, more capricious, and far less stable.[11]

Of course it is difficult to argue with much of this. From a British perspective, and especially one of the British upper class, the argument is not easy to refute. South American governments were generally capricious, corrupt, irresponsible and firebrand, as are many which are just beginning to set about to rule difficult and divided nations. And the Cuban government in place in 1902 was certainly to be all of those things, although again US controls blunted any tendency for it to be irresponsible and firebrand on the international stage at least. Once again, however, Churchill exaggerates greatly the degree of rejection of independence within 'impartial' Cuban ranks. After all, Churchill himself argues that the 'best blood' of the island has already gone over to the insurgents, at least in terms of political outlook.

Churchill afterwards turned on the rebels with arguments straight from the Spanish propaganda he would have heard relentlessly on his recent trip:

A graver danger presents itself. Two-fifths of the insurgents in the field, and by far the bravest and best disciplined part of the rebel forces, are pure negroes. These men, with Antonio Maceo at their head, would, in the event of success, demand a predominant share in the government of the country. Such a demand would be indignantly resisted by the white section, and a racial war, probably conducted with bitter animosity and ferocious cruelty, would ensue, the result being, after years of fighting, another black republic, or at best a partition of the island, as in San Domingo. This is the situation to produce which the richest island in the world is to be ruined; and it is to bring about such a state of things

that it is suggested that England should quarrel with its oldest and most
faithful ally …

The result of a head full of Madrid's propaganda or not, and granted the
obvious racism of the day so powerfully present here, the analysis has
nonetheless some striking features. Churchill is certainly understating the
presence of blacks in the Liberation Army. It would have been far over
40 per cent and might have reached close to two-thirds or even greater
especially if multiracial people were included in the figure.[12] But he would
have had no way of accurately gauging this and obviously the rebel leaders
were in no hurry to broadcast such a black and multiracial dominance of
their forces as they tried to win over undecided and often fearful whites to
the independence cause.

He is once again, however, very correct in suggesting both that with
victory the blacks would wish a share in government and the benefits of
a new country, and that whites would fight back ferociously to deny them
any such thing. The virtual race war of 1912 was thus a result that Churchill
foresaw clearly, and he was one of very few analysts who did.

His assertion that Spain was England's oldest ally is of course very wide
of the mark. While Portugal can and does claim that status, and few would
contest Lisbon on the matter, Spain's historic and even current relationship with Great Britain was hardly that of an ally, much less the oldest one.
Madrid had, it is true, been allied briefly with London in the years when
Spain was fighting against Napoleon for its own independence. But for
most of the long years of conflict between the Revolutionary Wars beginning in 1792 and the end of the Napoleonic Wars in 1815, Spain was either
on France's side or a neutral. Before that, in the eighteenth century, Spain
was almost always on the side of England's enemies. And in the sixteenth
and seventeenth centuries, Spain was a constant enemy of, and threat to,
England. Lastly, as we have seen, Spain was generally happy about British
handling of issues related to Cuba, but hardly considered the island nation
anything other than 'friendly', the adjective Suárez Valdés himself used
to describe the relations between the two nations to Churchill in their
first interview.

In March, Churchill wrote specifically of the US dimension of the war in
another article for *The Saturday Review*, entitled 'American Intervention in
Cuba'. He underscored the obvious interest of that country in the destiny

of an island only 300 miles away (sic) and suggests that 'the rebels have a powerful backing in New York and Washington'[13] and the island 'is much frequented as a winter and pleasure resort by all classes of Americans, and its troubles and disasters not unnaturally attract attention and excite interest throughout the States'.[14]

While it is true that Weyler had just taken over a short while before, his methods were already known to Gollan and his French and US colleagues in Havana. Churchill had of course left the island when the gentlemanly hand of Martínez Campos was on the helm and he knew little of the new regime. Thus his statement on the current Spanish prosecution of the war must be taken in that light:

> Another argument which carried great weight with Congress (in the recent debate on the recognition of Cuban belligerence) was the alleged cruelty and barbarity of the Spaniards. Personally, I do not believe that there has been any unwarrantable exercise of severity during the present war. The Spanish government have offered ample and sweeping reforms, and well-directed intervention might easily obtain adequate guarantees that they would be carried out. But Spain refuses, and rightly refuses, to treat with rebels in arms, a principle which is maintained by other civilized States ...
>
> When the sacrifices Spain is making to maintain an exasperating struggle are considered, it will be apparent that her moderation is extremely creditable ... Certainly when one recalls the methods of South American republics in dealing with their frequent Revolutions, and speculates on the terms which the administration of a 'Free Cuba' would offer to rebels, one cannot feel much indignation ...[15]

Churchill had of course been with a fighting column moving through extremely sparsely settled country, both on the way from Sancti Spiritus to Arroyo Blanco and from that village to the front and beyond. He had seen little of the treatment meted out to Cuban civilians by the Spanish Army even under the regulations and procedures applied by Martínez Campos, and he had seen nothing of the new measures taken by Weyler who had already by then started the infamous *reconcentración* of people in the countryside into defended villages, towns and cities. The idea here was to take the farming communities' populations and transfer them to those defended localities, thus cutting the *mambises* off from their support base for intelligence, supplies and recruits. But cut off from their farms, overcrowded in urban centres, without proper sanitary facilities, where they knew no one and with a supply system rickety at best, thousands starved or fell victim to disease.[16] It must have been especially galling to insurgent sympathisers to hear this Englishman talk about things he had not seen. Spanish treatment of prisoners was not something of which Spain could be proud. And, while this subject is always fraught with problems of interpretation, it seems likely that in general Cuban insurgent treatment of their prisoners of war, with the exception of Cuban-born soldiers serving in Spanish *guerrilla* or *voluntario* units who were almost always considered traitors and shot or hanged immediately, was better than that given by Spain to its prisoners. And Cubans could argue with great force that, after almost a century of promises, more assurances of supposedly sweeping Spanish reforms had an unconvincing ring to them.[17] Here, however, we are skirting the border between military and political issues.

To sum up, Churchill's knowledge of Spanish government in Cuba, while impressive in some ways, was far from total. His sympathy for the Spanish here again led him to a conclusion which he himself did not have a chance to verify, and there is a clear situation here of his giving the Spanish the benefit of the doubt.

Churchill had his first direct exposure to a context deeply requiring statesmanship in 1895 in Cuba. While not called upon to show his statesmanship at this time, he was asked to comment on what was required of others. His comments about compromise from both sides in order to return to peace, the need for reform from Spain and patience from Cuba, and rightly or wrongly a future role for the United States in the destiny of the colony showed that he was already able to enter the lists of discussions of statesmanlike solutions to the major issues involved, showing the promise of great things to come.

The demand for sophisticated political analysis placed by his leadership and ministerial positions for almost half a century from his first Cabinet post as President of the Board of Trade in 1908 was immensely greater than that to which he had to respond as a junior war correspondent in Cuba in 1895. Despite the many ups and downs of his political career, he was to hold many Cabinet and other senior posts, becoming prime minister twice but passing through First Lord of the Admiralty, Minister of Munitions,

Secretary of State for Air and for War, Home Secretary, Colonial Secretary, Chancellor of the Duchy of Lancaster, Chancellor of the Exchequer, Minister of Defence and others. All required a more impressive deployment of his skills of political analysis than did his Cuba trip. But it was in Cuba that he first honed those skills, put them to the test of public viewing, and gained the confidence to move on without reserve towards those other levels of engagement.

CHAPTER 9

THE YOUNG CHURCHILL AS MILITARY ANALYST

War is mainly a catalogue of blunders.

Churchill went to Cuba as a correspondent and an observer, of course. But it is worth remembering that he was a war correspondent and a military observer, as well as a serving officer in the British Army. It is therefore to be expected that his aim would be to give especially good analysis of the military situation in the colony more than the political. In spite of his age, he was exceptionally well suited to give such analysis: he was keen on politics, and had been for some years, but he was avid about things military, and had been since childhood.

He had come to see a war, to experience a war and to comment on a war; only incidentally was he there to see, experience and comment on the political context of that war. Little wonder then that it is in his military analyses made in Cuba that we get a better insight into the sort of man he was at the time, the things that interested him and the degree to which his eyes were open, taking in the sights around him and understanding them.

The war was a complicated one and its military aspects were no less complex than its political ones. Churchill's commentary fairly bristles with his impressions of a war unlike the ones he had studied in his books or his courses on military history. The Cuban insurrection of 1895 was indeed unlike almost anything European armies had experienced in the nineteenth century, despite the vastly diverse military experience of colonial expansion and its accompanying wars outside the old continent, involving the armies not only of the major colonial powers of Britain and France but also those of Germany, Russia, Austria-Hungary, Italy, Spain, the Netherlands, Portugal and even tiny Belgium.

The Cuban war, however, was an example of something unknown in European late nineteenth-century experience, that of a 'settlement' colony that was made up overwhelmingly of a European population, that is, Spanish, of whom over half were white, rising against its mother country. While the British had had such an experience, of course, well over a century before, in the American Revolution of 1775–83, and the Spanish had also experienced vast revolutions that shook all of Spanish America, from Mexico in the north to Chile and Argentina in the south, from 1808 to 1826, those experiences were far away in time by 1895. In the meantime the British had, more or less, understood that when a 'people numerous and armed' decide on independence from your rule, it is probably better to yield to that demand and find a way to a friendly relationship with them after that status is achieved. The Spanish had learned no such lesson from the loss of their American empire and adopted a colonial system even more corrupt, oppressive and exclusionary than the one they had applied before.

In the last quarter of the nineteenth century, the British faced sporadic risings in Africa and on the North-West Frontier of India, the French in North Africa, the Portuguese and the Germans to a small extent in southern Africa, the Italians in eastern Africa, and the Dutch in the East Indies. But these were related to the usual conquest and questionings of the rule that followed that conquest, and normally involved people whom the BBC was to later call 'dissident tribesmen' rather than settled subjects of their own sovereign, merely distant from and misruled by their mother country. Only the Boer War, breaking out at the very end of the century and involving white settlers, although not those from the metropolitan power against whom they fought, had more than a few similarities with Cuban events.

The Spanish Army now faced a colony no longer festering with revolt in only its eastern and poorer regions, but open and widespread revolution in all of the east and centre of the island. The invasion would mean the carrying of the war to literally the whole of the colony, from the traditional realms of revolt in the east to the town of Mantua, in westernmost Pinar del Río, in popular lore the place where Cuba ended. That rebellion would have significant support not only in Cuban exile communities abroad but even among the general population of the United States and the neighbouring British territories of the Bahamas and Jamaica. The only improvement in

Spain's international position vis-à-vis this insurrection, compared with the last, was that Latin American support for this rebellion was now very slight, fearful that Madrid's rule would merely be replaced by Washington's in the case of a rebel victory. In this war Cubans could not look to the automatic support of their fellow Latin Americans as they had done in the first. But this was in the end to be of precious little real help to Spain.

The Spanish Military in Cuba

Cuba insula est. And as was discovered in the first independence war, control of the seas around the island was essential if assistance for the rebels coming from abroad, in men, weapons and ammunition, was to be intercepted. As in the previous war, the lack of ammunition, and to some extent weapons, was the Achilles heel of the rebellion. The Spanish system of intelligence in the neighbouring countries, as we have seen, was very good indeed. But, in the final analysis, naval resources able to do the actual interception of rebel supplies was just as key in ensuring that this rebel vulnerability was fully exploited.

The navy had a major role in the first war and Spain deployed significant naval resources to the war effort then. An effective system of intelligence abroad, intelligence on the island and naval deployments and activity repeatedly put paid to insurgent schemes not only of supplying themselves but broadening the war. Spain in that first war had enjoyed a modern fleet of gunboats but Rear Admiral Delgado Parejo, the newly appointed commander of naval forces in Cuba and former commander of the Mediterranean fleet, who had arrived in Havana in June 1895, could count on no such support. His force, described by a prominent Cuba historian as so weak that Spain had little option but to count on US efforts to intercept expeditions and its own 'efficient network of espionage', led that same historian to conclude that 'there was no doubt that Spain's worst enemies in the war were to be found in the Cabinet'. In his words, Delgado Parejo had been given a 'badly mixed collection of vessels, true shells in some cases, which of warships had only the name'.[1]

This had already ended in tragedy. Stung by criticisms earlier in the war by the press in Madrid, the admiral had taken matters into his own hands and, hoping to outwit rebel spies in Havana, had sailed out of the harbour some weeks before Churchill arrived, at night and with no lights on his ship, the light cruiser *Sánchez Barcáiztegui*, to intercept a suspected rebel expedition. No sooner had he rounded the tip of land at the narrows leading out of the port than the ship collided with a coastal vessel, the *Mortera*, and sank, carrying the admiral, the captain, and thirty-two members of the crew to the bottom. This was 18 September, the same date on which the transport ship *Ensenada* sailed from Cádiz to Scotland to pick up the first consignment of new gunboats for this war. This would prove yet another example of too little too late and was still the talk of the town when Churchill arrived in the city.

If the navy was ill supplied to do its needed work, the army was less so. It had, as we have seen, a new rifle, a good artillery piece and plenty of men. But without doubt a major problem was that it had in large part the wrong sort of men. Instead of a fully regular army, it had a mixture of units, some very good, like the battalions in the column with which Churchill marched, and some very bad, the latter almost always made up of unwilling young farmers or urban labourers conscripted into the army, in the terribly corrupt Spanish system, and sent to Cuba with little adequate training, no acclimatisation and less understanding of why there were there. Their being brought into the army by this means, the *quinta* as it was called, the conscript soldier being termed, often disparagingly, but sometimes with sympathy for his plight, a *quinto*, was part and parcel of a context which explains in large part why, with the tens of thousands of troops Spain had on the island, and with its resultant total numerical superiority over the insurgents, it still could not suppress the rebellion and bring peace again as it had done in 1878.

The Cavalry Question

Although many authors have not placed great emphasis on this matter, no discussion of Churchill's considerations of the military situation in Cuba in 1895 can begin without a look at the state of the cavalry presence in Cuba in 1895 and for the whole of the war. The mid-nineteenth century had seen changes in military technology that had placed the horse in a much more vulnerable position, in so far as its status as a highly useful and integral component of the forces on the battlefield was concerned, than at any time in history. The rapid-fire, rifle-barrelled musket, loaded from the breach, or 'rifle' for short, had by the late 1860s replaced the single-shot, muzzle-loaded musket in use in one form or another for centuries. That rifle, with ranges of around 1,000m, could fire several times the distance, much more rapidly and with much more accuracy than muskets of the past.

This made the horse much more vulnerable to the fire of infantry than it had ever been. Infantry had for long understood that they offered tempting targets to cavalry when they were in line or column formations, their flanks or rear being favourite spots for cavalry attack. The solution, at least for solid infantry, was to form in squares and thus not 'offer' any flanks or rear for an enemy's cavalry to exploit, and use volley fire to break up attacks against it. Otherwise the infantry's chances could be very slim indeed since cavalry mobility would tend to find the offered flanks, or the even more vulnerable rear, and close, charge home and rupture their cohesion, turning them into a routed force more vulnerable still to the cavalry, now in hot pursuit of men on foot, whose broken formation would not afford them any protection.

This arrangement functioned, however, because even the best infantry could only get off perhaps four rounds a minute and those rounds were only effective at an absolute maximum range of about 100m. Now trained infantry, especially those with a rifle that used a multi-round 'clip', could fire many more rounds each minute and up to ten times the distance normal in the past. This rate of fire, added to this range of possible engagement, would slowly but surely sound the death knell of the cavalry except in highly particular circumstances.

Along with rapid-firing, long-range, rifle-barrelled weapons for the infantry soldier came the first machine guns, the Gatling gun being very tentatively introduced into the US army by the end of the Civil War in 1865, and the *mitrailleuse* reaching the French army by the end of that decade and at least theoretically ready for use in time for the Franco-Prussian War of 1870–71. This added firepower, soon to revolutionise battle and end for a time mobility on the battlefield, was likewise to shatter the traditional place of cavalry in combat. Finally, as if these other two breakthroughs were not enough, the development of the rapid-fire, breach-loaded, rifle-barrelled artillery of the end of the century added its powerful sound to the cacophony of modern battlefields where the cavalry would soon not find much of a place.

In response, there had been regiments of heavy cavalry (*carabiniers, cuiras-siers* and heavy dragoons), medium cavalry (usually dragoons but sometimes lancers as well) and light cavalry (hussars, light dragoons and at times lanc-ers) or their equivalents in all major armies. The heavy cavalry, larger men on larger horses, would engage in major events such as cavalry charges aimed at breaking the enemy. Medium cavalry would be slightly smaller men on slightly smaller mounts, often armed with a carbine and able to work as infantry as well, and capable of tackling many of the jobs of heavy or light cavalry. And then there was light cavalry, mounted on even smaller horses and manned by even slighter men, responsible for reconnaissance, pursuit, harassing, liaison, other communication and flank protection duties.

With the developments mentioned, however, the jobs of heavy and medium cavalry were becoming impossible for them to perform and only the light cavalry seemed to be destined to keep a place, however small, reserved for itself in modern warfare. And this place seemed even smaller for men raised on the stories of horsemen of old. This was the context for cavalry that people like Churchill, a romantic in these matters and newly arrived in the legendary 4th Hussars, were busy telling themselves could not be true.

Cuba, as it turned out, proved that there were still places where the new rules of the game did not yet apply. On the long and often relatively flat island, stretching nearly 1,400km from the westernmost tip of Cape San Antonio to the easternmost of Cape Maisí, movement by land was difficult at the best of times. The distances between points, the climatic conditions and the difficult topography meant that movement by horse was in the main the only practical means of getting about, except for short trips.

The Cuban farmer was accustomed to his horse, or at least those who could afford one. And the small and sure-footed Cuban pony to which Churchill referred more than once offered another enormous advantage to the peasant or soldier in that he did not know the concept of fodder and ate wherever he stopped and on whatever was available. A group of Cuban military historians recently published an excellent analysis of the island's small horse of the time, which was 'no longer the Arab beauty that [the sixteenth-century Spanish explorer] Hernando de Soto brought to Cuba'. But it grazed exclusively on grass and even the shortest stops for feed and rest seemed to provide the energy to continue on long marches and support its rider in combat. Another great advantage it offered the rebels was, logi-cally enough, its total acclimatisation.[2]

A number of other factors contributed to cavalry remaining the main arm of the rebel army and not merely an important adjunct. For one thing, superior mobility was the only way to ensure a fighting chance of avoiding the many columns, dominated overwhelmingly by foot soldiers, the Spanish sent after the invading Cuban forces in 1895 and later. Invading columns made up entirely of infantry would soon have been brought to battle by the superior numbers of the metropolitan forces and surely beaten decisively if levels of mobility between the two armies had been the same.

It is important to be clear here for our discussion of Churchill's views on the war. The same group of Cuban military historians insists, doubtless with reason, that the dominance of cavalry was also losing ground in Cuba and the main 'rebel victories were where infantry and cavalry cooperated well'. But for the *mambises* to go where they needed to go, transport what they needed to carry, conduct the only kind of war open to them, and fight and flee in order to fight again another day, mobility was the key and that mobility could only come from cavalry. The Spanish, by this analysis, 'lost from view that they were facing a guerrilla army and that, in counterinsurgency fighting, mobility is an essential factor'. Cavalry was thus the key to gaining and keeping both the tactical and the strategic initiative. And the Spanish, lacking in cavalry, were never able to get that initiative at either level. Gómez, especially in the 1895 invasion, was willing to give up infantry if he could get cavalry, and mounted as many infantrymen as possible, because cavalrymen could and did fight as infantry, but without a horse an infantryman could only fulfil his one assigned role. Such was the security the Cubans felt when riding around the country that the generalissimo, when moving about, kept an escort of only 100 men, all cavalry.

Nonetheless, the Cuban cavalry had a firm respect for the Mauser and its speed of fire and effective range. They made sure that, where possible, the distance between them and enemy infantry was kept to the minimum if they were going to be asked to cross it against that rifle's fire. This required cavalry to cooperate more closely with infantry than in the past, adopt a more open order offering less of a concentrated target to the enemy, and above all to move more quickly and employ speed, audacity and surprise. Even so, casualties among horses and men were often high when infantry were engaged. After Churchill's departure, in the action at Saratoga of 11–13 June 1896, some 100 of the total 350 horses fell in the fight.[3] A last point worth mentioning at this stage is that, munitions often being short in the rebel ranks, there were times when cavalry charges, however dangerous and costly, were the only option for commanders at key points in battle when a critical situation needed saving.

The Spanish general preference was to adopt the European standard idea of one cavalryman for every six infantrymen in a campaign. But, while perhaps accepted in theory in the old country, this was never applied in Cuba. Even at the height of the expansion of cavalry numbers under Weyler after Martínez Campos was long gone from the Cuban scene, the ratio was never anywhere near this. Instead, cavalry would be about one to fourteen infantrymen and these figures rarely included the infantry-heavy volunteer corps. This meant that the supposedly 'mobile' columns, to which reference was and is so often made, is a misnomer. They were only as mobile as infantry could march and waggons could roll over terrible terrain and bad or frightful roads. Artillery, available in significant quantities for the African wars, was rarely deployed in any strength in part because it was just too difficult to move about, and only lightweight and easy transportable mountain guns were sent at all. They proved useful on occasion but were rarely a decisive factor in action, although at times they could play a useful role, as we saw in the action at La Reforma, even when not available in large numbers.

Three weeks before Churchill arrived in Cuba, the chargé d'affaires in Madrid wrote to the Foreign Office with the following figures of Spanish strength:[4]

Infantry	59,000
Marine Infantry	2,700
Cavalry	3,886
Guardia Civil	4,400
Artillery	1,853
Police	976
Engineers	1,415
Guerrillas	1,152
Total	76,282

These figures do not give us the total number of mounted *guerrillas* mobilised for service. But merely taking into account the regular cavalry and regular infantry shows roughly less than 6 per cent of the combined force is cavalry rather than the 14 per cent that would have been normal for operations in the European style. Even if one were to assume, against all known evidence, that all the *guerrillas* were mounted, the figure would only improve to just under 8 per cent. And the point here is that Spain needed more than the ratio of one to six: it needed a figure that would allow the cavalry, through their mobility and speed, to force the Cubans to give battle once and for all. Essentially they had here a totally infantry-dominated army in the field, in a counter-insurgency war, and with mobility squarely on the side of the insurgents.

The Cuban Liberation Army

The Liberation army (Ejército Libertador) was a different matter altogether. Raised in 1868 on a highly regionalist basis, with rank, especially higher rank, usually more related to local status than to military knowledge, that regionalism permitted the construction of the army but also carried with it many of the seeds of eventual defeat. Troops from one province often felt very unhappy in being used to liberate others. The fact was that the force was, in its 1895 form, completely dependent for its rank and file on ex-slaves, poor labourers, the recently swelled ranks of the unemployed, landless peasants and the like. While some officers, especially senior ones, had experience of war from the 1868–78 revolution, most other ranks were new recruits, usually illiterate and with nothing like a military background.

Troops often reflected a situation known even today. Cubans rarely like the idea of military service and recent decades of required conscription have been accepted as a necessary evil only by generations of youth called upon to do their two or three years of national service with the colours. On the other hand, Cubans tend to make very good soldiers. With the Castro Revolution of half a century later, and the current Fuerzas Armadas Revolucionarias de Cuba (the Cuban Revolutionary Armed Forces), which were formed after its success in 1959, Cuba has shown that it can build a very impressive military, one capable of besting the 1961 US planned, armed, trained and in part directly supported invasion, and later a Western-backed South African force thousands of miles from home, with the Cubans having little local knowledge.

While that modern force takes its inspiration and much of its history from the rebel forces of 1868–78 and 1895–98, there is little in common between them. Other than the determination of its 1895–98 leadership and many of its men, and of course its great strength in cavalry, it was not an impressive body. It was rather a typical Latin American insurgent army in that, for example, it lacked heavy weapons like artillery altogether. Some almost humorous attempts were made, with considerable originality, to address that particular weakness, but little was achieved. It also lacked properly trained heavy infantry, although what it had as light and irregular troops on foot could surprise the Spanish on occasion with their steadfastness and hardiness. Las Villas province especially had developed something of an infantry tradition in the first war and continued it in the 1895 conflict.

The Liberation Army lacked proper logistics and lived off the land almost exclusively, the main exception being the occasions when the expeditions from abroad arrived to succour them. 'Off the land' meant, in reality, that the army was dependent on what it could obtain from raiding villages and towns, looting what could be taken, especially but hardly completely from Spanish merchants, on extortion of funds from landholders, and on what could be obtained from a more or less willing peasantry. The system functioned because of the large number of unarmed men who accompanied the force as it moved, filling tasks of acquisition of supplies, cleaning, carrying extra equipment, minding the horses on occasions and many other duties. And often the columns were accompanied by swarms of camp-followers who, as we saw at La Reforma, could cause real problems for the mobility of the column as a whole.

With such a 'system' of logistics nothing was easy. One enormous complication was the simply vast array of different basic weapons with which the rebel force was equipped. While all might have the machete, even the cavalry, the variety of rifles and even old-fashioned muzzle-loading muskets were part of the Achilles heel of ammunition supply and remained so throughout the war. For not only was ammunition hard to come by, to say the least, but such supplies as there were needed to respond to a huge range of different firearms: Remington single shot, Spanish model .43; Mauser Spanish 7mm; Mauser Argentino 7.65 (usually captured from the Spanish or obtained in raids on arsenals); US Remington and Remington Lee 7mm; Springfield .45; British, French and Belgian rifles, and even 1865 US models such as Sharps and Peabody .44.[5] If the Spanish thought they had problems because some *voluntario* units still had Remington's the Cubans would not have been impressed.

The army also had serious discipline problems. At the higher level, they tended to stem from either racial questions such as whites not wishing to take orders from superior black officers or from regionalist issues as seen in the first war. At lower levels they tended to be related to the general rejection of the need for formal discipline among much of the rank and file. The kind of war being waged, the hunger that often haunted the rebels' ranks, the lack of proper uniforms and the absolute need to conduct raids in order to secure booty of all kinds meant that a degree of similarity did exist between banditry and the reality of the war being conducted. The purposes were certainly very different but the actual conduct of the fighting, especially as seen by town dwellers so often attacked by the rebels, did come close to banditry or so it seemed to many.

Many of these issues Churchill addressed in his letters to *The Daily Graphic*, his letters home, his articles for other journals or his correspondence with other third parties. And the degree to which he addressed so many key aspects of the war showed clearly his keenness for and understanding of military affairs.

The Young Military Analyst

Churchill's very first written comments on the war were in his letter to his mother of 19 October. He was incorrect in his suggestion that the Spanish were building up their forces in Havana before heading up country to quell the rebellion, since they were quite capable of landing their forces anywhere they wished and thus avoiding the quite considerable difficulties of transporting them from the capital to the war zones.[6] And, since until the very end of the war following the US intervention in April 1898 the rebels were never able to take and hold a single town, the ports remained entirely available for Spanish troop movements as desired.

On arrival, however, and as a result of Churchill's duties, and perhaps some reading into the situation, thanks to the materials General Chapman had given him, his reporting became much more exact. While it is a pity that he did not look into the defences of Havana a little more carefully upon his initial arrival on the island, he did comment on Morro Castle and the lack of an atmosphere of war in the capital, both of which comments were accurate and important. It is also fascinating to note that of all the incidents of the war so far upon which he could comment, he discussed the arrest and trial of a junior officer for 'neglect of duty'. And even though the event was six months in the past, he spent time and space on it:

> Here it was that the sentence of death on Lieutenant Gallegos was carried out in May last. This officer had the charge of a small post with some fifty soldiers, and was unfortunate enough to be breakfasting in a café when the insurgents happened to pass, and so was taken prisoner, with all his men. The rebels let them go, but kept their arms, and the court-martial sentenced the lieutenant to be shot for neglect of duty.[7]

This story, old as it was, impressed Churchill. Yet it is interesting that he did not share his views with the readers of the 'letter' despite the fact that there are at least three interesting points mentioned here and indicative of things of importance in the conflict:

> there were instances of unprofessional conduct in the army; the rebels would often let government troops go when captured, doubtless because they did not have the means to take care of prisoners of war since they were constantly on the move and could often hardly feed themselves; and the measures taken to ensure officers and men conducted themselves correctly could be draconian.

As an aspiring young officer, the story must have made him think about his career. But he did not go further than merely relating what had happened. And another such incident, not ending quite so tragically for the young officer and to which reference will be made later on, occurred near where his column was operating.

His main comments on the military soon after arrival were those on the *voluntarios* who he saw that first evening in Havana. He was impressed and said so, in this first assessment of soldiers he made in print:

> During the evening which I passed in the capital some volunteers marched in from the front, preceded by a band and surrounded by a great crowd. They were a fine lot of men – young, but well developed – and

though they looked tired, marched jauntily, and were evidently much
pleased with themselves. Their uniform was made of white cotton and
they wore large straw hats of limp material, twisted into every conceivable
shape. They were very dirty and did not preserve much order, but for all
that they looked like solders and were well armed. These 'volunteers', of
which there are about 25,000 in all, take it in turn to garrison the different outlying towns, afterwards coming back for duty in Havana.[8]

Recruited in large part, especially in this second major war, from Spanish-
born young male immigrants, dependent for their livelihood in general on
the more *integrista*, and also usually Spanish-born part of the population,
these *voluntarios* joined up to show their loyalty, to protect their privileges
as *peninsulares*, and often enough merely to have the opportunity to impose
themselves on the native-born population. It is a somewhat curious but
easily explained fact that these Spaniards, having come to Cuba to make
their fortunes as Churchill himself pointed out, often hated the locals
whom they felt considered themselves superior to their fellow subjects
from Iberia. Cuban urban society, especially that of Havana, was much more
cultured and refined than the places in the peninsula from which most of
these reservists came. And the Cuban people they dealt with at work could
probably read and write, were often polished urbanites as Havana still pro-
duces, and did not feel inferior to this class of Spaniard, ill educated and
often from the most backward areas of a backward country.[9] There were
many more than the figure of 25,000 volunteers Churchill gives on the
whole island now that war had broken out again. And at least in the capital
they could cause havoc if something happened they did not like, especially
if the Captain-General of the day appeared to be adopting any policy other
than 'search and destroy' to the enemy. Despite his formal power they could,
and did, make or break these officers on occasion.

In this war the Cuban element of this corps was much less loyal than
in the first. The misgovernment of the interwar years had had its effect on
bodies of troops from the island itself just as it had on the population of the
island as a whole. Desertions to the insurgent camp, almost unknown in
the first war, were numerous in this one. Even units of proven loyalty over
many years could, with the effects of the invasion, turn on their employers
and pass over to the enemy. Churchill did not have enough time to get to
know these troops, their exceptional intransigence and the special problems

they posed to the government and the prospects for a compromise peace. But he was impressed with them, as we can see, and there is no doubt that, as a mobilised auxiliary force to the regulars, they were of great value not only in allowing regulars to be freed up for less static duties than the ones they usually performed, but in participation in a wide range of full-scale military operations.

Churchill turned his attention in his first letter to the military situation with respect to transport as it appeared as he left the station in the train he took to Santa Clara and Martínez Campos' headquarters, especially the part of that journey after Colón. The enemy clearly struck wherever they wished and the huge deployments of men for duties in the small forts, blockhouses guarding railway bridges and other defensive works did not greatly deter them. On the other hand, while they had a number of tricks (Churchill called them 'dodges') in their use of dynamite, he wrote that 'the insurgents appear not to understand its employment, as only two explosions have taken place so far, though there have been many attempts'. He likewise could not resist the temptation to take a first jibe at supposed rebel lack of courage when he says 'At Santo Domingo a pilot engine and an armoured-car are added to the train, as the rebels often indulge in target practice – from a respectful distance.'

He then reflected upon the determination of the Spanish in this war but also on the advantages the rebels have in having access to 'accurate intelligence', and the 'sympathy of the entire population'. His assessment of the rebels' strategy in using incendiary weapons, however often he criticised them for their excesses and negative effects, was nonetheless one of admiration for its effect in potentially crippling the Spanish war effort. And, as we have seen in the discussion of the *jubo*, he was correct in emphasising these effects.

His next letter, dated 23 November, from Sancti Spiritus, now that he had seen more of the war zone, was even more clear-headed and analytical. His discussion of the railway journey from the port town of Tunas de Zaza to Sancti Spiritus showed his information-gathering capacities as well. He spoke of the 30 miles of railroad between the two places as 'the most dangerous and disturbed on the whole island'. This may be an exaggeration, as was the suggestion, already discussed, that in the Escambray Mountains, which he was skirting, there were some 15,000 to 20,000 rebels operating. In fact, there were only just over 17,000 total enrolments in the insurgent army by the end of 1895 and the percentage of them in this region would have been small if nonetheless significant.[10] There were many other parts of the island which might have claimed the status of more dangerous, but this was certainly an exposed and difficult example as well. What struck him especially was that in this small part of the war, the requirement for troops and emplacements was massive. A full 1,200 troops were deployed along this short line of track, yet, despite this, 'communication is dangerous and uncertain'. This was surely an important part of his assessment – huge deployments of troops for small tasks and even then they did not achieve fully the objective set them. The fact that the speed of the train in which he travelled was reduced to a mere 10 miles per hour shows the kind of impact the mere thought of a rebel threat could produce on the Spanish defensive deployment island-wide.

He was also right in insisting on writing about what might appear a small incident but one that was to have considerable impact. He described briefly an attack, led by Máximo Gómez himself, against one of the small forts the Spanish had everywhere. The place in question was the small outpost of Pelayo, 18km south-east of Sancti Spiritus, garrisoned by a small detachment of troops, forty from the Regimiento de la Unión and seven Guardia Civil. The post's commander was Lieutenant Quinciano Feijóo and he had his men deployed in the post's four outer small blockhouses and one large central one. Churchill would doubtless have said, as he did about Lieutenant Gallego in his first letter, that this lieutenant was also unfortunate. For on 17 November, three days before Churchill's arrival in Cuba, the main column commanded by Máximo Gómez himself, who, it will be recalled, was west of the Trocha in order to pin the Spanish down and permit an easy passage of that defensive line by Maceo, approached the lieutenant's small command with a very large force. The Cuban version of events is that Gómez called on the Spaniard to surrender and after a parley it was agreed that he would surrender but only after honour was saved and that therefore the Cubans would have to fire a few shots prior to the fort raising the white flag. This sort of arrangement was hardly original in such circumstances.

The Cuban version of the story is that nonetheless when Gómez and his forces approached the fort after the formalities had been observed, the garrison opened fire and wounded three insurgents and some horses. It is likely that this occurred not through perfidy but because some of the soldiers either did not understand they were to surrender or that they did not agree with the decision taken and wished to continue resistance. Be that as it may, the storming of the fort now began, and the Spanish lieutenant then sur-rendered properly. All the Spanish troops were released and it was they who Churchill saw, and of whom he wrote:

> About a week ago they took one of the small fortified posts which I have described to you. Maximo Gomez himself directed the attack. Fire was opened on the fort from a hill distant about 500 yards. As soon as the attention of the defenders was drawn to this point two fresh bodies of the enemy opened upon them on each flank, and, at the same time, a fourth detachment, about 100 strong, assaulted the gate, and had it down in an instant. The garrison, numbering fifty, surrendered promptly, and after being deprived of arms and ammunition were allowed to go free. They marched in here in a body looking very crestfallen, and it is reported that the officer will be brought before a court-martial.

Clearly Churchill had been given a different version of events by the Spanish. At his court martial Feijóo presented a declaration saying that there were 4,000–5,000 rebels and that, in the face of Gómez's invitation to sur-render, 'I answered roundly no and in no way, and then a little more than 800 rebels presented themselves attacking the fort, I defending myself for two hours of firing from four to six, and the fort being reduced to ashes.' He said that it was only in the face of 'certain death' that he had surrendered his post and his men.[11] What is curious about this story is that the implication in what Churchill wrote seems to be that he saw these men but in fact the deposition to the court martial is dated 18 November, the attack took place on 17 November, and therefore it is difficult to imagine how Churchill could have seen the men march into Sancti Spiritus when he only arrived there on 23 or, more likely, 24 November. Be that as it may, Churchill is surely right in suggesting that the rebels in the area were giving the Spanish 'a great deal of trouble lately'. And the Spanish must have been extremely embarrassed by this event, which was the talk of the town in Sancti Spiritus when he and Barnes arrived. The Spanish version of great courage on the part of the subaltern officer resisting hours against hopeless odds, and only surrendering when his post was in ruins, must have been required to salvage national honour at that moment.

Another interesting comment from this letter is the suggestion that disease was mostly affecting the poor and the troops. And it is here that

Churchill suggested the impossible figure of 15,000–20,000 insurgents outside the town, an exaggeration which the Spanish may have given as the reason why they were not having much success.

Writing in more detail of intelligence and such matters in this war, he then gave a description of the advantages guerrillas have in this kind of insurgency that could have come from a twentieth century textbook on the subject:

> The great advantage the insurgents have is the detailed and constant information which they receive. Their only uniform is a badge. This can be taken off at will, and when so removed it is impossible to tell a rebel from an ordinary peasant. Hence they know everything: the position of every general, the destination of every soldier, and what their own spies fail to find out their friends in every village let them know.[12]

In his last letter before his 21st birthday, dated 27 November, in Arroyo Blanco, he was recounting his march with the column up to that fortified village and most of his comments on the military context were more tactical than strategic. He wrote with great sense of a military situation in which the difficulties of tactical movement are many impassable roads, dependence on convoys for supplies, long detours through the country, the difficulties of moving with the column having to 'straggle over a couple of miles of ground' and its inevitable vulnerability at such times. As seen he summed it up with a phrase many later commanders of counter-insurgent forces would understand about the situation they faced as well: 'As a rule it is impossible to do more than to go straight ahead, and often it is difficult to do that.' This quality of observation was remarkable for an officer of his age and experience, unable to easily communicate with his colleagues on the march and, as a rule, unable to see the enemy.

At Arroyo Blanco he described the defensive arrangements of the village with clarity and told of the troops there having had a 'brush with the enemy the day before yesterday' (almost certainly 26 November). He had been learning well the lessons of his first day in Havana, where he wrote with a lovely turn of phrase, 'it was explained to me that while the Spanish authorities were masters of the art of suppressing the truth, the Cubans were adepts at inventing falsehoods. By this arrangement conflicting statements and inaccuracy are alike assured.' A week later, with all his new experience, he did not accept at face value assertions from either side and said merely that the garrison 'claims to have killed and wounded over twenty rebels, including a "chief"'.

This is just as well. Recent research suggests that the real story was rather different although such an action did take place. When General Luque's column was near Arroyo Blanco shortly before Churchill's arrival, they were harassed by Colonel Rosendo García's rebel forces, essentially the Honorato Cavalry Regiment, a local Sancti Spiritus unit. During that operation there was an action on 26 November in which the rebel leader (*jefe* or chief) Pío Cervantes was killed. But it is unlikely that there were anything like the casualties inflicted on the rebels that the garrison in Arroyo Blanco claimed to the young British subalterns.[13] It is interesting but hardly surprising that the Cubans suggested they turned back this column from more far-reaching operations and the action was therefore a victory for the rebels and thus the Spanish had no reason for boasting to the British.

Be that as it may, it is this *mambí* cavalry regiment, the Honorato, and its commander, Rosendo García, who almost certainly have the honour of having engaged the column in what was Churchill's baptism of fire.[14] Rosendo García Medrano was a cavalry commander from Puerto Príncipe, capital of the province of Camagüey, the classic home of Cuban cavalry (Puerto Príncipe has now been renamed Camagüey). He was 40 at the time of the engagement with the Suárez Valdés column and had fought, virtually as a child to begin with, in the Ten Years War, going into exile after having resisted the Pact of Zanjón agreements ending the war in 1878. By the middle of 1895 he was back in Cuba as a full colonel and given command of the Regimiento de Caballería Honorato. This man, who had such a major role in Churchill's development (if undocumented and hitherto unknown), is hardly ever mentioned, nor are the actions which preceded the La Reforma fighting of 2 December; they are never linked to the Churchill experience in a direct fashion. Research on him is sometimes more complicated because of later accusations as to his real loyalty to the insurgent cause.[15]

Leaving this aside, Churchill's account continued to brim with interesting points on the war and what he was seeing. He was now noting his first real signs of the war's effects and referred to the rebel forces' harassing tactics and the constant presence of their reconnaissance elements; he suggested that the troops were able to kill a couple of these men on 26 November, though Spanish official reports mention no such success. They do, however, confirm that the Spanish lost one man in fighting that day. The key point though is that the column was being observed by the insurgents for much of the time.

Then Churchill began a well-argued though brief assessment, for an audience of illustrated daily paper readers, of the strategic situation and what the Spanish were up against:

> To-day, however, we have news that Maximo Gomez is encamped with 4,000 men a couple of leagues to the east, and early tomorrow we start after him. Whether he will accept battle or not is uncertain, but if he does not want to fight the Spaniards have no means of making him do so, as the insurgents, mounted on their handy little country-bred ponies, knowing every inch of the ground, possessed of the most accurate information, and, unimpeded by any luggage, can defeat all attempts to force a battle.[16]

He demonstrates his understanding of the context of the war in its essentials, that is, the lack of mobility of the Spanish forces, combined with exceptional potential in that field on the part of the rebels, joined with their very special intelligence conditions, leaving almost automatically the initiative in the hands of the insurgents. They gave battle when they pleased, refused to do so when they did not please, and left the Spaniards slow to react, out-manoeuvred constantly and with all the frustrations of a large regular force with size but few other advantages over a smaller enemy which held the initiative. And, with the invasion, this enemy now held that initiative in the decisive area of the country and not just in the ignored east.

Winston also certainly had his eyes and ears open for information on the rebels. As we have seen, he had heard that the chief problem for them was the lack of ammunition, suggesting they often went into action with only two or three rounds a man. In addition, as already alluded to, he found them 'very bad shots'. It is here that he then discussed the machete. This sword-like instrument, which he called the 'national weapon' of the islanders, deserves a bit more discussion since Churchill is so obviously impressed by it as to spend more time on it than on the Mauser or any other weapon he mentioned. One of the keenest Spanish military observers in Cuba, Colonel Camps y Feliú, certainly agreed with Churchill, calling the machete 'the best combat weapon in Cuba', and adding that it 'works to defend oneself in the countryside, it serves to cut branches in the wild, it serves to clear land and it is of indisputable practical use for any soldier on foot or on horseback, in the attack, in the woods or small meadows'.[17]

Another source, agreeing with Churchill's observation that one of the main problems the Spanish had was that their columns tended to debouch from the trails they were following into the open in single file or two abreast, meaning that they were in the worst possible formation to resist attack or ambush, commented on the machete at greater length and in ways with which the British officer would undoubtedly have agreed:

> the machete, which in open country cannot compare with the bayonet; fighting in the midst of woods, on the other hand, assuming a clash with them, one can assume that it will occur with both sides in open order or in defilade; in the first case, groups or pairs, and in the second, the lead persons, will have to fight more or less individually, using bayonets which will easily get caught in the vines, bushes and other underbrush, being very difficult to extricate in those moments and, on the other hand, machetes cut through such obstacles speedily. Advancing or withdrawing, with a machete one opens the way everywhere and a bayonet is merely a hindrance.[18]

It is also important to note that the negative morale effect of the machete was great among Spanish troops. They feared the dreadful wounds the weapon produced on those unlucky enough to be struck by one, especially in the hands of a *mambí* soldier. The rebels knew of this effect and with it their own morale would rise. It is then interesting to note that, despite the almost mystical fame of the cavalry charge with the machete (the '*carga al machete*') in Cuba, even to his day, they were rarely employed by commanders who could avoid having recourse to them. In the face of the Mauser, they were simply too expensive in human lives. But this does not change the fact that in the hands of horsemen or infantry, as Churchill quickly seized upon, the weapon itself was extremely useful and much respected.

In his fourth letter, Churchill noted but made no further comment on what was in effect the emasculation of Suárez Valdés' column in Arroyo Blanco as one force was sent off with the rations for a north-western garrison, taking with it two battalions and what was doubtless only loosely describable as a squadron of cavalry as escorting troops. This left the general with only just under half of his original force, 1,290 men, although Churchill mistakenly thinks he has 'about 1,700', and only seventy of those mounted. In addition, rather oddly, he referred to those seventy men as 'two squadrons', which of course would have been far from the case since a single full squadron of regular cavalry would normally have been made up of more men than that. The state of enemy intelligence was again referred to, if only obliquely, in Churchill's comment that, once the main column heard their fellows in the ration column come under fire just as soon as both headed out of the village, Suárez Valdés ordered his own troops to wheel about and 'For about two miles we retraced our steps in the direction of Iguara, in order to deceive the enemy's scouts, and then struck off to the left and marched due east.'

He then gave the account of the enemy party of twenty-five, doubtless cavalry, who were watching the column's movements and who headed off rapidly towards the protection of some woods when they were seen by the Spanish. Even with the best will in the world, the Spanish were in their usual position of not being able to close with the enemy. But they at least tried to resist the traditional rebel effort to keep them from sleeping as Churchill's words show:

> The cavalry remounted and pursued those fellows with the greatest promptitude, but they were unable to catch them before they reached the edge of the forest, into the depths of which it was impossible to follow. It was evident that the enemy was very close, and in order to prevent the camp being disturbed by his fire during the night no fewer than four companies of infantry were posted on the edge of the woods, and numerous other precautions taken to avoid a surprise.[19]

The next sections of the letter referred to the heavy going involved in marching through the local terrain and the impact of this factor on reconnaissance, an issue to which he came back more than once given its centrality. It is curious, however, that Churchill did not inform the readership of the context here, one in which the enemy was slowing the advancing Spaniards by taking up highly temporary firing positions to harass the column, then giving ground and moving farther back upon his base at La Reforma. It may well be that Churchill did not know that such a tactic was likely because the briefings from his hosts were of the usual Spanish 'best case analysis' type. As at other times, even if he were allowed to attend a briefing, his lack of Spanish would have limited his ability to follow the overall picture. But this is conjecture. Perhaps the most telling comment came from his incident at the riverside, where, in his description of that in some ways humorous scene, he put in an aside of real importance for the conduct of guerrilla warfare: 'Of course they had their rifles – in this war no soldier ever goes a yard without his weapon.' Less convincingly, and curiously, he also remarked that 'After about half an hour the insurgents had enough, and went off carrying their wounded and dead away with them', adding that they had 'killed and wounded several soldiers about the camp'. It does appear that there were some wounded at this stage of the march, but no dead, and there is no evidence to suggest the rebels lost dead at this time either. On the other hand, it was almost always the case that reports from both sides in this war minimised friendly casualties while exaggerating those of the enemy.

As the main action was joined, he made some other interesting comments: for example, 'To describe ground shortly is always difficult, and to describe it at length is futile, as no one ever takes the trouble to read the description carefully enough to understand it.' Many war correspondents and military historians can attest to the validity of Churchill's statement here, although he then went on to give rather a good and useful description of the very ground across which they were moving. And it must be said that his description of the action itself is as good as one could hope in a short article of this kind. What is also interesting to note is that his sketch of the battlefield shows the ground very well and it is really rather easy to imagine the tactical context from it. He would not have known, however, that it would be published alongside the article he wrote, so he could not assume that the reader had a visible image to refer to when reading the account.

From his description of the fight, several conclusions about his analysis of the Spanish and rebels can be inferred. One is of course the great personal courage of General Suárez Valdés, which Churchill and Barnes could not avoid emulating as they remained under the same fire, which was heavy at times. Another is the professionalism of the infantry. And yet another is the obvious vigour of the Spanish troops in the advance under fire. Less clear is why he suggested that casualties among the staff, which were minimal, as for the column as a whole, were 'out of all proportion to those of the rest of the force'.

Then there is a contradiction with points he makes in his fifth and last letter to London, one which it is important to address here. He had first written, 'The infantry advanced and occupied the enemy's position. Pursuit was impossible owing to the impenetrable nature of the woods in the rear, and as the force had only one day's rations left we withdrew across the plain to La Jicotea.' Yet, in the next letter, he criticised at length and sharply the decisions made at the end of that day:

> The Government troops had taken a week's hard marching to find the enemy, and, having found them, had attacked them promptly and driven them from their position. The natural course was to have kept in touch at all costs, and to have bucketed them until they were forced to either disperse or fight. No pursuit was, however, attempted. Honour was satisfied, and the column adjourned to breakfast, after which we marched to La Jicotea, and the men went into cantonments. It seems a strange and unaccountable thing that a force, after making such vigorous marches, showing such energy in finding the enemy, and displaying such steadiness in attacking them, would deliberately sacrifice all that these efforts had gained. Such tactics make the war interminable. Here you have a General of Division and two thousand of the best troops in the island out for over ten days in search of the enemy, overcoming all sorts of difficulties, undergoing all kinds of hardships, and then being quite contented with killing thirty or forty rebels and taking a low grass hill which was destitute of the slightest importance. At this rate of progress it would take the Emperor William, with the German Army, twenty years to crush the revolt.[20]

This is Churchill's only major assessment of the overall scene he had witnessed over those few days with the column. It is noteworthy on several points. First, despite an increasingly pro-Spanish ring to his writing, this attack on their strategy and tactics is obvious. It is difficult to find fault with what he wrote in the sense that, as a good cavalry officer and as someone with at least a good deal of book learning about the military, he would have expected Suárez Valdés to have pressed home his advantage and pressured the Gómez–Maceo column to the greatest extent possible, giving the rebels no rest and pinpointing their position while he assembled forces to give them the coup de grâce.

If it was so important to stop this invasion, then why, he was asking, did the one force that was in contact with the enemy, and which had just 'driven them from their positions', stop right there and do no more? These are fair questions and it is interesting that he did not find in his own analysis any answers, thus leaving the criticisms standing. Churchill's training as a cavalry officer and his lifelong interest in things military would have taught him that under circumstances like those the Spanish faced on the late morning and early afternoon of 2 December, the initiative should not be lost. The enemy was attempting to move westwards and it was vital to stop him from doing so as early as possible, both for tactical reasons and because the propaganda value of his enjoying an unimpeded continued advance was very great indeed in a war where propaganda, and its objective of public opinion, was of the essence in achieving victory.

That same training and love for military history should perhaps have made him look a little more deeply into the context of the column with which he was serving, the orders his general had almost certainly received, and the simple relative strengths and capacities of the two forces that had met that day at La Reforma. General Suárez Valdés, for reasons of increased mobility for his slow fighting column, had been obliged to reduce the rations of his troops for this operation to only four days. This meant he could not imagine successfully keeping in touch with the enemy, much less 'bucketing them' or even less forcing them to disperse or fight. While Churchill was certainly right that the textbook of military tactics would have suggested such an approach, the real context in which Suárez Valdés was working did not allow for such a thing.

Instead, he found himself not only constrained by the issue of remaining rations but infinitely more by the fact that he was vastly outnumbered and totally outclassed in terms of the required mobility to engage the enemy in the fashion his second-lieutenant critic advised. Even if with more rations he could have continued to operate for several more days, he would not have been able to achieve what Churchill suggested. Churchill acknowledged that his column's commander certainly did not have more than 1,700 men available and we now know that the figure was in fact slightly less than 1,300. The enemy's strength was reported as at least 4,000 and in some reports even more. And he had just seen that the enemy's impedimenta suggested strongly that this figure was accurate. But these total figures were in many senses neither here nor there: what mattered was the number of horsemen that were available. They alone would have provided the mobility for Suárez Valdés to keep contact with the enemy, 'bucket him' and put such pressure on him that he would be forced to fight or disperse. That cavalry was neither in the Spanish column nor available on call at any foreseeable time in the future. It could even be argued that such mounted strength was not available on the island as a whole, much less locally. Instead the general had the ridiculously small mounted force of some seventy cavalry, who were not going to be able to achieve any of the goals Churchill discussed and would simply have been swept aside by mounted troops over forty times their number in any kind of attempt to force into fight the rebel column or even simply shadow it effectively. And Spanish infantry plodding along, however well, could do little to help in this.

Even in infantry terms, the situation was not all that good. Suárez Valdés was not to know that the column was about to lose 1,000 men from its infantry force when it was detached shortly thereafter for duties to the south-west in the attack on the Trinidad area. He himself had only slightly more than that number, some 1,130, and from them must be taken the light casualties of the day and the two previous days. His two small artillery pieces did little to address this vast imbalance in the forces of the two armies present.

To some extent this is to quibble. The objective here is to assess the quality of the military analysis of a 21-year-old subaltern, himself, as we have seen from the *New York World* article of a few days later, 'knowing only the amount of strategy necessary for the duties of a second lieutenant'. In spite of Churchill's deep study of military history, this is largely accurate. Second lieutenants were and are taught tactics, not strategy. While they may have learned the principles of war, generally acknowledged to apply at both tactical and strategic levels, they do not have opportunities to see them in application except at the lower of those two strata of operations. Churchill knew what should have been the strategic and tactical precepts applied in this case but he knew them as part of an ideal case.

In the actual situation of that afternoon of 2 December, his column's commander, not in a position yet to attempt to bring together sufficient force to do the things Churchill suggested, did what he had to do. He left the slow-moving column behind, moved as fast as possible to get into a position where he could be overall commander in the region, and so left on horseback the next day for Ciego de Ávila to take the train immediately for the coast, to take ship for Cienfuegos and thence back to his headquarters, in order to pull together the size and type of forces that might actually achieve the things that, he would have agreed with Churchill, now had to be done. This thinking is confirmed by his draft messages that very day to his commander-in-chief in Santa Clara, two of which are extant in the Spanish military archive although it is impossible to know which was actually sent:

[Version 1]

I left for Ciego de Ávila with a guerrilla ... and I came here [Tunas de Zaza] with a gunboat in order to continue on to Sancti Spiritus, with the objective of organising a column to leave as soon as possible for Iguará, where I think there should be established a force to join the operations of the Navarro and Aldecoa columns, and I believe it would be of great convenience that Remedios send another strong column towards Tobosi to avoid among the four of them that the enemy achieve without difficulty his objective, which according to news is nothing other than to advance via the territory of Las Villas towards the western part of the island as far as is possible.

[Version 2]

Considering that it is urgent to organise columns from Sti. Spiritus to combine them with those mentioned and contain the advance of those bands [Maceo and Gómez], I have gone with my escort to discuss with General Aldave [commander at the Trocha] and I have come here by sea to advise you of the measures I am taking and to await your orders.[21]

It is also confirmed in the General Order issued by General Suárez Valdés to his troops of the column when he left them the next day at Jicotea before he, his escorting *guerrilla* (presumably the Yero), and Churchill and Barnes left that morning for Ciego de Ávila: 'The necessity to organise in my district forces to engage in the operations against Gómez and Maceo obliges me, much to my regret, to separate myself momentarily from the column.'[22] This was his priority and this is what he did. It was not to carry on at the head of a slow infantry column attempting to hold onto the extreme tail of a rapidly advancing and large enemy column that had to be stopped, not 'tailed'.

Churchill may also simply not have been sufficiently well informed of what the strategic stakes were to be able to make a fully accurate assessment. The Spanish, as we have seen, knew that things were going badly. And, though they probably did not know he was writing for a major newspaper in Britain while with them as a military observer, they certainly knew he was an officer from an important army and country, and the son of an aristocrat of note. They would not have wanted him to know too much of the simply dreadful context in which they found themselves with the feared invasion of the west on its way, the army's columns woefully inadequate, despite their numbers of men, to defeat it, and political pressure mounting against their Commander-in-Chief and even some of his more junior generals.

It must be said that Churchill gave in his military analysis proof of a major gift for understanding military issues, a powerful ability for expression of that understanding, and a clear thirst for knowledge of what was going on about him. From small points on morale to large ones on approaches to guerrilla warfare in general, the young correspondent showed promise of the highest order. Humour, intelligence and balance already characterised his writing and would continue to do so when he addressed military affairs.

Perhaps the views of one of the very few Spanish sources who have looked at the military aspects of Churchill's analysis of things in Cuba at the time will help us to measure the value of his work. Colonel Blas Piñar Gutiérrez, a Spanish infantry colonel and former army attaché at the embassy in Buenos Aires and commentator on the sole Spanish-speaking translation of the letters for *The Daily Graphic*, sums up the young Winston's military analysis as follows:

> [while] one cannot deny an enormous ingenuity and frankness, which goes with his youth, in his descriptions and considerations, that do not always follow along the same narrative line, but rather change in rhythm and in argument, the whole is impregnated with a notable knowledge of military affairs, a frank, positive, open and in some way didactic attitude, and an obvious capacity for reflection before a reality that breathes before him day after day.[23]

Churchill and Guerrilla Warfare in Cuba

The major flaw in the analyses Churchill made of the military context in Cuba was surely in the area of some elements of his understanding of the type of war the Cuban rebels were conducting. Churchill was a young and keen regular officer, in his first ever exposure to a military operation. He came from a highly traditionalist army and was himself an aristocrat, conservative and a decided imperialist. He was not likely to be keen on the kind of warfare he saw the rebels engaging in during the revolution against Spain that he witnessed for those eighteen days. He was also the guest of another regular army and was enjoying very much being, to use the modern term, 'embedded' with the Suárez Valdés column and being considered in general by the Spanish as something of a celebrity guest.

As he himself admitted, he was at first in considerable sympathy with the rebellion and his criticisms of Spanish misgovernment abound. But he also soon suggested that such sympathy was reserved for the rebellion and not the rebels themselves. He found their tactics disturbing, to say the least, and not those of gentlemen. The policy of torching property, leading to the ruin of the island, he found particularly unacceptable. This did not mean that he did not find what the rebels were doing sound strategy, as we have seen.

He was especially impressed with the ability of the Cubans, avoiding action when it did not suit them, and waiting always for only the most favourable conditions before ever engaging the Spanish in open warfare, to choose when and where to fight. Several authors suggest that Churchill did not really understand the Cubans' use of guerrilla warfare. Manchester wrote that he had 'failed to grasp the essential nature of guerrilla warfare'. Isaac Pitrulla and many others agree. But this is not entirely fair. He certainly understood many of its principles: for example, mobility, fighting only when conditions favoured such action, the importance of propaganda, making war against the economic structures of the state.

Churchill does not seem, however, to understand that this type of war involved a different kind of courage on the part of the soldiers engaged in it. As a regular he does not seize on why the rebels must, in his words, be 'masters of the art of running away' or other damning phrases of the kind. He was wrong when he wrote in *The Saturday Review* that the insurgents 'cannot win a single battle or hold a single town'. They won many battles before getting to La Reforma or they would not have made it that far. And they won others while Churchill and Barnes were still in Cuba and while they sailed home, during what was a triumphal march westward, the beginnings of which the two officers had witnessed. And it can be forcefully argued, from what we have seen, that the action at La Reforma itself was a victory, since the Spanish were unable to stop the invasion or even appreciably slow it down. While they could not hold a town for any signifi-cant period, such a goal did not form part of their strategy although they would certainly have liked to hold one in order to settle their revolutionary government and increase the chances of international recognition. Cuban rebel soldiers often fought with great gallantry but Churchill saw them only in a hit-and-run role, and in a rapid withdrawal from a fight. Given who he was, he was unlikely to be impressed. But he should have been able to draw consistently conclusions more closely related to the facts of the case as he does on occasion. For example, while sarcastic about rebel valour in one of his articles for the British press, he does situate their approach to fighting within the insurgent strategy: 'I admire the rebels for the quickness and rapidity with which they get over the ground … soon out of sight. I make no reflections on their courage, but they are well versed in the art of retreat. Of course the secret of their strength is the ability to harass the enemy and carry on a guerrilla warfare.' Churchill's firm professional understanding of why the rebels do what they do is here, as often elsewhere, at war with his disgust with their unmannerly way of doing it.[24]

The Sketches

It is not clear whether the idea of sketches to accompany the Cuban articles was Churchill's or his editor at *The Daily Graphic*. It would have been per-fectly logical for either of the two men to have suggested them, Churchill because he wanted to write for an illustrated paper, and Thomas and Heath Joyce because that was what they most wished for in order to provide draw-ings to accompany the articles in their newspaper.

Winston's training as a light cavalry officer would have included some instruction in drawing. Hussars routinely reported back to their command-ing officers and the latter to their higher formation commanders on what they discovered on reconnaissance duties, in traditional intelligence terms, 'on the other side of the hill'. Such reports frequently included sketches of enemy positions, troop movements, fortifications or just terrain features of interest to higher commanders at all levels, which helped them visualise much better than mere texts what the report was referring to and thus be in a better situation to understand the context in which they found themselves and to prepare plans for future action. In order to better do such sketches all light cavalry officers were expected to develop at least the rudiments of drawing and of linking by text an understanding of what was seen with what was said in their reports. Churchill also almost certainly had some basic drawing lessons in some of the fortifications courses he so enjoyed at Sandhurst before joining his regiment.

It is also true that there are at least some references to Churchill liking drawing at a much earlier age, and of turning that interest to military themes. In what William Manchester call's Winston's 'first surviving attempt in the arts', as a 16-year-old he had made a sketch of Kaiser Wilhelm II, in London to visit a special exhibition at the Crystal Palace. Winston had gone there to see him with Count Kinsky, his mother's Austrian lover, and had brought a sketchbook for the occasion. He described the Emperor's uniform to his brother Jack in a letter, where he said the large brass helmet of His Imperial Majesty was accompanied by a 'polished steel cuirass & a perfectly white uniform with high boots'.[25] Thus Winston's first such effort was of a military figure in the most glorious of uniforms, perfectly in keeping with the boy's interests and passions.

While in Cuba, Churchill did at least sixteen sketches, some or perhaps all of which are still extant in some form and in safe keeping at the Churchill Archive at Churchill College, Cambridge.[26] They are of immense interest to historians dealing with the uniforms and weapons of the day, battle scenes such as his own at La Reforma, troops moving and being inspected, river and other obstacle crossings by elements of the column, arrivals and departures of the column from places such as Arroyo Blanco, warships, fortifications, parts of the Trocha, scenes of military life in the column, senior officers and much else. Contemporary renderings of the Cuban flag, the *mambí* badge which served as their uniform in so many cases, the Spanish railway defensive posts, the armoured trains they used constantly and the types of locomotive that towed them, the blockhouses of the Trocha, both Spanish regular soldiers and voluntarios, a staff dinner scene on campaign, cavalry on the march, the town of Sancti Spiritus and the village of Arroyo Blanco or at least parts of them, Martínez Campos himself inspecting newly arrived troops at the quayside, close sketches of officers and soldiers, troops at rest, and the actual action at La Reforma: these sketches form a valuable piece of heritage for both Cuba and the Churchill story. The fact that it was Winston himself who drew them, even if they were subsequently greatly 'doctored' by specialists, makes them priceless.

It is, however, very difficult to judge how good at drawing Churchill was from these sketches. As mentioned above when discussing the way the *Daily Graphic* and other illustrated papers dealt with their business, Churchill would doubtless have sent the sketches with his letter for publication. Standard practice was then for a staff artist to improve sketches for publication. We have no idea as to how good or bad the initial work was although it is clear that it was good enough to invite publication, kudos from the editor and pay for work done. And we know nothing about the staff artist except for his name: Mr T.C. Crowther.[27] It would be fascinating to know more about these drawings from his first adventure abroad given his later sketches accompanying his Boer War articles and his future interest in painting.

Churchill's need to do military analysis in depth grew over most of his career and outstripped anything he was required to do on the island. His analysis of the Boer War just four years later is impressive to this day. Carlo D'Este wrote, 'What is less explicable is how a young man of his limited education and experience, untrained as he was in strategy and high command, could have achieved such a deep understanding of the Boer War.'[28] This was the case in Cuba but not to the same degree as in South Africa, much less in the working up to the First World War, the interwar years or the great trials of the Second World War. And we cannot see anything in Churchill's thinking about war in Cuba that would lead us yet to Manchester's assertion that 'In fact, his military thought was so extraordinary that others simply could not grasp it.'[29] But for a 21-year-old lacking experience, it was frequently exceptional in its breadth and its flashes of deep intelligence, and very often in its originality.

CHAPTER 10

THE IMPACT OF THE CUBAN ADVENTURE

> Continuous effort, not strength or intelligence,
> is the key to unlocking our potential.

Churchill arrived back in England on 21 December. It was one of the few wars from which he was to be, to use the now infamous phrase, 'home for Christmas'. He had had a comfortable crossing on the *Etruria*, untroubled by the weather that had kept him from writing his final letter, as he intended, from on board the *Olivette*, the week before.

Thus everything had almost gone better than Churchill could have imagined. In the gestation of the idea, planning of the trip, obtaining of the requisite permissions, travel to and through the United States and on to Cuba, meetings in Havana, travel to the 'front', interviews with the captain-general, joining up with the Spanish Army column, marching with those troops, observation of the fighting alongside them under considerable fire themselves, travel back to Havana, and then to Tampa, New York and back to the United Kingdom: there had hardly ever been a hitch. When there had been one, as when trains were missed in Cuba, it was all to the good, and nasty experiences were in fact avoided through those connection problems, as he wrote to his mother shortly after his return to Havana. In short, as so often in his life, Churchill had been exceptionally lucky.

And he had achieved all he had set out to do. He had, most importantly, had the 'private rehearsal' of his baptism of fire, and, if it was nothing like the leadership and battle test he was to have two years later on India's North-West Frontier, it was no less real, with a real dose of fire over a couple of days, sustained danger over long hours the day of the La Reforma action, including several minutes highly exposed to quite heavy fire.[1] And here in Cuba he and Barnes were alone, not surrounded by British troops and the British Army. Churchill had discovered that the dangers of war, if not always its discomfort, were 'suited' to his personality, as he had gone to Cuba to check. As Robert Lloyd George put it, Cuba 'was his first taste of front-line action, and he loved it'.[2]

If war did indeed suit his personality, he was subsequently to see much of it, fighting in several of its manifestations: the Indian North-West Frontier, the Sudan, the Boer War and the First World War. He was also to have a major politico-military role in the last of these, as well as in the work-up to the Second World War. And last and most dramatically, he was to lead not only the United Kingdom, the Commonwealth and the empire in that great struggle but in many senses to be the inspiration of the war efforts of all the democracies. Even in his last term as prime minister, from 1951 to 1955, he had to address questions of the management of Britain's wars in Korea and Malaya, a near-insurgency in Kenya and a military intervention in British Guiana. Wars and conflict made up much of his life and, as all his biographers have agreed, he thrived on it. Cuba introduced him to them. In 1895, in his own words, he had found it 'cruel but magnificent'. Over time he would find it 'cruel and squalid'.[3]

He had also shown courage under fire as demonstrated by his decoration for bravery, the Red Cross of Military Merit. This confirmation of his courage was clearly very important for him; it was only the first of a large number of medals, orders and decorations he was to receive over his life, but it *was* the first and it was specifically for courage and steadiness under fire, just the attributes of personality he most wished to have and to show. It would be annoying to have the War Office not allow him to wear such medals but he would find a way to do so occasionally.[4] In an army like the Spanish, where decorations were given away with such ease, and as a foreign officer who might be getting them as much for his name and country as for his own comportment, it was reassuring to know that beyond doubt he had behaved with calm and distinction under fire. If his leadership skills remained untested, his courage had passed the first of many tests.

It is impossible to deny that he was then, and for some time, what the army disparagingly called a 'medal hunter'. He did not deny it but he remained convinced that it was personal courage on the battlefield which was the shortest route to national renown and thus to political office. Instead of being merely the son of Lord Randolph Churchill, Winston had begun to carve out his own niche of personal fame.

This was the only time that Churchill served with a foreign army, far from the things with which he was most familiar, though, of course, he served alongside other armies, such as the French and Belgians, and dealt with any number of them: Dominion and colonial forces, Americans, Czechs, Dutch, Egyptians, Germans, Moroccans, Norwegians and Poles, amongst others. He fought against Afghans, Boers, Germans and Sudanese. And he was to go on to serve with a variety of British and colonial units – the 17th Lancers, the Grenadier Guards, the Royal Scots Fusiliers and the 31st Punjab Infantry.[5] But he was only ever commissioned into three: the 4th (Queen's Own) Hussars, the Queen's Own Oxfordshire Hussars and the South African Light Horse, the last of these only as a temporary and local measure to permit his activities in the Boer War. He was only, as was right and proper, considered to have been a full member of the first two. The 4th Hussars was of course his regular regiment with which he served those four years and from which he had obtained leave to go to Cuba. To it, perhaps belatedly, he showed great loyalty after he left it formally, and visited its troops at least three times as honorary colonel even in the dark days of the Second World War.[6] But, almost uniquely for someone so active, he had never actually seen active service with this regiment, having always been detached from it for those more momentous times.

He also later showed exceptional loyalty to his reserve regiment, the Queen's Own Oxfordshire Hussars (QOOH), the one in which he served, although only on a part-time basis, from 1902 to 1916, and rejoined in 1922. He was of course an officer of some distinction by the time he joined the regiment and, so pleased as they were to have him, he was immediately made second-in-command of a squadron, going on to command one and receiving promotion to major before the coming of the First World War. It was in the uniform of this unit that he went off to war in November 1915, having left the government in May after negative reactions to his role in the Gallipoli campaign. He also became this regiment's honorary colonel and ensured that it was given proper roles in the Second World War when it was threatened with being broken up and fed into the line as mere drafts for other units. Winston was both a regular and a reserve soldier and in the latter role was known for loyally undergoing training, and executing command, even when he was hard pressed with official duties and writing.[7] Little wonder then that Churchill went on to be considered in both regiments as 'the Greatest Hussar', a title he now enjoys in all hussar regiments of the Commonwealth.[8]

In his drive for public attention, Churchill had also written articles for the press, not just as a correspondent but as a war correspondent, during his time on the island. Those first articles were published by a major newspaper read by many thousands of people, and not just the aristocracy, in the most important city and country in the world. Others were published after his trip by one of the most important weeklies in the world where political analysis was concerned, and a journal to which many very important writers, and very few minor ones, contributed. Not only were they read but also appreciated.

In one highly laudatory comment, from no less than Joseph Chamberlain, then Colonial Secretary in the Salisbury government, who had been sent a copy of one of Winston's *Saturday Review* articles by Lady Randolph, he wrote back to her describing it as 'the best short account I have seen of the problems [with] which the Spaniards have to deal', adding that it also 'agrees with my own conclusions. It is evident that Mr Winston kept his eyes open.'[9] This must have been gratifying to Winston. But if he was to repeat the success, as he very much hoped, his newspaper bosses too had to be happy with his work, and say so. Thus equally pleasing must have been the note from T. Heath Joyce, the editor of both the *Daily Graphic* and *The Graphic*, who wrote on 10 January 1896, 'I may say that your letters and sketches have been extremely interesting and were just the kind of thing we wanted.' This letter was followed four days later by one from the manager W.L. Thomas, who as we have seen, was also a man of considerable prestige and influence in the newspaper world, saying:

> Allow me to compliment you on the result [as I imagine of your first experiences] as a Special Correspondent & artist combined. Your letters were very interesting and to the point and the sketches useful … I am sorry that your time was so limited and so preventing your sending more'.[10]

This kind of reaction was just what Winston needed for his future attempts to repeat the Cuban experience.

This of course means that he had also had success in his first journalistic experience. And the editor and manager of the paper had no reason to say such things out of mere courtesy. The articles that Churchill had sent were good, very good, and Chamberlain and these professional newspapermen were right in praising them. If we have seen some flaws, that is hardly surprising for a man of Churchill's age on his first assignment, dealing with complex political and military issues, and without the local language. Now Churchill could see a way to become better known to the public, to find the adventure he craved and show the courage he now knew he had, and he now knew he could write well and impressively, and be paid for it, a constant concern for the young officer. Journalism, and specifically war journalism, was to become a major part of his life for some time. This would allow him to develop and hone those skills which by his next war would mean a book published of his experiences. Cuba had opened the door to all this self-discovery and all these options.

Churchill simply could not afford either a military or a political career without some outside income. Almost all cavalry officers had the support of family in order to stay the course of service expenses in that corps. Politicians in the Britain of this era were paid very little, by any standard, on the assumption that it was an honour to take part in the direction of public life, and that men who expected to enjoy that honour would find the money to do so. This meant, however, that only those with incomes from outside their parliamentary duties could stand for a seat there. The appeal of writing for profit, however badly it might have appeared to many in the upper class of the time to see an aristocrat and political figure working in this way, was thus a major one.

The success of these first offerings from Cuba opened the door to newspapers and other sources of income for written work to which Churchill applied himself in the years after 1895. Without that breakthrough it is uncertain what the future of the young Winston's writing career would have been. As readers will know the quality of Churchill's writing has always been a subject of debate. Some argue that it is some of the finest in the English language while others say that it is good but not of world-class stature and there are those who even suggest that rewards for his writing were given more for his status as the recognised greatest hero of the free world than for their intrinsic value. Frederick Woods argues that a variety of 'facts seriously weaken any assertion that he was a great writer or a great stylist. He was always a powerful writer, an exciting writer, a persuasive writer, even a moving writer …'[11] For a man as multi faceted as Churchill, this may be praise enough.

Keith Alldritt's more recent assessment of Churchill's writing speaks of 'an outstanding literary quality which unquestionably belongs in the canon of English literature in this century' but that his work was uneven and tending to 'grand but pretentious language'. Nonetheless he goes on to suggest that the work produced before the 1940s deserves praise for its 'prose by wit, subtle human insights, pace, drama and a poetic richness' beginning with his work on the Siege of Malakand (India) and does not mention his articles in the press of journals on Cuba. But this may be due to the fact that they have been much harder to access until recently, whereas the Malakand, Sudanese and Boer War writing came out in book form.[12]

In any case, for our purposes, his writing at 21 was good enough to please demanding editors of first-class newspapers and intellectual journals. That was praise of the highest kind and an excellent beginning to a life that was of letters, reflection and action of a Renaissance man of the first order, as Manchester asserts.[13]

The Other Advances

As a Spanish biographer has said, 'The Cuban adventure had opened the expectations of Churchill. He had participated in real combat which placed him in a position of superiority above the rest of his companions from Sandhurst who would soon give him the nickname of "the Cuban hussar".' And, while clearly feeling that his subsequent Afghan experience was going to be even more important, even Con Coughlin, the biographer of that later campaign, suggests that 'In Cuba, Winston had taken a significant step towards his goal of fame and fortune, one that he would seek to replicate in Afghanistan.'[14]

Churchill had clearly taken a giant step towards becoming his own man. In the regiment, though still a subaltern, he was an officer who had now seen more action than most, including those much more senior. In his family, it was now clear to Lady Randolph that her role was to back a man on the move and not move him herself. As her biographer put it, referring to the chances she would have of being the head of the family and of keeping her grip on Winston, 'the Cuban escapade at least illustrates how increasingly difficult it would be for Jennie to exercise such control'.[15] But she seems to have quite readily taken to the role of provider of constant solid support for her eldest son, especially in his projects for the future, just as she had done for Lord Randolph, whatever the state of their marriage at a particular time.

The results were immediate and life-changing. Winston was in a position to take advantage of much because, although his leave was over, his last months in the army at Aldershot, only 32 miles from London, were full. The duties he had to perform with the regiment were minimal and there were no time-consuming activities which could keep him from the capital for long. The 4th Hussars were off to India and that meant a relaxing last few months in the mother country of empire, months which Churchill enjoyed to the full.

He finished up his articles for *The Saturday Review*, accepted a commission to write another, on life at the Royal Military College Sandhurst, for the same journal, and apparently took on some undocumented requests to speak on Cuba. He wrote further on the subject for both British and American publications and these articles were generally well received.

He was, after his return from the island, increasingly invited to dinners and social events where his views on the colony's present and future were eagerly sought. But his fear that the posting to India would cloud his chances for the future, as he would be so far away from where things that mattered would be happening, grew markedly as it became clear that the posting would be to Bangalore and not the north. There was unlikely to be much action in the sleepy southern garrison town even if things did become, as they so often did, unruly on the North-West Frontier. Instead he might expect to have his energy atrophy in the heat, dust and boredom of a 'useless and unprofitable exile'.[16]

Being sought after over his Cuban experiences, especially by highly placed former friends and political associates of his father, such as the Prince of Wales, members of the Rothschild family, Joseph Chamberlain, Lord Wolseley himself again, Arthur Balfour and Herbert Asquith, allowed Churchill to actively seek ways of avoiding his posting to the sub-continent, something unlikely to have pleased either his new colonel or his army colleagues. He tried to get leave to cover the Greek Cretan Rebellion against Turkey, recently broken out, then the Egyptian punitive expedition, and

Matabeleland, where his friend and support Frederick de Moleyns would be decorated for the first time. But, even for Churchill, the chances were slim. It was simply unheard of for a young officer to avoid being sent abroad with his regiment for the first time. The Secretary of State for War Lansdowne refused his request and now Lord Wolseley did the same, whatever his connection with the Churchills.[17]

After all, this was supposed to be the time that any young officer had been dreaming of, with his own soldiers to command for the first time, when his own responsibilities with the regiment he was supposed to love were given the opportunity to grow, and when he would have his first real opportunity to get to know his men, his messmates and the army. To try to get out of it would be badly seen even by those who liked Churchill most. And there were plenty who already did not like him, who now felt this attempt to avoid colonial service was even more proof that Winston was not a loyal army man or even, the greatest of scandals, was disloyal to his regiment. Rumours of his endeavours to skip out of regimental service were, as Manchester put it, 'causing talk'. And this is hardly surprising because he essentially tried everything he could think of, and especially his mother's considerable influence, to duck what he saw as the whole Indian trial.[18]

As usual, however, his luck held out. He had the protection of his old commanding officer, Colonel Brabazon, until early summer 1896, and even Lieutenant-Colonel William Alexander Ramsey, who took over the 4th from the dashing 'Bwabs', showed a marked willingness to be patient with his rather upstart young subaltern. Described by Con Coughlin as 'a quiet and unspectacular officer who suffered the misfortune of never having seen active service in nearly thirty years of military service', Ramsey's taking command must have seemed yet another reason for Winston to dread India, especially Bangalore, and crave for a more exciting time elsewhere. But Ramsey appears to have backed Winston in several of his unorthodox schemes and to have remained more or less resigned to his young subaltern always having some hare-brained scheme that involved missing regimental duties. And though it is reasonable to imagine that he would have been the first to wish to curb this temperamental youth who had already seen more active service than his commanding officer, just the opposite was true and he was, if anything, generally indulgent towards Winston. Though, as Coughlin put it, surely accurately, 'Presumably Colonel Ramsay encouraged the desire to acquire martial experience among his junior officers',[19] he did not have to do so with Winston, yet he did have this approach strained by the many difficulties caused by Churchill's entirely unorthodox ways of going about it, not only in the months after Cuba but for most of his command until Churchill finally left regiment and army in 1899.

Churchill had been a 20-year-old officer very recently arrived in a cavalry regiment of the British Army, just beginning his military career and with precious little experience of life, no wartime experience at all, who had never been anywhere near the place he was about to go, who had absolutely no practical experience in journalism, much less in the especially taxing world of war correspondents, without local knowledge or any linguistic skills pertinent to his destination, without knowledge of any significant kind of the stakes or the issues involved for either of the two parties in the war. He had nonetheless planned and executed what really was a daring plan of adventure before, during, and after his Cuban trip.

It was Winston who conceived the trip from its beginnings, Winston who won over Barnes, Winston who, with the support of Reggie and the adjutant got the support of his colonel, Winston who wrote himself to the British ambassador in Madrid asking for key assistance and introductions to the major actors on the military stage in Cuba. It was he who cajoled and convinced his reluctant mother into not only backing but paying for the scheme, but also making the contacts that would allow him to see and gain permission from Lord Wolseley, Commander-in-Chief of the British Army, he who saw not only that senior officer but also his head of intelligence and convinced them that he could be trusted with a serious mission even if a highly unofficial one, and he who made the contacts with the press that led to his being taken on as a war correspondent of a major British publication. It was Winston who actually went to the island, carried it all off, endured the hardships of his first campaigning, showed real courage in action, won his first medal, wrote the letters to his newspaper, and came back to a controversy which by any standards he handled well and supremely better than one could imagine a by then 21-year-old doing.

Prior to his Cuban trip, Churchill was merely the son of a well-known politician and aristocrat. By the end of his adventure he was one of the few officers in his regiment who had seen action and was sought after to speak on the war in Cuba, valued for his opinions on both political and military matters by some of the most important people in the land, an acknowledged journalist who had written and sketched for two of the most important publications in Britain, with new contacts made by himself, *not* inherited from his parents, with a delicate mission for the War Office behind him, respected as never before by his mother and family, and reassured as to his own abilities, courage and future.

No longer was he just another young subaltern, or someone unclear as to what he wanted to do. If, before Cuba, he had had doubts about the army, now they seemed entirely cleared up. He would stay in the army for now, though doing his best to avoid the peaceful Indian military scene, still believing that the way to success in public life was by doing noteworthy things as a man of distinction and adventure. He was firmly on his way to that life, and he had greatly improved his 'hand' for the game of politics in which he would later be in engaged. And he was only just 21.[20]

The Impact on Others

Alas, there is nothing much to go on in order to discover the impact of the Cuban adventure on Churchill's ever-patient and loyal friend Reggie. He went back to his duties as assistant adjutant and, as we have seen, went on to a long and distinguished military career, and the acquisition of many of the medals Winston would doubtless have loved to have received.

In India the two officers became even closer friends, largely because Winston began to play well on the polo field and both were key members of the regimental team as it went from one victory to the next in the British Army of the great colony. Reggie, when later promoted adjutant with De Moleyns' departure, was able to support Winston in his attempts to get to any fighting there was, and did so without envy or reserve, according to all sources. He retained the new commanding officer's confidence and Winston was certainly grateful. When Churchill was given permission to go north for the 1897 Malakand Field Force's campaign, he wrote to his mother, 'Barnes behaved splendidly about my leave as he would have loved to go himself and it was due to his efforts as adjutant that I got it.'[21]

Politics was not for Reggie, though he was made Deputy Lieutenant of Devonshire in 1927, a county where he would spend ever more time as he grew older. He was one of the longest-serving honorary colonels of the 4th (Queen's Own) Hussars, doing that job from 1919 to 1941, and then handing over to Churchill in 1941. Winston held the position from

1941 until 1958 when the regiment amalgamated with the 8th King's Royal Irish Hussars to form the Queen's Own Royal Irish Hussars. Barnes retired from the regular army in 1921. One of his sons was Sir George Reginald Barnes, principal of the University College of North Staffordshire. Another was killed in the desert in North Africa in June 1941 with the Coldstream Guards. Barnes himself died in 1946.

The Cuban Situation after Churchill Left

Churchill continued to write on the Cuban situation for several months, and to speak on it for even longer. Indeed, it is no exaggeration to say that the experience was never forgotten and Cuba remained a country for which he had a special regard. When Churchill sailed from Havana, probably on 8 December 1895, he left a city and country in an exceptional state, a condition whose cause he had witnessed at first hand over the previous two and a half weeks.[22] The crossing of the Trocha by the rebels, followed closely by the action at La Reforma, the Battle of Iguará and the advance of the insurgent infantry on Trinidad and cavalry on the west of Las Villas province were key moments in the invasion programme Gómez was now earnestly conducting. The Spanish, and especially the local commander in Las Villas, Suárez Valdés, and his Commander-in-Chief in Santa Clara, Martínez Campos, were having some of the worst days of their lives trying to cope with the turn of events that Barnes and Churchill had experienced.

Columns were organised in all the main garrison towns west of the Trocha and sent out to try to pinpoint the whereabouts of the rebel columns and, if possible, bring them to battle. But Gómez continued with his well-proven tactics of engaging his enemy only when he had a virtual certainty of victory. The key elements were to burn the cane fields and thus disrupt the colonial economy, and to carry the war as far west as possible showing the populous western provinces that the goal of independence was indeed possible, that the Liberation Army was not a black horde determined on vengeance over the whites who had held them down so long, and that the Spanish were not going to win this war.

The rebel successes in all these areas ensured that political pressure in both Spain and Cuba caused a change of command on the island. Martínez Campos was exhausted. He had seen all his successes in bringing the Ten

Years War to an end with his Pact of Zanjón of 1878 brought to nothing by the unwillingness of successive governments in Madrid to bring real reform to Cuba, and thus this new war had started seventeen years later. And he had at best only half-heartedly headed out to the island again and with grave doubts about the prospects of victory this time.

Unable to bring about that victory quickly in Oriente, and himself defeated and nearly killed in an early battle of the campaign in the east, he was a shaken man by the time he deployed his headquarters to Santa Clara on 4 November, a little over two weeks before Churchill's arrival. He had been on active campaign for nearly seven and a half months by then, having arrived in Santiago from Spain on 16 April.[23] From there he watched every attempt to defeat decisively Gómez west of the Trocha and Maceo east of it come to nought. He then had to contemplate Maceo's crossing of the Trocha to join Gómez for the invasion without being able to do anything effective to stop the movement. There were times, such as at the Battle of Maltiempo on 15 December, when Gómez decided to accept battle, but it was only when he was sure to profit from it. The government forces were never able to force him into a fight.

Inexorably the rebels approached and crossed into Matanzas province, entering the province of Havana on New Year's Day 1896. They skirted the capital itself, driving deep into Pinar del Río, the island's westernmost province. Gómez, using the same strategy as in November, tied down the Spanish in Havana province while Maceo, with a cavalry column of over 1,500 men, drove rapidly westward to capture, on 22 January, the town of Mantua and secure the propaganda coup of having taken the revolution from the furthest east to the furthest west of Cuba. The dream of the independence movement, frustrated for three decades, had come true. And the Spanish reeled from it all, sending columns of slow moving infantry hither and yon with little prospect, as Churchill had assessed, of bringing the rebels to an open battle where they could be defeated.

Under these circumstances the impact on the Spanish high command could hardly be expected to be minor. Calls for Martínez Campos to be removed won out, despite the fact that neither the War Minister nor the Queen Regent wished to take that very drastic step. On 17 January, with the rebels not far from Havana, though still incapable of seriously threatening the capital itself, Martínez Campos resigned and power on the island was transferred provisionally to General Sabas Marín. The former captain-general issued a general order and also addressed the troops suggesting that the whole responsibility for defeat so far lay with him, and that in any case a large part of public opinion wished him to go and he had no wish to divide the nation on the issue at such a time.

In fact, he had already expressed to his superiors the view that only the most draconian military and civil control measures could hold Cuba at that time for Spain and that his moral principles would not allow him to take those measures. He had suggested that, if the government were prepared to go to those lengths to keep the island, he would recommend Valeriano Weyler as next captain-general as he would be able to adopt such measures and perhaps end the rebellion. His recommendation was accepted and Weyler was called to command in the colony. He was effective in bringing the rebels' victorious march to a close but he was unable to bring the revolution to an end. In fact, his excesses swelled insurgent ranks with furious people who beforehand had been indifferent to the independence cause or who had viewed it as an impossibility. The Autonomist option, which lasted from New Year's Day, 1898, until the US take-over of the island exactly one year later, failed because it was once again too little, too late, in terms of reform and regaining Cuban confidence in any solution that implied the slightest continued loyalty and connection to the mother country.

Martínez Campos sailed for Spain on 21 January. With him sailed many officers who were to mark Spain's twentieth century. One was Juan O'Donnell, Churchill's very temporary guide to things Cuban in Santa Clara in November. Another was Primo de Rivera, later, in the 1920s, to become Spain's dictator. Others affected included Suárez Valdés, who became military governor of Havana, although he would soon be back in command of troops trying yet again to find and destroy Maceo and Gómez. In Spain, Churchill's benefactor from afar, the Duke of Tetuán, resigned in sympathy with Martínez Campos.

Cuba would become independent four years later, and even then only in name. The US occupation, beneficial on many fronts such as health, communications and development, ended only when the control of the new republic could be guaranteed by a new government, unstable to be sure but under direct threat of US intervention if it did things unpalatable to Washington. By then Cuba's economy, ruined by the many years of war, had come to be totally dominated by the United States, a mirror of what had happened at the political level. This situation, where the great calls for real independence were to be frustrated for several decades, opened the way to yet another revolution, sixty years later, that attempted to finally make independence a reality. The highly charged and emotional political context of Cuba in the first decades of the twenty-first century leaves open the question of the degree to which that attempt was worthwhile but certainly it was achieved at last with Fidel Castro's new government in January 1959.

CONCLUSION

It has been the argument of this book that the nature of the formative experience Churchill underwent in the conception, preparation, conduct and aftermath of his Cuban adventure of 1895 is such that it can properly be said that through it he 'came of age' in the full sense of that term, and that therefore this experience is worthy of greater interest and attention from historians dealing with the development of this great man.

As a statesman who had enormous stature, possibly the greatest of his age, Churchill was to go on to operate on the most important stages for much of the twentieth century. But his first direct exposure to its challenges, and his first study of its pitfalls, was during and after his Cuban trip.

As one of the great adventurers and soldiers of fortune of an age of adventurers and soldiers of fortune, Churchill was to undertake such adventures many times in his life, especially in the years immediately after 1895. But his first foreign adventure was in Cuba that year.

As one of the most impressive students and practitioners of politics of his era, Churchill was to hold several Cabinet posts, including prime minister at a time of great national and international peril, and live the great game for most of his life. But his first opportunity for serious political analysis came with his visit to the Caribbean island.

As a military analyst of great skill, he was often called upon to make, or thrust himself into making, decisions based on those analyses, over the many years of his military career and military-related political life. But the first occasion where such skills were brought to bear in a public arena, and counted, was in Cuba in 1895.

Churchill was to become one of the most renowned, and best paid, war correspondents at the turn of the twentieth century.[1] But his first experience of that exciting field of work was his reporting for the *Daily Graphic* during the unsuccessful Spanish campaign to suppress the second major Cuban independence war.

Churchill is surely almost unique in being a man who was to be minister of all three armed services at one time or another over his political career and closely connected with the forces for almost all his life. Yet his first assignment from the War Office came with the request that he study and report on the Spanish rifle round being used against the Cuban insurgents in the rebellion of 1895.

Churchill is known for always dealing with those at the top, whatever his own rank and position, and using fully his connections as well as those of his father and mother and the rest of the family. The first deployment of those skills, thereafter something of a system or formula for him, was in order to obtain the permissions and make possible his trip to Cuba with Reggie Barnes.

Related to this, it is extraordinary how often in his life he dealt with the great, from those he met through his father to those who made his funeral the spectacular event it was. But it was in connection with the Cuba trip that for the first time, and as a result of his own efforts, he came into contact with some of the great men of three countries and of the period.

And related to that, Churchill had a life peppered with coincidences which brought him into contact with the great events of the day. In Cuba, he had his first of these when he found himself in the middle of the invasion of the west, the most decisive event in what was then a 27-year-old story of conspiracy and revolution, and only a short distance from two of the greatest figures in Cuban, and indeed Latin American, history.

Winston has become the symbol of resolution and 'not giving in' to many not only of his own time, and especially during the Second World War, but to this day. This trait was first visible to the public in his handling of the obstacles to this visit.

Just as much as for resolution, Churchill is known for personal courage of the highest order. He deployed it on innumerable occasions ranging from Cuba through North-West Frontier of India, the Sudan, South Africa,

Antwerp and right up to and through the 'blitz'. His first personal test of that courage, however, was still his baptism of fire on 1–2 December 1895 during the actions around La Reforma.

Winston became one of the most decorated figures of the modern world. The medals he received were from many countries and for many services and he treasured them all his life. His first, for steadiness under fire, was awarded him during and for his service in Cuba.

Churchill later felt that you were known by your enemies: if you did not have any, the chances were you did not stand for anything. In his case, a subject of controversy for all of his public life, that aspect of his life appeared for the first time in dramatic form as a result of the Cuban experience.

That controversial side of his life was also present in a diplomatic sense. Churchill spent a life dealing with complex and delicate diplomatic contexts. In Cuba, serving 'with' an army engaged in repressing a revolution generally supported by the British public, made for his first exposure to the more dicey side of international life.

A powerful writer, author of 58 books, 842 articles and 9,000 pages of printed speeches, Churchill went on to win the Nobel Prize for Literature.[2] But his first writing was done for *The Daily Graphic*, the newspaper that commissioned him, for *The Saturday Review*, and for other papers in Britain and the United States while covering the political and military events of late 1895 Cuba.

Winston, especially after the Dardanelles debacle of 1915, began to sketch and paint in an increasingly serious way, and became an accomplished painter. But his first serious and published works of art were his sketches, admittedly improved by professionals, for *The Daily Graphic*, done in the rebellious colony.

Churchill travelled all over the world during his life and must be considered a truly great traveller, even well beyond his days as a young adventurer. But his first trip outside the tranquil life of north-west Europe was to the far from tranquil Caribbean island of 1895.

Winston found in his mother an ally of great value, and one now totally devoted to his advancement. But the support she gave him for the Cuban adventure's success was to mark the beginning of this new phase in their relationship and her acceptance that further control of her son would be unlikely. From Cuba on, he was solidly in the driver's seat in his new formula for bringing her skills into a firmly supporting role for his future endeavours.

These are only some of the 'firsts' associated with Churchill's planning and execution of his Cuban adventure. A proper list would include his first 'near death experiences', at least as an adult, his first military operation, his first coming to the notice of foreign royalty in his own right, his first time serving with a foreign army, his first public shows of what was to become the enormously famous 'Churchill wit', his first time working in a sustained way in a foreign language, and his first real exposure to Cuban cigars and to the invaluable practice of the siesta.

On 30 November of that year, Churchill had his 21st birthday as he moved along rural Cuban roads to his baptism of fire the next day. In almost every sense, it is in the Cuba of 1895 that he comes of age.

THE CUBAN ADVENTURE CHRONOLOGY

1895

August	4th Hussars advised of Indian posting the next year
Late September	The idea of a visit to a war zone begins to germinate in Churchill's mind
Early October	Churchill writes to Sir Henry Drummond Wolff to get him Spanish permission
4 October	Churchill writes to his mother announcing his intentions to travel to Cuba
8 October	Sir Henry obtains the Spanish Minister of War's permission
18 October	Churchill has interview with Lord Wolseley, C–in–C of the British Army
20 October	Churchill has interview with General Chapman, Director of Military Intelligence
2 November	*Etruria* sails from Liverpool with Churchill and Barnes aboard
9 November	Major Wilson visits the Foreign Office to advise them that the two officers go 'privately' *Etruria* arrives in New York
17 November	Churchill and Barnes leave New York by train for Tampa
18 November	Arrival Tampa Bay

19 November	*Olivette* sails from Tampa for Cuba with two officers aboard
20 November	*Olivette* arrives in Havana Check-in at Gran Hotel Inglaterra Meeting with Consul-General Alexander Gollan Meeting with General Arderíus, second in command in Cuba
21 November	Train journey to Santa Clara via Colón, Cruces and Santo Domingo Meeting with General Martínez Campos, captain-general, in Santa Clara HQ Train to Cienfuegos and night there. First 'letter' to the *Daily Graphic* written
22 November	Trip by coastal steamer to Tunas de Zaza Failed attempt to join a train to Sancti Spiritus; spent night in Tunas de Zaza
23/24 November	Rail journey from Tunas de Zaza to Sancti Spiritus Meeting with General Suárez Valdés Second 'letter' dated
24/25 November	Column leaves Sancti Spiritus for Iguará with Churchill and Barnes
26 November	Column arrives in Iguará
27/28 November	Column arrives in Arroyo Blanco Third 'letter' dated
30 November	New fighting column leaves Arroyo Blanco
1 December	Churchill has his baptism of fire
2 December	Advance to and action at La Reforma; night in Jicotea
3 December	To Ciego de Ávila with Suárez Valdés and then by rail to Júcaro By gunboat *Cometa* from Júcaro to Tunas de Zaza (late night)
4 December	By gunboat *Ardilla* from Tunas de Zaza to Cienfuegos (very early morning) By train to Santa Clara; night in Hotel Santa Clara Fourth 'letter' written
5 December	By train to Havana By chance meeting with Martínez Campos

8 December	*Olivette* to Tampa Bay
9 December	Train to New York
10 December	Arrival in New York
13 December	First 'letter' published in *The Daily Graphic*
14 December	*Etruria* sails for Liverpool
	Fifth 'letter' on this date (uncertain)
17 December	Second 'letter' published in *The Daily Graphic*
21 December	*Etruria* arrives in Liverpool
	Train to London, dinner for four with Lady Randolph

NOTES

Preface

1. The book was Peter Clarke's *Mr Churchill's Profession: Statesman, Orator, Writer*, London, Bloomsbury Press, 2012.
2. Corsairs and pirates constantly raided Cuba, and even took Havana more than once, during the long wars with Spain of the sixteenth and seventeenth centuries. Indeed, the famous Morro Castle at the entrance to the harbour of Havana, mentioned with admiration by Churchill in his first article, written in 1895, is often referred to as Drake's Castle as its construction was in part to deter a further attack on the city by that famous corsair and pirate. And the British had attempted a more formal attack to establish a foothold in eastern Cuba in the ill-fated expedition of Admiral Edward Vernon in 1740–41.
   For these stories, see Francisco Pérez Guzmán, *La Habana: clave de un imperio*, Havana, Editorial Ciencias Sociales, 1997; and Olga Portuondo Zúñiga, *Una derrota británica en Cuba*, Santiago, Editorial Oriente, 2000.
3. Celia Sandys, Sir Winston's granddaughter, is herself a prolific author on the subject of her distinguished relative's life. Her works include the highly engaging *Chasing Churchill: The Travels of Winston Churchill*, London, Unicorn Press, 2014, which includes an interesting chapter on Cuba.
4. Lourdes Méndez Vargas' book, subsequently supported by the British Embassy in Havana, was published in Spanish in March 2014 by Editorial Luminaria, a provincial press in Sancti Spiritus, with the title *Arroyo Blanco: la ruta cubana de Churchill*.

5. To mention just two examples of this key moment escaping attention, neither Tuvia Ben-Mosha in his study of Churchill as a strategist nor James Lawrence in his book on Churchill and empire even mentions his time in Cuba where he made his first public comments on both those subjects. See Ben-Mosha, *Churchill: Strategist and Historian*, Boulder (Colorado), Lynne Rienner, 1992; and James Lawrence, *Churchill and Empire*, London, Weidenfeld & Nicolson, 2013.

6. Cubans term the economic warfare conducted against them by the US since 1960 a 'blockade' but for obvious reasons the US prefers the term 'embargo'. For the Canadian role here, see John Kirk and Peter McKenna, *Canadian–Cuban Relations: The Other Good Neighbor Policy*, Gainesville, FL, University Press of Florida, 1997.

7. Douglas Russell, *Winston Churchill, Soldier: The Military Life of a Gentleman at War*, London, Brassey's, 2005.

8. See Hal Klepak, *Cuba's Military 1990–2005: Revolutionary Soldiers in Counter-Revolutionary Times*, New York, Palgrave Macmillan, 2006; and Hal P. Klepak, *Raúl Castro and Cuba: A Military Story*, New York, Palgrave Macmillan, 2011.

Chapter 1 1895: A Year and a Context

1. William Manchester, *The Last Lion: Winston Spencer Churchill, Visions of Glory 1874–1932*, New York, Delta, 1989, p. 7.

2. Francisco Castillo Meléndez, *La Defensa de la isla de Cuba en la segunda mitad del siglo XVII*, Sevilla, Padura, 1996.

3. Alfred Thayer Mahan, *The Influence of Seapower upon History, 1660–1783*, Boston, MA, Little Brown, 1893.

4. *Guerrilla* means 'little war' in Spanish.

5. '*La siempre fiel*' (always loyal) was in some ways the motto of Spanish Cuba. The island had indeed earned such a description. Colonial militias had fought hard against pirates and foreign military expeditions sent against them over the centuries and had done quite well in harassing the British during the invasion of 1762. And the colony had remained steadfastly loyal in the face of calls by the continental colonies, especially Mexico and Colombia, for it to rise up, as they had done, and fight for independence. See Jaime Rodríguez, *The Independence of Spanish America*, Cambridge, Cambridge University Press, 1998; and Roberto Hernández Suárez, *Capitanía General de Cuba: guerras de independencia en Hispanoamérica, 1800–1830*, Havana, Editorial Política, 2011, pp. 7–30.

6. See the interesting Gloria García, *Conspiraciones y revueltas*, Santiago, Oriente, 2003.

7. See the Chilean and Peruvian chapters of Adrian English, *Armed Forces of Latin America*, London, Jane's, 1984; and Robert Scheina, *Latin America: A Naval History, 1810–1987*, Annapolis, MD, Naval Institute Press, 1987.

8. Enrique de Miguel Fernández, *La Correspondencia de Azcárraga con Weyler sobre la Guerra de Cuba (1896–1897)*, Valencia, Soler, 2010, p. 15.

9. Hugh Thomas, *Cuba: The Pursuit of Freedom*, London, Eyre and Spottiswoode, 1971, especially pp. 233–44 and 293–309.

10. The term *mambí* was first used as a denigrating term by the Spanish and loyalist forces to describe the Dominican resistance during Madrid's attempt to reinsert the Dominican Republic into the empire in 1861–65. It became a source of pride for insurgents there and was taken over by the Cuban rebels in the Ten Years War. It remained a means of describing those who fought against Spanish rule until independence.

11. For a very good study of the race issue in Cuba over these years, see Ada Ferrer, *Insurgent Cuba: Race, Nation and Revolution 1868–1898*, Chapel Hill, NC, University of North Carolina, 1999.

12. Mildred de la Torre, *El Autonomismo en Cuba 1878–1895*, Havana, Ciencias Sociales, 1998. The *integristas* also formed a political party at this time, the Partido Conservador, or conservative party, supported essentially by Spaniards resident in the colony or by Cubans loyal to the Crown.

13. For an excellent overview of the role of these interest groups in decision making on Cuba in Madrid, see María del Carmen Barcia, *Elites y grupos de presión: Cuba 1868–1898*, Havana, Ciencias Sociales, 1998.

14. Ferrer, *Insurgent Cuba*, pp. 153–4. Please note: the term multiracial is used throughout to refer to someone with black and white ancestry. The outdated term 'mulatto' is used frequently in nineteenth-century texts.

15. José A. Piqueras, *Cuba, emporio y colonia: la disputa de un mercado interferido 1878–1895*, Havana, Ciencias Sociales, 2007, especially pp. 57, 62 and 210–38.

16. Ibid., p. 181. In this process there were winners and losers, with many of the great *hacendados* (landholders) ruined when they could not adjust to the new and rapidly evolving context, while others became massively more prosperous.

17. John Kirk, *Martí: Mentor of the Cuban Nation*, Gainesville, FL, University Press of Florida, 1983.

18. The Spanish had been extremely successful in the first war in using white Cuban fear that the blacks, who made up the majority of the

rebel army, wanted a black republic on the Haitian model, and that race war would inevitably be the result of independence and would lead to the destruction of the island's peace and prosperity. A similar stance by the Spanish, with some truth to it, was to ask Cubans if what they really wanted was merely to join the rest of the Latin American republics of the time in having an independent nation but one constantly wracked by civil strife, instability and racial conflict, because that would inevitably be what awaited them if they opted for independence. See Yoel Cordoví Núñez, *Máximo Gómez: en perspectiva*, Santiago, Editorial Oriente, pp. 19 and 65.

19. Quoted in José Miró y Argenter, *Crónicas de la guerra, Vol. 1: La Campaña de la Invasión*, Havana, Moderna Poesía, 1909, p. 92.
20. Gustavo Placer Cervera, *Inglaterra y La Habana 1762*, Havana, Ciencias Sociales, 2007, p. 200. At the time of Churchill's visit, however, disease among Spanish troops was not nearly as high as it was to become since the war was so recently begun and the number of troops deployed still relatively low. Even so, Spain had 2,887 fatal casualties through disease in 1895, mostly from yellow fever. See Yolanda Díaz Martínez, *Vida y avatares de los hombres en contienda: la subsistencia en la Guerra del 95*, Havana, Editora Política, 2008, p. 125.
21. For a full discussion of insurgent health issues, see Ismael Sarmiento Ramírez, *El Ingenio del mambí*, Vol. 2, Havana, Editorial Oriente, 2008, especially pp. 296–304.
22. Manchester, *The Last Lion*, pp. 129–30.
23. Carlo D'Este, *Warlord: A Life of Winston Churchill at War, 1874–1945*, New York, HarperCollins, 2008, pp. 33–5.
24. Randolph Churchill, *Winston S. Churchill, Vol. 1: Youth 1874–1900*, Boston, MA, Houghton Mifflin, 1966, p. 265.
25. The post of honorary colonel of a regiment in the British and Commonwealth tradition is that of a senior officer or member of the Royal Family who takes a special interest in the well-being of the unit and defends it in high places. Normally an officer named to this honorary position will have previously served in the regiment or will have a family or similar connection.
26. Winston S. Churchill, *My Early Life*, London, Eland, 2000, p. 61.
27. Quoted in D'Este, *Warlord*, p. 35.
28. CHAR 28/21/1–2 Letter WSC to Lady Randolph 11 January 1895.
29. There is some confusion about the actual dates here. Manchester (*The Last Lion*, p. 210) gives the date of Churchill reporting for duty as the 18th and his commissioning as the 20th. Churchill writes to his

mother from Aldershot for the first time on the 19th. See also letter WSC to Lady Randolph quoted in Randolph Churchill, *Winston S. Churchill*, p. 235.

30. This idea of giving the new officer basic cavalry (or other corps) training as if he were a mere soldier is an old and honoured one in many regiments of the British Commonwealth to this day and is often thought to be the best means to ensure the new officer does not get above himself but rather knows what the soldiers he or she is to command know of their job and will therefore be vastly better prepared to be their leader than if he or she does separate training not so aimed. The pip system is the rank designation basis for British Commonwealth armies: one pip designates a second-lieutenant, two pips a lieutenant, three a captain. At higher ranks pips accompany crowns and laurel wreaths to designate more elevated status.

31. Manchester, *The Last Lion*, pp. 155, 215. See also pp. 98–100.

32. Randolph Churchill, *Winston S. Churchill*, p. 257. Coughlin refers to him at the time as 'the head of a relatively impoverished family of a somewhat tarnished reputation'. See Coughlin, *Churchill's First War: Young Winston at War with the Afghans*, London, St Martin's, 2014, p. 19.

33. Ibid., p. 257; Martin Gilbert, *Churchill*, London, Houghton Mifflin, 1967, pp. 827, 928; and interview with Major David Innes-Lumsden, Regimental Secretary, Queen's Royal Hussars, London, February 2014. He was not finally to clear his initial tailor's bill for six years, a situation not at all rare in the officer corps of the day. Tautz & Sons are perhaps best known for inventing not only knickerbockers but waterproof tweeds. See 'Die Workwear', www.dieworkwear.com.

34. The first of these was derisorily referred to as 'A Subaltern's Advice to Generals' on a number of occasions wherein Churchill was again called a 'medal snatcher', a view not reserved to senior officers but often shared by fellow subalterns as well. For more on Churchill at the time, see Richard Harding Davis, *Real Soldiers of Fortune*, New York, Scribner's, 1910, pp. 77–117, especially 82, 90, 91. The last quote here is from p. 117.

Chapter 2 Cuba: An Idea and a Plan

1. Most modern readers will doubtless find such lengthy leaves difficult to understand in a standing army. But the nature of pre-motorised

warfare was such that this leave did not appear to be in any way excessive. The key factor was that cavalry and transport horses consume in a day several times the weight of what a soldier does. This means that winter campaigning is virtually impossible as there is little if any fodder available for the horses and this implies that what is needed must be brought along with the army in waggons. Those waggons must be pulled by horses who themselves are part of this logistics nightmare. It is this reason, and not the Hollywood-inspired idea that somehow officers needed to be back in their capitals for the social season, which reduced earlier warfare generally to campaigning only in the late spring, summer and early autumn months when fodder was plentiful.

2.   Michael McMenamim and Curt Zoller, *Becoming Winston Churchill*, New York, Enigma Books, 2009, p. 69.

3.   Letter from WSC to Lady Randolph 16 August 1895, quoted in Coughlin, *Churchill's First War*, p. 67. See also Manchester, *The Last Lion*, p. 233.

4.   Quoted in Manchester, *The Last Lion*, p. 259.

5.   Letter WSC to Lady Churchill dated 24 August 1895, quoted in Randolph Churchill, *Winston S. Churchill*, p. 250; and Coughlin, *Churchill's First War*, p. 19.

6.   Ibid., p. 124.

7.   The Battle of the Somme cost the British Empire 419,654 casualties, the highest by far in a single battle in its entire history.

8.   See Mark Grotelueschen, *The AEF Way of War*, New York, Cambridge University Press, 2007, pp. 285–6.

9.   Churchill's quote is from his speech to the 4th Hussars Association Dinner of 1938 when Winston was guest of honour and is quoted in the 'Association Notes' of the regimental journal of that year. Barnes also seems to have got something of a name for kindness and fair play. See Julian Putkowski and Mark Dunning, *Murderous Tommies*, Barnsley (Yorkshire), Pen and Sword Books, 2012.

10. The Regiment's Polo Book traces the main matches in which both Barnes and Churchill played over the early years of Winston's service with the 4th Hussars. Barnes was apparently an especially good 'back'.

11. 'The Regimental Association Dinner', *Journal of the IV Queen's Own Hussars*, 1946, p. 29. The dinner in question was that in honour of Churchill's naming as honorary colonel where Barnes said, with characteristic charm, 'what a very good friend' Churchill was and that, 'When I was colonel of the regiment, I always felt that there

could only be one real colonel of the regiment and that was Winston Churchill.' The keen reaction of Barnes to the Cuba idea is recorded in Churchill, *My Early Life*, p. 69.

12. Quoted in Ralph G. Martin, *Lady Randolph Churchill: a Biography*, Vol. 2, London, Cassell, p. 59.

13. CHAR 28/21/71/72 Letter WSC to Lady Randolph dated 4 October 1895.

14. Letter Lady Randolph to WSC, written from France and dated 11 October 1895, quoted in Randolph Churchill, *Winston S. Churchill*, p. 254.

15. See Martin, *Lady Randolph Churchill*, p. 59.

16. CHAR 28/21/71/72 Letter WSC to Lady Randolph dated 4 October 1895.

17. The purchase and selling of commissions was a constant feature of the old British Army before the practice was abolished in 1871 as part of the Cardwell reforms. It ensured that a man had the financial wherewithal to keep up an officer's station, had a stake in the status quo and would have access to money on retirement. But its abuses were many as were its obvious disadvantages.

18. Churchill, *My Early Life*, pp. 60–64; and D'Este, *Warlord*, p. 57.

19. Shortly after his return from Cuba, Churchill faced nasty suggestions of wrongdoing and even of homosexual improprieties as a result of treatment meted out to a prospective officer wishing to join the Hussars but who was not wanted by some subalterns, including Churchill. The matter was settled with Churchill entirely exonerated. See Manchester, *The Last Lion*, pp. 212–13.

20. Richard Holmes, *In the Footsteps of Churchill*, London, Basic Books, 2009, p. 39.

21. D'Este, *Warlord*, p. 29.

22. See throughout Sir F. Maurice and Sir George Arthur, *The Life of Lord Wolseley*, London, William Heinemann, 1924.

23. Ibid., p. 341.

24. Manchester (*The Last Lion*, p. 220) quotes him as protesting that 'he wasn't against change. He favored it … when there was no alternative.'

25. W/P 24/53 Letter Lord Wolseley to Lady Wolseley 23 June 1895.

26. There was the heaviest pressure for him to accept the prized diplomatic post including from the new prime minister, Lord Salisbury, and even from Queen Victoria herself. See W/P 24/89/2 letter from Lord Salisbury of 7 August 1895. Even Lansdowne's letter

seemingly offering the job of Commander-in-Chief to Wolseley mentioned how disappointed the Kaiser would be if Wolseley did not go to Berlin. Wolseley was having none of it, such was his keenness on having the job for which he had been looking forward for twenty years. See W/P 24/89/2 letter from Wolseley to Lord Lansdowne of 9 August, and W/P 24/58 letter Wolseley to Lady Wolseley of 30 June 1895.

27. WP Documents 1 through 4 of Wolseley's correspondence with Lord Randolph dated 8 October 1885, 13 November 1888, 12 December 1888 and 11 July 1890.

28. WP/M1/110/33–35. Letter Wolseley to Lady Wolseley of 5 November 1885.

29. The book on Marlborough's early life was published in 1894 as *Life of the Duke of Marlborough* and received considerable acclaim leading to its author being invited to become a member of the Literary Society and being asked to take part in a number of activities reserved for major figures in British letters. His autobiography was entitled *Story of a Soldier's Life* and was published in 1903. It did not receive the same favourable reaction. See Maurice and Arthur, *The Life of Lord Wolseley*, pp. 333–6.

30. WP 24/61 Letter from Lord Wolseley to Lady Wolseley 3 July 1895. Unfortunately for Wolseley, at this early date Lansdowne did not appear to be in any hurry to name a commander-in-chief.

31. Ibid., secret cable 10 August 1895.

32. NA 30/40/2 'Ardagh Papers', Letter from Wolseley to Ardagh 4 October 1895.

33. WP 24/120 Letter Lord Wolseley to Lady Wolseley 9 October 1895.

34. WP 24/121 Letter Lord Wolseley to Lady Wolseley 21 October 1895.

35. WP Correspondence of Queen Victoria No. 9, 20 October 1895.

36. CHAR 28/21/73 Letter WSC to Lady Randolph 19 October 1895.

37. CHAR 1/14/3 Letter from J. Duncan Daly at War Office to WSC dated 19 October.

38. CHAR 28/21/74–75 Letter WSC to Lady Randolph dated 21 October 1895.

39. FO 88/6657 documents relating to speeches by General Chapman, 31 July 1895.

40. CHAR 28/21/74-75 Letter WSC to Lady Randolph dated 21 October 1895.

41. See http://www.ballisticstudies.com7x57; http://www. Mauser+7x57+cartridge=+qs; and http://americanriflemean.org.

42. Osprey, *The Spanish-American War*, Men at Arms Series No. 437, London, Osprey, 2010, pp. 24, 33–5.

43. Most of what follows is from Martin Pugh, in various sources including his *The Tories and the People, 1880–1935*, London, Blackwell, 1986.

44. The other members were John Gorst and Arthur Balfour.

45. The Primrose League eventually had a million members, or at least Winston was to claim so in his biography of his father. In any case it remained in existence into the 1950s.

46. See Sir Henry Drummond Wolff, *Rambling Recollections*, London, Macmillan, 1908.

47. This was shrewd analysis. Spain had faced the almost united opposition of Latin American public opinion and government policy during the Ten Years War, when pro-Cuban sentiment was generalised in the region. But by the time of the second independence war, the fear of US expansion southward was such that nationalists across the area tended to support Spain against the Cuban rebels in the belief principally that Cuba would necessarily fall into US hands if it were free of Spain. Only Ecuador continued to support Cuban independence openly. See FO 72/2003 Note from Sir Henry Drummond Wolff to Lord Salisbury No. 60, dated 18 March 1896; and Sergio Guerra Vilaboy, *América Latina y la independencia de Cuba*, Caracas, Ediciones Ko'eyu, 1999, esp. pp. 96–8.

48. Christopher Hall, *British Diplomacy and United States Hegemony in Cuba 1898–1964*, London, Palgrave Macmillan, 2013, pp. 25–6.

49. AHN, Ultramar Cuba-gobierno, No. 304 Report on Jamaica Weapons Seizure dated 26 June 1895.

50. FO 72/1993 Note from Admiralty to Under-Secretary of State at the Foreign Office No. M8484 dated 9 November enclosing dispatches from commander of *HMS Partridge* of 20, 23 and 24 October 1895.

51. 'Filibusters' was the name given by Spanish Americans initially to US informal attempts to annex Central American and Caribbean states to the Union in the years before the US Civil War. The Spanish later used this term to denigrate the efforts of Cuban insurgents and make it look like they were not really fighting for independence but for annexation to the US. While of course a good many actually were, most were doing no such thing and fought for full independence for the island.

52. FO 72/1993 Cable 46 from C-in-C North America and West Indies Station to Admiralty dated 21 October 1895. See also Dispatch

17846/95 from R.H. Meade, Colonial Office, to Under-Secretary of State at Foreign Office (Sanderson).

53. FO 72/1993 Note from FO (Sanderson) to Colonial Office dated 4 November 1895.

54. AHN, Ultramar-gobierno, Notes numbers 175 of 13 April 1895 and 182 of 15 April 1895.

55. FO 72/1979 Despatch FO 259 Drummond Wolff to Lord Salisbury dated 27 August 1895.

56. FO 72/1979 Despatch FO 271 (Confidential) Drummond Wolff to Lord Salisbury dated 11 September 1895. Actually, for Spanish purposes, the French press was even more important than the British at this moment as Madrid was trying to raise a major loan on the Paris Bourse. But French journalists were as a rule seen to be much less pro-Cuban than the British who were viewed as 'shamelessly' anti-Spanish. Churchill almost alone was considered pro-Spanish. See 'Churchill y la Guerra de Cuba', in *Foro de Historia Militar*, www.elsemanaldigital.com.

57. This is of course the same British ambassador Pauncefote who signed the Hay–Pauncefote Treaty of 1901 with John Hay, the US Secretary of State. This treaty abrogated the Clayton–Bulwer Treaty of 1850, which had retained essentially US–British parity in Central American affairs, and provided for neither country building its own interoceanic canal in the area. The new treaty gave the US the right to do just such a thing and in effect accepted British inferiority in Central America and the Caribbean where US interests were concerned. For the events related to Howard in Cuba, see FO 72/1991 Ramsden to Pauncefote dated 30 September 1895.

58. FO 72/1993 Sanderson to Lord Carlisle dated 7 November 1895. Refers to despatch from Gollan of 25 October where Ramsden had advised that Howard had arrived in Santiago on 23 October and was leaving on 26 October.

59. FO 72/1987 Lord Salisbury to Gollan No. 5 dated 23 November 1895.

60. See his interesting defence of his government's actions in his *Apuntes del ex-ministro de estado, Duque de Tetuán, para la defensa de la política internacional y gestión diplomática del gobierno liberal-conservador desde el 28 de marzo de 1895 a 29 de septiembre de 1897*, Madrid, Péant, 1903.

61. For the extraordinary story of Britain and the Royal Navy's role in suppressing the slave trade in Cuba see David R. Murray, *Odious Commerce: Britain, Spain and the Abolition of the Cuban Slave Trade*,

Cambridge, Cambridge University Press, 1980. For Azcárraga, see Fernández, *La Correspondencia de Azcárraga con Weyler*, pp. 17–18.

62. CHAR 1/14/1 Letter Drummond Wolff to WSC dated 8 October 1895.

63. CHAR 1/14/4 Letter of introduction for WSC from Lord Salisbury sent to him on 31 October 1895.

Chapter 3 The Multifaceted Adventurer

1. Even Carlo D'Este (*Warlord*, p. 44) suggests as much.

2. FO 72/1993 internal memo A. Laveron to Sir Thomas Sanderson No.70 dated 9th November 1895.

3. This is mostly from Keith Neilson and T.G. Otte, *The Permanent Under-secretaries for Foreign Affairs, 1854–1946*, New York, Routledge, 2009, pp. 92–122.

4. See the first section of David Stafford, *Churchill and the Secret Service*, Woodstock, NY, Overlook Press, 1998.

5. Douglas S. Bissell, *The Orders, Decorations and Medals of Sir Winston Churchill*, Hopkinton, NH, The International Churchill Societies, 1990.

6. A guinea was an oft-used term, especially among the upper class, for £1 1s. The pound was divided into 20 shillings so would be expressed today as £1.05.

7. The quotes here are from http://Spartacus-educational.com/jthomasL.htm.

8. Manchester, *The Last Lion*, pp. 165–6.

9. See Peter Harrington, 'Images and Perceptions: Visualizing the Sudan Campaign', in Edward M. Spiers (ed.), *Sudan: The Reconquest Reassessed*, London, Routledge, 2013, pp. 82–101; and Peter Clarke, *Mr Churchill's Profession: Statesman, Orator, Writer*, London, Bloomsbury Press, 2012, pp. 37–8.

10. In fact, there was not much Akers could do when Winston arrived as he was in Venezuela at the time. But, as we shall see, Winston needed precious little further help than what he had already garnered from so many senior sources. See CHAR 1/14/5 letter Makenzie Wallace to WSC dated 31 October 1895. Needless to say, given the Spanish view of the biases of the British press in favour of the insurgents, such information might have had some effect on the nature of the welcome given to Churchill.

11. A very large number of sources have Churchill leaving for Cuba from Key West after the rail journey from New York. But the only railway company serving southern Florida in 1895 was the Florida East Coast Railway. Churchill used this line to get as far south as he could since Key West had no rail service of any kind or indeed any other land-based route through the Florida Keys that reached as far as this 'Southernmost point in the USA'. Railway service to the island was only established in 1912. See Jefferson Brown, 'Key West Mail and Steamship Service', in *Key West: The Old and the New, 1912*, in Floridpedia, University of South Florida, 2004.

12. Charles Wrigley, *Winston Churchill: A Biographical Companion*, Santa Barbara, CA, ABC-Clio, 2002, p. 146.

13. This part of the story is the only one that has previously received adequate attention, so little space has been given to this part of Winston's trip.

14. Letter WSC to his brother Jack dated 15 November 1895, quoted in Coughlin, *Churchill's First War*, p. 78.

15. CHAR 28/21/90–91 Letter WSC to Lady Randolph dated 20 November 1895.

16. Donald H. Dyal, *Historical Dictionary of the Spanish-American War*, undated, Santa Barbara, CA, Greenwood Press.

17. The *Olivette* met a sad fate. It went aground in thick fog and sank on 12 January 1918 while a general cargo ship still on the Key West-Havana run. For the ship's story, see Dennis Casey, 'A Little Espionage Goes a Long Way', www.fas.org/irp/agency/aia/cyberspokesman/99-11/history1.htm, and http://www.ebay.com/itm/SS-Olivette-Built-a887-Cuba-tampa-Key-West-Mail-Steam. For its sinking see 'Key West Ship Ashore', *The New York Times*, 13 January 1918, which describes the dramatic rescue of its seventy-four passengers from the disaster.

Chapter 4 Cuba: Arrival and Deployment

1. Churchill, *My Early Life*, pp. 69–70.

2. See throughout Placer Cervera, *Inglaterra y La Habana 1762*.

3. See for example, *Diario de la Marina*, for this and next quotes, for 2 and 12 November 1895. It is true, as Lourdes Méndez Vargas argues in her look at Churchill in and around her village of Arroyo Blanco, that much of the unofficial press, or at least those less inclined to political news such as *El Figaro* or *La Habana Elegante*, did not carry the story. But the newspapers that mattered politically and militarily most

certainly did. Méndez Vargas, *Arroyo Blanco: la ruta cubana de Churchill*, Sancti Spiritus (Cuba), Luminaria, 2014, p. 48.

4. FO 72/2013 Despatch Gollan to Lord Salisbury No. 4, dated 2 January 1895. He was not to get any in 1896 either.

5. Of the eighty Spanish generals who served in the thirty years of off–on conflict known as the independence wars, eighteen were actually Cuban-born. René González Barrios, Lecture to María Loynaz series on Cuban military history, 'El Alto Mando español en las guerras de independencia', February 2014.

6. This is from http://referendumparacubaya.blogspot.co.uk/2013/05, but some other non-academic sources refer to this meeting as well. Miró Argenter (*Crónicas de la guerra*, pp. 274–86) refers to Arderius in his often sarcastic and usually unflattering terms as an excessive worrier and 'panic artist', as the term goes in the army, in the later preparations for the defence of Havana against rebel attack.

7. BRDW, Winston S. Churchill, 'Letters from the Front', 1, *The Daily Graphic*, 13 December 1895. This state of affairs led to almost laughable estimates of rebel strength. The same letter refers to such estimates as ranging from 50 men to 18,000.

8. *Diario del Ejército*, 21 November 1895, p. 1, col. 5.

9. Churchill, *My Early Life*, p. 70.

10. See Gómez's complaint to Maceo that, while he never had more than 7,000 Cubans 'apt for service' during that war, Spain could count on some 30,000 who 'fought in defence of the metropolis'. Quoted in René González Barrios, *El Ejército español en Cuba, 1868–1878*, Havana, Verde Olivo, 2000, p. 79. By 1895 and especially as a result of the 'invasion' of the west, of which Churchill witnessed the beginning, this figure was never reached again and many more examples of the desertion of Cubans from the royalist forces occurred than were dreamed of in the first war.

11. Churchill, *My Early Life*, p. 219.

12. SHM, DIR0016 MC, Personal File, Arsenio Martínez Campos.

13. It was also rumoured that he was taking too many stimulants which, while hardly surprising given the task he had been given, cannot have helped much under the circumstances. See FO 2875 Drummond Wolff to Lord Salisbury dated 5 October from San Sebastián with the court. Martínez Campos was said to be in poor health and 'he partakes more of stimulants than is good for him'.

14. The Trocha Júcaro–Morón was the 68km trench line stretching from the port of Morón in the north to Júcaro in the south and pivoting

on the garrison town of Ciego de Ávila in western Camagüey province. It was lined with barbed wire, centred upon sixty-eight blockhouses at 1km intervals, backed up by a military railway, and had cleared fields of fire to the front for some distance to allow for easy spotting and interception of Cuban rebel forces. It was to be greatly enhanced in the years after Churchill left.

15. BRDW, Churchill, 'Letters from the Front', 2, 23 November 1895, *The Daily Graphic*, 17 December 1895.

16. The Battle of Las Guásimas is the largest battle ever to take place on Cuban soil although the 1961 defeat of the Bay of Pigs invasion is sometimes cited as more important on a number of scores. See Francisco Pérez Guzmán, *La Batalla de las Guásimas*, Havana, Ciencias Sociales, 1975.

17. BRDW, Churchill, 'Letters from the Front', 5, 14 December 1895, *The Daily Graphic*, 13 January 1896.

18. Quoted in Francisco Pérez Guzmán, 'La Revolución de 95: de los alzamientos a la campaña de la invasión', in Instituto de Historia de Cuba, *Las Luchas por la Independencia Nacional, 1868–1898*, Havana, Editora Política, 1996, pp. 430–80, 455.

19. BRDW, Churchill, 'Letters from the Front', 3, 17 November 1895, *The Daily Graphic*, 24 December 1895.

20. Louis Perez, *Cuba between Empires 1878–1902*, Pittsburgh, Pittsburgh University Press, 1983, p. 105.

21. Ibid., pp. 105–6.

22. CHAR 28/21/73 Letter WSC to Lady Randolph dated 19 October 1895.

23. It is curious that Churchill has Captain O'Donnell written down a mere lieutenant in his *My Early Life*, pp. 70–1, and indeed a young one at that. In fact, O'Donnell was 11 years older than Winston. His confusion, other than brought about by 35-year-old memories, may have been caused by the fact that the two British officers also met other young Spanish subalterns at the headquarters in Santa Clara.

24. AGMS/CELEB/Caja119,EXP.6 Juan O'Donnell y Vargas.

25. Churchill, *My Early Life*, p. 71. All later authors accepted the rank as lieutenant but it would have been very odd indeed for a general of Martínez Campos' importance to have an ADC of such low rank and the Spanish archive reference noted in fn.109 is clear on the matter.

26. BRDW, Churchill, 'Letters from the Front', 1, *The Daily Graphic*, 13 December 1895.

27. BRDW, Churchill, 'Letters from the Front', 2, 23 November, *The Daily Graphic*, 17 December 1895. The village is sadly now in terrible shape although the pier is still there, as is a painting of it by a local artist in its former splendour of roughly the time of Churchill's visit. The railway station, just as in Churchill's day, is still standing, more or less.

28. It is difficult to credit that Suárez Valdés had reported incorrectly such vital dates to his commander in Santa Clara and his subordinates west of the Trocha. His wire and other correspondence in the *Servicio Histórico Militar* is crystal clear on the matter. See SHM Caja 3953 Campaign Operations Santa Clara November 1895, correspondence Suárez Valdés to Martínez Campos of 22, 24 and 26 November and to commanders of gunboats *Cometa* and *Ardilla* for passage to General Aldave of 22 and 26 November 1895.

29. Interview with Sancti Spiritus city historian Dra. María Antonieta Jiménez, Sancti Spiritus, 24 January 2014. Churchill's report on disease there was certainly correct. One of the city newspapers reported 1,062 dead from smallpox and yellow fever in the city alone during the period August–December 1895. See *La Fraternidad*, XI, No. 512, 1 May 1896.

30. Spanish archives have repeated references to the effects of this rain, and indeed some significant storms, over the time of Churchill's visit.

31. SMG, Caja 3953, Campaign Operations Santa Clara, November 1895, unnumbered cables Suárez Valdés to Martínez Campos of 22 and 24 November 1895.

32. Francisco Pérez Guzmán, *Radiografía del Ejército Libertador*, Havana, Ciencias Sociales, 2005, p. 169.

33. AGMS/1a/3437S,EXP.0. Alvaro Suárez Valdés. He was to be promoted lieutenant-general in 1896 and went on to become President of the Supreme Council for War and the Navy, and a senator. He died in 1917. See also SHM Caja 3787 Campaign Operations 1896–98 for Suárez Valdés' actions before he joined this story.

34. Churchill, *My Early Life*, p. 72.

Chapter 5 Oh Bliss! Coming of Age and Coming under Fire

1. Churchill, *My Early Life*, pp. 72–3. Churchill thought the area held some 15,000 to 20,000 rebels. This was certainly a wild exaggeration

as this would have been more or less equal to the whole insurgent army throughout the island at the time. And the main force under Maceo had yet to cross the line and enter the province. Nonetheless the threat was a major one for the column. See BRDW, Churchill, 'Letters from the Front', 2, 23 November, *The Daily Graphic*, 17 December 1895.

2. SHM Caja 3953 Campaign Operations Santa Clara November 1895, cable Suárez Valdés to commander of *cañonero Ardilla* (Lieutenant Bausá) in Tunas de Zaza for General Aldave dated 24 November; Suárez Valdés to General Luque via Lieutenant-Colonel Santander in Iguará dated 24 November; and Suárez Valdés to Martínez Campos dated 22 November 1895.

3. Ibid., Bausá on *Ardilla* from Aldave, cable 25 November; and from gunboat *Cometa* in Tunas de Zaza from Aldave as well, dated later that day, No. 12, 25 November 1895.

4. René González Barrios, *El Ejército español en Cuba, 1868–1878*, Havana, Editorial de las FAR, 1988, quote from Máximo Gómez, p. 159.

5. Churchill, *My Early Life*, p. 74. Churchill kept up the practice of taking a siesta for the rest of his life. Indeed, Cuban historians have joked with the author on this subject suggesting it was actually Cuba that won the Second World War. Their argument is that, since Churchill believed he was able to do the essential work of wartime only because of the boost the siesta gave him at midday thus making him able to work late into the night, and since without Churchill the war would most certainly have been lost, it follows that, since Cuba introduced him to the siesta, it should have the credit for the victory. This assertion is usually made only after several of the 'rum cocktails' (the '*runcotelle*' of Churchill's memory which should be spelled as it still is in Cuba as '*ron cocktail*') or similar libations have been consumed. While there is of course precious little support for such an assertion, Carlo D'Este (*Warlord*, p. 328) reminds us that there is some: 'He [Churchill] attributed his ability to cram a day and a half into a single day to his long time habit of napping "like a child" in the afternoon for an hour of deep, untroubled sleep in the nude, a prerequisite, he said. The key to a successful day was a combination of his nap and proper eating.'

6. Quoted in D'Este, *Warlord*, p. 458.

7. Churchill, 'Letters from the Front', 3, 17 November 1895, in *The Daily Graphic*, 24 December 1895; and Churchill, *My Early Life*, p. 75. In fact they did not 'go after him' until two days later than this suggests, on 30 November and not the 28th.

8. BRDW, Churchill, 'Letters from the Front', 3, 17 November 1895, *The Daily Graphic*, 24 December 1895.
9. Churchill, *My Early Life*, p. 69.
10. AGMS/*Hojas de servicio*, Antonio Díaz Benzo.
11. BRDW, Press, Churchill, 'Letters from the Front', 3, 17 November 1895, *The Daily Graphic*, 24 December 1895.
12. Quoted in Larry Morales, *Máximo Gómez al oeste de La Trocha*, Havana, Ediciones Unión, 2003, p. 71.
13. Bernabé Boza, *Mi Diario de la Guerra*, Vol. 1, Havana, Ciencias Sociales, p. 161. 'La Bayamesa' was the hymn of the insurgent cause of independence from Spain. It is now the national anthem of Cuba.
14. See, for example, SHM, Caja 3700, Movements of Forces, 1895–98, Cable from undisclosed officer to Commander 1st Division complaining of still having to mix in one force two companies of troops with Mausers and five with Remingtons and the need to organise things in a way to ensure that supply of ammunition can be achieved. The success of Gómez in keeping the Spanish busy, as well as the frustrating requirement to act in small ad hoc forces rather than in formed battalions, is attested to in un-numbered cable, Commander Sancti Spiritus Brigade of Operations to Commander 2nd District, SGM Caja 3953, Telegrams of actions, dated 21 November 1895.
15. General García, a hero to his fellow Tuneros, from today's province of Las Tunas (not to be confused with Tunas de Zaza many hundreds of kilometres to the west) was active in what many observers considered sedition against the legitimate government and military command structures of the revolutionary movement in the last stages of the first war. He was, however, without doubt an effective commander and a man of great courage. See Victor Manuel Marrero, *Vicente García: mito y realidad*, Havana, 1992.
16. AGMS/Hojas de servicio, General José García Navarro, pp. 2–9,
17. SHM, Caja 3700, Movements of Forces, 1895–98, Captain-General to all divisional commanders dated 2 and 9 November 1895.
18. AGMS/Hojas de servicio, General José García Navarro, pp. 10–14.
19. SHM, Caja 2700, Movements of Forces, 1895–98, Arderíus to General Moreno dated 7th November 1895.
20. See http://www.spanamwar/spanishkrupp75.htm.
21. SHM Caja 3700 Movements of Forces, unnumbered cable dated 9 November 1895 General Moreno to Arderíus; Cable No. 1, dated 11 November 1895 Navarro to Moreno; and cable No. 59 dated 9 November 1895 Arderíus to Moreno.

22. SHM ibid., Draft unnumbered cable Arderíus to Moreno dated 7 November (11.30 a.m.).

23. SHM, Caja 3701 (Guerrillas), unnumbered message Captain-General to Commander 4th District dated 25 September 1895.

24. Boza, *Mi Diario de la Guerra*, Vol. 1, p. 20.

25. These optimistic rumours held that the insurgents were of about 4,000 men but of these 3,500 were infantry and only 500 cavalry. Given what the Spanish knew about Gómez's style of warfare, and objectives in this campaign, it is difficult to think the Spanish high command took the breakdown into infantry and cavalry contained in such reports seriously. See Anonymous, *Crónicas de la guerra de Cuba*, Havana, Editorial Figaro, 1895, p. 52.

26. Spanish officers and other observers tended to denigrate Gómez as just another *cabecilla* (rebel chief). There were, however, honourable exceptions. It is interesting to note that Gollan, the British consul-general, had no such thoughts. He wrote to London of Gómez's 'military skill of a high order' speaking also of his 'tenacity of purpose' as keys to his success. FO 72/7024 Cable 2 (Political) Gollan to Lord Salisbury, dated 10 January 1896.

27. Caja 3953 Campaign Operations Santa Clara November 1895, Suárez Valdés to commander *Cometa* (in Tunas de Zaza) for forwarding to General Aldave (in Ciego de Ávila), dated 26 November 1895. See also note with much of the same message, dated previous day to Martínez Campos.

28. BRDW, Churchill, 'Letters from the Front', 4, 4 December 1895, *The Daily Graphic*, 24 December 1895.

29. See Churchill, *My Early Life,* p. 74.

30. See Sandys, *Chasing Churchill*, pp. 219–21. Some of this is from a conversation with Celia Sandys, London, October 2013. But see also Churchill, *My Early Life*, p. 12. Manchester (*The Last Lion*, pp. 171–3) almost certainly went too far in suggesting that French was 'a language that he detested'.

31. Churchill, *My Early Life*, pp. 74–5.

32. Ibid., p. 75.

33. Ibid., p. 76. This is taken as certain evidence for the date of 30 November as his baptism of fire by Randolph Churchill, although it is interesting that Gilbert (*Churchill*) mentions no such event occurring on that day.

34. BRDW, Churchill, 'Letters from the Front', 4, 4 December 1895, *The Daily Graphic*, 27 December 1895.

35. Ibid.
36. SHM, Caja 3954 Operational Diaries, December 1895. Suárez Valdés to Martínez Campos report on column's activities dated 2 December 1895.
37. BRDW, Churchill, 'Letters from the Front', 4, 4 December 1895, *The Daily Graphic*, 27 December 1895. Cuban accounts do not mention any casualties from this attack.
38. Churchill, *My Early Life*, p. 77.
39. BRDW, Churchill, 'Letters from the Front', 4, 4 December 1895, *The Daily Graphic*, 27 December 1895.
40. There is much written, but mostly in Spanish, on these two generals. See for Gómez, Juan Bosch Gómez, *El Napoleón de las guerrillas*, Havana, Ciencias Sociales, 1996; and for Maceo, José Luciano Franco, *Antonio Maceo: apuntes para una historia de su vida* (2 vols), Havana, Ciencias Sociales, 1975.
41. Pérez Guzmán, *Radiografía*, pp. 17–18.
42. J.L. Tone, 'The Machete and the Liberation of Cuba', *Journal of Military History*, 1998, pp. 1–28.
43. Escolante Colás et al., *Diccionario enciclopédico de historia militar de Cuba, Vol. 1: Biografías*, Havana, Ediciones Verde Olivo, 2001, pp. 342–3.
44. CHAR 28/21/79091 WSC Letter to Lady Randolph dated 6 December 1895.
45. BRDW, Churchill, 'Letters from the Front', 4, 4 December 1895, *The Daily Graphic*, 27 December 1895.
46. SHM, Caja 3954 Operational Diaries, December 1895. Suárez Valdés to Martínez Campos report on column's activities dated 2 December 1895. Not too much should be made of the fact that the column was not fired upon over this route given that the enemy had already moved off in the opposite direction, making good their break with the Spanish force behind them.
47. Bernabé Boza, *Mi Diario de la Guerra*, Vol. 1, pp. 51–2. Cuban accounts usually refer to the action at La Refoma as a well-planned and -executed 'ambush' into which the Spaniards fell that morning. This idea is, to say the least, far-fetched as Suárez Valdés was moving to engage Gómez and knew the insurgent camp was at La Reforma.
48. Miró Argenter, *Crónicas de la guerra*, pp. 94–6. The author goes on to make a strong criticism of the tactics of Suárez Valdés in this action. On some of its points Churchill might have agreed, which will be discussed later. Brigadier-General José Quintín Bandera Betancourt, commander of the invasion infantry at the beginning, was another

of the black senior officers of the insurgency, fought in all three independence conflicts, and was famous for his machete charges, although he was usually with the infantry by this stage of his career.

49. See Aisnara Perera Díaz, *Antonio Maceo: Diarios de campaña*, Havana, Ciencias Sociales, 2001, pp. 13–14.

50. Churchill of course uses that next great adventure to write an actual book of his experiences and not just articles for the press. See Winston S. Churchill, *The Story of the Malakand Field Force: An Episode of Frontier War*, London, 1898.

51. *Significo a V.E. con el mayor gusto la serenidad e interés con que los oficiales del ejército inglés Mister Spencer Churchill y Reginald Barnes han seguido todos los incidentes de las operaciones y del combate al que asistieron a mi lado.* See SHM, Caja 3954 Operational Diaries, December 1895. Suárez Valdés to Martínez Campos report on column's activities dated 2 December 1895.

52. CHAR 28/21/79091 Letter WSC to Lady Randolph dated 6 December 1895.

Chapter 6 The Sequel: Immediate and Long Term

1. BRDW, Churchill, 'Letters from the Front', 5, 14 December 1895, in *The Daily Graphic*, 13 January 1896.

2. These would have been recommendations for citations or decorations for these officers' bravery and conduct in the fighting. See again SHM, Caja 3954 Operational Diaries, December 1895. Suárez Valdés to Martínez Campos report on column's activities dated 2 December 1895.

3. For the Captain-General's reply, see Caja 3954 Operational Diaries December 1895. Cable Martínez Campos to commander *Ardilla* (Bausá), No. 38, for onward transmission to Suárez Valdés, dated 3 December 1895. For Gollan's comments, see FO 72/1987, Gollan to Lord Salisbury, Political No. 35, dated 13 December 1895.

4. René González Barrios, *Los Capitanes generales de Cuba, 1868–1878*, Havana, Verde Olivo, 1999, especially pp. 240–2.

5. Escalante Colas et al., *Diccionario enciclopédico de historia militar de Cuba*, pp. 187–8.

6. This huge figure was, for example, mentioned in the report by Colonel Ramos, the commander in the central town of Cabaiguán, to his counterpart in Armas, saying he had got the figure from General Oliver himself. See Caja 3809 Telegraphic news, unnumbered cable Ramos to Armas dated 8 December 1895. Oliver was at that

time in Placetas, almost 50km to the west of Sancti Spiritus and a place where rumours were as rife as anywhere in those shocking days. For what Suárez Valdés knew of the enemy at this point see the same documents, cables Nos 75 and 77 from Generals Luque and Oliver to their superior dated 7 December 1895.

7. See flurry of signals from and to all of these in Caja 3809, 'Telegraphic News', dated 6, 7 and 8 December.

8. See the useful Carlos Abreu López et al, *Síntesis histórica provincial Sancti Spíritus*, Havana, Editora Historia, 2011, p. 121.

9. Gollan even suggested that the strength of the rebel forces was at least 30,000 men. While again this is doubtless an exaggeration, it does say something of the kind of near panic the arrival of the insurgents must have caused among loyalist elements of the population, particularly in Havana, and in the high command. There was also a report of very widespread destruction not only of the *zafra* (sugar harvest) but also of other property including major damage to British-owned railways. See FO 72/1987, Cable No. 35 Gollan to Lord Salisbury.

10. *Diario del Ejército*, Special Supplement, 1 December 1895; and SHM, Caja 3703, Captaincy-General of Cuba, Undated 'Situation of Forces', General Staff Campaign Section.

11. It was very common for small towns and villages in the Cuban countryside to have a Spaniard as the principal citizen, usually the owner of the general store or some other commercial establishment. These people were usually very loyalist and would be happy with the arrival of columns of troops supporting Spanish rule. Their visit was also usually good for business. See BRDW, Churchill, 'Letters from the Front', 5, 14 December 1895, *The Daily Graphic*, 13 January 1896.

12. SHM Caja 3954 Operational Diaries December 1895, draft cables Suárez Valdés (Tunas) to Martínez Campos dated 2 December 1895.

13. CHAR 1/14/13 General Staff Letter, Army of Operations in Cuba, Martínez Campos, open letter to column commanders, dated 20 November 1895. This was the day before the Captain-General met them himself but after word from General Arderíus of their arrival in Havana was received at the headquarters in Santa Clara.

14. Letter Winston Churchill to Bourke Cockran dated 20 November 1895, quoted in McMenamin and Zoller, *Becoming Winston Churchill*, p. 79.

15. The chargé d'affaires in Madrid, G.F. Bonham, despatch to Lord Salisbury No. 303, dated 8 November 1895, gave these details. Drummond Wolff had left on leave on 15 October and did not

return to duty as ambassador until 17 November. Not everyone in the Foreign Office administration seemed to know of this request for leave. See also FO 72/1979, Cable 309 Drummond Wolff to Lord Salisbury, 17 November 1895.

16. Quoted in Enrique de Miguel Fernández, 'Azcárraga y la conducción de la guerra de Cuba', PhD Thesis, University Jaume I de Castelló, 2011, p. 370.

17. *Diario de la Marina*, 'Tunas de Zaza', 7 December 1895.

18. Isaac Pitrulla, 'Winston Churchill en Santa Clara', *El Camajuense*, XVIII, 1997, p. 53'. This article was provided to the author by Mr Arnaldo Díaz, a journalist and television producer in Santa Clara.

19. *Diario de la Marina*, articles 'De Santa Clara' and 'Noticias oficiales: grandes acciones', dated 4 December 1895.

20. SHM, Caja 3810 (Noticias Telegráficas), November–December 1895, Requests by two correspondents of 3 and 4 December 1895 with annotated approvals in ink.

21. See, for example, *Correspondencia Militar*, issues of 29 and 30 December 1895.

22. Anonymous, *Crónicas de la guerra de Cuba*, p. 117; and Escalante Colas et al., *Diccionario enciclopédico de historia militar de Cuba*, Vol. 2, p. 425.

23. AGM, Sección 1, Legajo E-1344. Quoted in Bissell, *Orders, Decorations and Medals*, p. 17.

24. *Diario de la Marina*, 'Sir Spencer Churchill', p. 2, column 6, 7 December 1895. The ship didn't sail that afternoon, and their names do not appear on the passenger list published in the same newspaper for the following day either. It is interesting to note that Churchill clearly understood the controversy raging at the time over the conduct of the war and, despite obvious temptations, carefully avoided leaping into it. This speaks volumes of his sensitivity to the diplomatic, political and military context surrounding him.

25. These are the surely strikingly accurate words of John Pearson, *The Private Lives of Winston Churchill*, Bloomsbury, NJ, Barnes and Noble, 2011, pp. 81–5, to describe this moment in Churchill's life where, if not in the exceptional fashion of later years, he is for the first time a regular feature of press interest.

26. For this and the following quote, see Martin Gilbert, *Churchill and America*, London, Pocket Books, 2006, p. 18.

27. Manchester, *The Last Lion*, p. 229.

28. Articles in the *New York World*, 15 December 1895; and the *New York Herald*, 14 December 1895, both quoted in ibid., p. 19.

29. John Tone, *War and Genocide in Cuba, 1895–1898*, Chapel Hill, University of North Carolina Press, 2009, pp. 220–1.
30. FO 72/1979 Drummond Wolff to Lord Salisbury, FO 320 dated 7 December 1895.
31. BRDW, Churchill, quoting *The Star*, 6 December 1895.
32. Ibid., quoting *The Sun*, 6 December 1895.
33. Ibid., quoting the *Glasgow Daily Record*, 6 December 1895. The same article appeared in *The Western Press* on that day.
34. D'Este, *Warlord*, p. 47.
35. Ibid., quoting *Eastern Morning News*, 7 December 1895. On roughly this date another undisclosed British newspaper from the collection of clippings Churchill kept, said that, 'Churchill had been in the country for some time, and he has now offered his sword to Marshal Martínez Campos … and the Marshal has accepted … Another scion of the British aristocracy is fighting with the Cubans. This is Hon. Cecil Howard.'
36. Ibid., quoting *The Newcastle Leader*, 7 December 1895.
37. Ibid., quoting *The Morning Post*, 'The Cuban Revolt: An Englishman's Experiences', 8 December 1895.
38. Ibid., quoting *The Glasgow Times*, 19 December 1895.
39. See 'Mr. Winston Churchill', article from the *New York Herald* reprinted in *Diario de la Marina*, 21 December 1895, where at least he is neither ennobled nor promoted greatly and is referred to as 'Hussar lieutenant of the Hussars of Great Britain'.
40. 'Lord Churchil', in *Diario del Ejército*, 22 December 1895.
41. In a letter of 3 October, Lady Randolph says how 'The boys are so delighted at the thought of ringing their own front door, they can think of nothing else'. Quoted in Celia Lee and John Lee, *The Churchills: A Family Portrait*, London, Palgrave Macmillan, 2010, p. 86. This was of course not quite true since we know that Churchill was about to write to his mother about his Cuban idea, and thus was most certainly thinking of *something* else, but there is no doubt that he liked the idea of a new and pleasant London home for the family and a place for his own future office and base. The former residence is now the Rose Court Hotel. Despite what has been said above about Churchill's French, it still seemed to be quite faulty as witnessed by his reference to a *parti carré* which should have read a *partie carrée*.
42. CHAR 1/14/22 and CHAR 1/14/23 Letters from Drummond Wolff to WSC, dated 17 and 24 February 1895. Churchill had suggested

that Spain might be guilty of 'senseless cruelty' in the war in the first article. The Latin verse, by Vergil, '*macte tui virtute puer*', which ends the second, favourable letter, is usually finished with '*sic itur ad astra*'. The usual translation of this phrase is 'Go forth with values, boy, this is the path to the stars.' An alternate translation is 'Blessings on your courage, boy, this is the path to the stars.' It was obviously meant to buck Winston up at the time and show him that, from Drummond Wolff's perspective, he was doing the right thing and would achieve a great deal in life, something to which he came back in 1908, in Winston's case, in his book *Rambling Recollections*.

43. Randolph Churchill, *Winston S. Churchill*, pp. 277–80.

Chapter 7 Myths and Realities: '*se non è vero è ben trovato*'

1. See Barry Singer, *Churchill Style: The Art of Being Winston Churchill*, New York, Abrams, 2012, p. 167.
2. Ibid., p. 30.
3. For the quote of Churchill scholar Larry Arnn, see Manchester, *The Last Lion*, p. 36. See Cita Stelzer, *Dinner with Churchill: Policy-Making at the Dinner Table*, London, Short Books, 2011. pp. 206–8.
4. See Celia Sandys' description of her meeting with Fidel Castro in *Chasing Churchill*, pp. 43–4.
5. CHAR 1/14/9 Letter Mr M. Shaw Bowers to WSC, 10 December 1895. See also Sarmiento Ramírez, *El Ingenio del mambí*, p. 116.
6. *Diario de la Marina*, 17 June 1896, p. 1., column 2.
7. The main myth, and the surrounding elements, are discussed in Méndez Vargas, *Arroyo Blanco*, especially pp. 34–5, 96–8, the book launched in the village in 2014.
8. Even today the *marabú* plant, a hefty bush of a dense wood that defies any clearance except the most tedious and labour intensive, is a problem on the island. Shortly after taking formal office in 2008, President Raúl Castro actually called the scourge Cuba's 'Number One Enemy', such is its effect on agricultural development.
9. See Sarmiento Ramírez, *El Ingenio del mambí*, especially p. 29.
10. See, for example, D'Este, *Warlord*, p. 43.
11. Richard Holmes, *Redcoat: The British Soldier in the Age of Horse and Musket*, London, HarperCollins, 2002, especially p. 226.
12. BRDW, Churchill, 'Letters from the Front', 1 *The Daily Graphic*, 13 December 1895.

13. Jiménez González, in his full treatment of the phenomenon of the *tea*, does not even mention the snake in question nor does any other source consulted on this subject including innumerable Cuban peasants who laughed at the idea. See Jiménez González, *Historia militar de Cuba*, pp. 270–5, and Jiménez González, Ángel et al., *Historia militar de Cuba*, Vol. 5, Havana, Editorial Verde Olivo, 2011, pp. 270–75, in its full discussion of the incendiary campaign, mentions no such means although it does address many other ways of conducting the incendiary warfare of the day.

Chapter 8 The Young Churchill as Political Analyst

1. Manchester, *The Last Lion*, pp. 121–2.
2. González Barrios, *El Ejército*, p. 20.
3. See for this and both the preceding quotes, BRDW, Churchill, 'Letters from the Front', 1, *The Daily Graphic*, 13 December 1895.
4. See throughout the classic Ramón Guerra, *Guerra de los Diez Años*, 2 vols, Havana, Ciencias Sociales, 1972.
5. BRDW, Churchill, 'Letters from the Front', 2, *The Daily Graphic*, 17 December 1895.
6. The dating and place of writing of this letter are both highly dubious. Churchill was sailing from New York on 14 December, whereas his letter of that date suggests he was still in Tampa Bay. This is more than just curious and this author has found no explanation for the obvious inaccuracy on both scores.
7. This, and the next three major quotes, are all from BRDW, Churchill, 'Letters from the Front', 5, *The Daily Graphic*, 13 January 1896.
8. See, for example, quote from Gómez in Antonio Piralta Criado, *Anales de la Guerra civil*, Vol. 6, Madrid, Editorial González Rojas, 1895, p. 177.
9. Ferrer, *Insurgent Cuba*, gives some discussion to this but the most complete work is that of Silvia Castro Fernández, *La Masacre de los Independientes de color en 1912*, Havana, Ciencias Sociales, 2002.
10. Perez, *Cuba between Empires*, pp. 376–86.
11. Churchill, *Saturday Review*, 17 February 1895.
12. Ibid., Ferrer, *Insurgent Cuba*, attempts to come close to finding the real figure. Pérez Guzmán, *Radiografía*, accepts that this is not possible. But certainly all modern sources give the figure as more than half. Hugh

Thomas gives estimates of others reaching as high as 80–85 per cent of total forces being black but doubtless including multiracial people. Of course this is before the exceptionally successful recruiting of whites that occurred after the invasion of the west was accomplished. See Thomas, *Cuba*, p. 323, and Ferrer, *Insurgent Cuba*, p. 230.

13. Ibid.
14. Ibid.
15. Ibid.
16. Many of the elements of this policy could be seen afterwards in British approaches to combatting guerrilla warfare in the South African War.
17. Both sides routinely accused the other of atrocities with prisoners and with the treatment of civilian populations. The Cubans were called brigands and thieves living off the booty they seized in raids on peaceful towns. The Spanish were accused of callous slaughter of thousands of *reconcentrados* and of shooting all prisoners as traitors to the crown. The story of the *reconcentración* is well told in Tone, *War and Genocide*.

Chapter 9 The Young Churchill as Military Analyst

1. See for this and the sequel below, César García del Pino, 'El Naufragio del crucero "Sánchez Barcáiztegui"', in his *La Habana a través de los siglos*, Havana, Ediciones Boloña, 2012, pp. 151–83, especially 165–6.
2. Ángel Jiménez González et al., *Historia militar de Cuba*, Vol. 5, Havana, Editorial Verde Olivo, 2011, p. 258.
3. Ibid., pp. 253–7.
4. FO 72/1979 Sir G. Bonham to Lord Salisbury No. 299 dated 26 Oct 95 No.299. Bonham was chargé in Madrid from August to December when Sir Henry Drummond Wolff was away either on leave or away from the capital. These figures were reported in the press but interpreted to Bonham by the German military attaché in Madrid. The report was in error in terms of its total figure, which should be 75,382.
5. Jiménez González, *Historia militar de Cuba*, Vol. 5, p. 330.
6. The rebels had tried to found a navy, or at least put to sea a corsair raider, in the first war for independence. The attempt failed for a variety of reasons and probably was quite far-fetched to begin

with. They did not get even close to this option in the 1895 war as conditions for such ships had changed entirely.

7. BRDW, Churchill, 'Letters from the Front', 1, *The Daily Graphic*, 13 December 1895.

8. Ibid.

9. For the fascinating story of these *voluntarios*, especially their early years, see Mercedes García Rodríguez, *Con un ojo en Yara y el otro en Madrid*, Havana, Ciencias Sociales, 2012, pp. 88–134; and Marilú Uralde, *Voluntarios españoles en Cuba*, Havana, Editora Historia, 2009.

10. Pérez Guzmán, *Radiografía*, p. 15.

11. For a Cuban version of these events, see Escalante Colas et al., *Diccionario enciclopédico de historia militar de Cuba*, Vol. 2, Havana, Editorial Verde Olivo, 2004, p. 291. For the court martial, see SHM Caja 3953 Campaign Operations Santa Clara November 1895, Declaration Lieutenant Quinciano Feijóo, dated 18 November 1895. And for Churchill's recounting see BRDW, Churchill, 'Letters from the Front', 2, *The Daily Graphic*, 17 December 1895.

12. This quote and the next are from BRDW, Churchill, 'Letters from the Front', 2, *The Daily Graphic*, 17 December 1895.

13. It is curious that neither this action nor Pío Cervantes makes it into the encyclopedia of Cuban military history (*Diccionario enciclopédico de historia militar de Cuba*, Havana, Verde Olivo, 2004), often quoted here and written under the direction of General Amels Escalante Colás, in either Vol. 1 (*Biografías*) or Vol. 2 (*Acciones Combativas*). However, see Luis F. del Moral Nogueras, *Serafín Sánchez: un carácter al servicio de Cuba*, Havana, Verde Olivo, 2001, p. 243, quoted in Méndez Vargas, *Arroyo Blanco*, pp. 102–3. See also Miró Argenter, *Crónicas de la guerra*, pp. 174–5.

14. See Méndez Vargas, *Arroyo Blanco*, p. 104. The author does not go this far but it is implicit in her assertions here and certainly seems highly likely to the author of this book that she is correct.

15. Pérez Guzmán, *Radiografía*, pp. 37–9.

16. BRDW, Churchill, 'Letters from the Front', 3, *The Daily Graphic*, 24 December 1895.

17. Colonel Camps y Feliú, quoted in Jiménez González, *Historia militar de Cuba*, p. 338. Many readers will doubtless be thinking of the famed Gurkha *kukri* while considering this weapon.

18. Colonel Jiménez Castellanos, quoted in ibid., pp. 338–9.

19. BRDW, Churchill, 'Letters from the Front', 4, *The Daily Graphic*, 27 December 1895.

20. BRDW, Churchill, 'Letters from the Front', 5, *The Daily Graphic*, 13 January 1896. It is interesting to note, as usual during this period, that the German army is taken as the example of the best, this on the basis of its exceptional success against Austria in 1866 and France in 1870–71. Churchill was to see it first-hand during manoeuvres in 1906 and 1909, as the guest of the Kaiser himself, and of course even more dramatically in the First World War.

21. SHM Caja 3954 Operational Diaries December 1895, draft cables Suárez Valdés (Tunas) to Martínez Campos dated 2 December 1895.

22. Ibid., *Orden General*, Jicotea, 3 December 1895, Suárez Valdés' column.

23. Blas Piñar Gutiérrez, 'Prólogo', *Churchill en Cuba 1895*, Buenos Aires, Editorial Nueva Mayoría, 1998.

24. Randolph Churchill, Companion Volume, p. 620.

25. See Randolph Churchill, Companion Volume I/1, pp. 256–7.

26. Nine of these sketches, through the kindness of Mr Allen Packwood of the Churchill Centre Archive, were published in this author's 'Cuba 1895: First Full Signs of the Man He Was to Become', in *Finest Hour*, No. 159 (Summer 2013), pp. 24–9.

27. One reference to Mr T.C. Crowther is in the Spanish translation of the texts Churchill sent to *The Daily Graphic*, done by Elena Patejuck for the *Editorial Nueva Mayoría*, in 1998 and to which reference has already been made. It reads 'In addition to his despatches, Churchill also sent to the *Daily Graphic* informal sketches. These were not used but were drawn anew by a member of the staff of the Graphic, T.C. Crowther, for their publication.' Piñar Gutiérrez, *Churchill en Cuba 1895*, p. 34. The second reference is in the work of Frederick Woods, *Artillery of Words: The Writings of Sir Winston Churchill*, London, Pen and Sword Publishers, 1992, Chapter 2, fn. 12.

28. D'Este, *Warlord*, p. 143.

29. Manchester, *The Last Lion*, p. 569.

Chapter 10 The Impact of the Cuban Adventure

1. For a detailed description of that next adventure see the highly readable Coughlin, *Churchill's First War*. For his comments on whether war suited him, see his discussion of this topic with regard to Cuba in Churchill, *My Early Life*, p. 69.

2. Robert Lloyd George, *David and Winston*, Woodstock, NY, The Overlook Press, 2008, p. 19.

3. Churchill, *My Early Life*, p. 58.
4. For example, he is photographed wearing his Spanish Red Cross medal in the well-known 1900 picture of him in the uniform of the South African Light Horse. See Bissell, *Orders, Decorations and Medals*, p. 16.
5. Manchester (*The Last Lion*, p. 202) has Churchill serving with the Oxfordshire Artillery and the Oxfordshire Yeomanry as well for an extraordinary total of nine regiments with which he supposedly served during his military career. But this is not quite the case. He certainly worked with artillery from the county but he did not serve with them, as the expression goes. And the Oxfordshire Yeomanry is simply another name for his reserve regiment, the Queen's Own Oxfordshire Hussars.
6. In a variety of sources, including the regimental journal of 1946, there is mention of four Churchill visits during the war to the Hussars. But Churchill spoke of only three (El Alamein, Cyprus and Italy) in his speech to the Regiment on the occasion of the Regimental Association Dinner of 1946, the first since before the war. See also David Scott Daniel, *4th Hussar: The Story of the 4th Queen's Own Hussars 1685–1958*, Aldershot, Gale and Polden, 1959. Churchill's son Randolph was to serve in the Regiment as well.
7. See two very interesting articles on his reserve service, previously hardly looked at, in Paul H. Courtenay, 'WSC: Eternal Hussar', in *Finest Hour*, No. 159 (Summer 2013), pp. 20–1; and in the same issue, Ursula Corcoran, 'Churchill, Woodstock and the Oxford Yeomanry Museum', pp. 22–3.
8. The commanding officer's tank is always named 'Churchill' in The Queen's Royal Hussars of today, where the prize for the best troop at tank gunnery is still 'The Churchill Cup'. The regiment, currently based at Sennelager, near the north German town of Paderborn, while still officially termed light cavalry, is now equipped and trained in the heavy armour role. Churchill's presence in the historical memory of the regiment is a major one as is, interestingly enough, that of Barnes.
9. Quoted in Gilbert, *Churchill: A Life*, London, Heinemann, 1991, p. 62.
10. CHAR 1/14/21 W.L. Thomas to WSC dated 14 January 1896.
11. Woods, *Artillery of Words*, p. 152.
12. Quotes are from a review by James W. Muller, in *Finest Hour*, 7 (Winter 1993–94), where the work cited is Keith Alldritt, *Churchill the Writer: His Life as a Man of Letters*, London, Hutchison, 1992.

13. Manchester, *The Last Lion*, p. 35.
14. See José Vidal Peláez, *Winston Churchill (1874–1965)*, Madrid, Editorial Acento, 2003, p. 32; Coughlin, *Churchill's First War*, p. 87. The author has not seen any other reference to 'the Cuban hussar'.
15. Martin, *Lady Randolph Churchill*, p. 63.
16. Quoted in Coughlin, *Churchill's First War*, p. 88.
17. Ibid., pp. 91–4.
18. Manchester, *The Last Lion*, pp. 233–4.
19. Both these quotes on Colonel Ramsay come from Coughlin, *Churchill's First War*, pp. 102, 124.
20. This is how he referred to his time in the army in his letter to his mother dated 16 August 1895, just before the Cuban idea germinated in his mind, as quoted in Randolph Churchill, *Winston S. Churchill*, p. 249. 'It is a fine game to play – this game of politics – and it is well worth waiting for a good hand before really plunging.'
21. Letter WSC to Lady Randolph Churchill, dated 29 August 1897, quoted in ibid., p. 124.
22. It is very curious that the usually accurate passenger lists for the *Olivette*, published regularly in the Havana press, include neither Barnes nor Churchill for 8 December. However, no other date seems feasible given other timings for Tampa and New York.
23. AHN Ultramar, Cuba-Gobierno, 1895, Martínez Campos, Nos 185, 204, 221, 240, 5 June 1895.

Conclusion

1. Manchester, *The Last Lion*, p. 12.
2. Figure provided in June 2014, by Ronald Cohen, specialist in Churchill's writings and publications about him. See also his definitive *Bibliography of the Writings of Sir Winston Churchill*, London, Thoemmes Continuum, 2006.

BIBLIOGRAPHY

Primary Sources

Archival Sources

AHN Archivo Histórico Nacional (Madrid)
      Libros Sección Ultramar (Cuba-Gobierno)
APSS Archivo Provincial (Sancti Spiritus)
CAC Churchill Archives Centre (Cambridge)
      BRDW   Broadwater Collection
      CHAR   Chartwell Papers
      CHUR   Churchill Papers
HL Hove Library
      WP Wolseley Papers
NA (British) National Archives (London)
      FO Foreign Office
      AP Ardagh Papers
AGM Archivo General Militar (Segovia)
SHM Servicio Histórico Militar (Madrid)

Memoirs

Boza, Bernabé, *Mi Diario de la Guerra*, Havana, Imprenta La Propaganda, 1900.

Maceo, Antonio, *Diarios de campaña*, Havana, Ciencias Sociales, 1960.

Miró y Argenter, José, *Crónicas de la guerra*, *Vol. 1: La Campaña de la Invasión* (3 vols), Havana, Instituto del Libro, 1970.

Tetuán, Duke of, *Apuntes del ex-ministro de estado, Duque de Tetuán, para la defensa de la política internacional y gestión diplomática del gobierno liberal-conservador desde el 28 de marzo de 1895 a 29 de septiembre de 1897*, Madrid, Péant, 1903.

Vesa y Fillart, Antonio, *Historial del Regimiento Caballería de Juraco y de su estandarte*, Havana, 1908.

Periodicals

Correspondencia Militar (Madrid)

Diario de la Marina (Havana)

Diario del Ejército (Havana)

La Fraternidad (Sancti Spiritus)

Eastern Morning News (Kingston-upon-Hull)

Daily Graphic (London)

The Glasgow Daily Record

The Glasgow Times

The Graphic (London)

The Morning Post (London)

The Newcastle Leader

The New York Herald

The New York Times

The New York World

The Saturday Review of Politics, Literature, Science and Art (London)

The Star (London)

The Sun (London)

The Western Daily Press (Bristol)

Secondary Sources

Books and Articles

Abreu López, Carlos, et al., *Síntesis histórica provincial Sancti Spíritus*, Havana, Editora Historia, 2011.

Alldritt, Keith, *Churchill The Writer: His Life as a Man of Letters*, London, Hutchison, 1992.

Anonymous, *Crónicas de la guerra de Cuba*, Havana, Editorial Fígaro, 1895.

Ben-Mosha, Tuvia, *Churchill: Strategist and Historian*, Boulder, Lynne Rienner, 1992.

Best, Geoffrey, *Churchill: a Study in Greatness*, Oxford, Oxford University Press, 2003.

Birkenhead, Earl of, *Churchill 1874–1922*, London, Harrap, 1989.

Bissell, Douglas S., *The Orders, Decorations and Medals of Sir Winston Churchill*, Hopkinton, NH, The International Churchill Societies, 1990.

Bosch Gómez, Juan, *El Napoleón de las guerrillas*, Havana, Ciencias Sociales, 1996.

Cardona, Gabriel, and Juan Carlos Losada, *Weyler: nuestro hombre en La Habana*, Barcelona, Planeta, 1998.

Castillo Meléndez, Francisco, *La Defensa de la isla de Cuba en la segunda mitad del siglo XVII*, Sevilla, Padura, 1998.

Castro Fernández, Silvia, *La Masacre de los Independientes de color en 1912*, Havana, Ciencias Sociales, 2002.

Churchill, Randolph, *Winston S. Churchill, Vol. 1: Youth 1874–1900*, Boston, MS, Houghton Mifflin, 1966.

Churchill, Winston S., *The Story of the Malakand Field Force: An Episode of Frontier War*, London, 1898.

—*Great Contemporaries*, London, Butterworth, 1937.

—*My Early Life*, London, Eland, 2000.

Clarke, Peter, *Mr Churchill's Profession: Statesman, Orator, Writer*, London, Bloomsbury Press, 2012.

Cohen, Ronald, *Bibliography of the Writings of Sir Winston Churchill*, London, Thoemmes Continuum, 2006.

Coughlin, Con, *Churchill's First War: Young Winston at War with the Afghans*, London, St Martin's, 2014.

Corcoran, Ursula, 'Churchill, Woodstock and the Oxford Yeomanry Museum', in *Finest Hour,* No. 159 (Summer 2013), pp. 22–3.

Cordoví Núñez, Yoel, *Máximo Gómez: en perspectiva*, Santiago de Cuba, Editorial Oriente, 2007.

Courtenay, Paul D., 'WSC: Eternal Hussar', in *Finest Hour*, No. 159 (Summer 2013), pp. 20–1.

Cowles, Virginia, *Winston Churchill: The Era and the Man*, London, Hamish Hamilton, 1953.

D'Este, Carlo, *Warlord: A Life of Winston Churchill at War, 1874–1945*, New York, HarperCollins, 2008.

De Diego, Emilio, *1895: La Guerra en Cuba y la España de la Restauración*, Madrid, Editorial Complutense, 1996.

De la Torre, Mildred, *El Autonomismo en Cuba 1878–1895*, Havana, Ciencias Sociales, 1998.

De Miguel Fernández, Enrique, 'Azcárraga y la conducción de la guerra de Cuba', PhD Thesis, Jaume I de Castelló University, Castellón (Spain), 2011.

De Quesada, Alejandro, *The Spanish–American War and Philippine Insurrection 1898–1902*, Men at Arms Series 437, London, Osprey, 2010.

Del Carmen Barcia, María, *Elites y grupos de presión: Cuba 1868–1898,* Havana, Ciencias Sociales, 1998.

Del Moral Nogueras, Luis F., *Serafín Sánchez: un carácter al servicio de Cuba*, Havana, Verde Olivo, 2001.

Díaz Martínez, Yolanda, *Vida y avatares de los hombres en contienda: la subsistencia en la Guerra del 95*, Havana, Editora Política, 2004.

Drummond Wolff, Sir Henry, *Rambling Recollections*, London, Macmillan, 1908.

Dyal, Donald H., *Historical Dictionary of the Spanish–American War*, Santa Barbara, CA, Greenwood Press, undated.

Emrys, Hughes, *Winston Churchill: Political Bulldog*, New York, Banner, 1955.

English, Adrian, *Armed Forces of Latin America*, London, Jane's, 1984.

Escalante Colás, General Amels, et al., *Diccionario enciclopédico de historia militar de Cuba* (3 vols), Havana, Editorial Verde Olivo, 2001–05.

Fernández, Enrique de Miguel, *La Correspondencia de Azcárraga con Weyler sobre la Guerra de Cuba 1896–1897*, Valencia, Soler, 2010.

Ferrer, Ada, *Insurgent Cuba: Race, Nation and Revolution 1868–1898*, Chapel Hill, NC , University of North Carolina, 1999.

Franco, José Luciano, *Antonio Maceo: apuntes para una historia de su vida* (2 vols), Havana, Ciencias Sociales, 1975.

García, Gloria, *Conspiraciones y revueltas*, Santiago, Oriente, 2003.

García del Pino, César, 'El Naufragio del crucero "Sánchez Barcáiztegui"', in *La Habana a través de los siglos*, Havana, Ediciones Boloña, 2012, pp. 151–83.

García Rodríguez, Mercedes, *Con un Ojo en Yara y el otro en Madrid*, Havana, Ciencias Sociales, 2012.

Gilbert, Martin, *Churchill*, London, Houghton Mifflin, 1967.

—*Churchill: A Life*, London, Heinemann, 1991.

—*Churchill and America*, London, Pocket Books, 2006.

—*Churchill: The Power of Words*, New York, Da Capo Press, 2012.

González Barrios, René, *Los Capitanes generales de Cuba, 1868–1878*, Havana, Verde Olivo, 1999.

—*El Ejército español en Cuba, 1868–1878*, Havana, Verde Olivo, 2000.

Grotelueschen, Mark, *The AEF Way of War*, New York, Cambridge University Press, 2007.

Guerra, Ramón, *Guerra de los Diez Años* (2 vols), Havana, Ciencias Sociales, 1972.

Guerra Vilaboy, Sergio, *América Latina y la independencia de Cuba*, Caracas, Ediciones Ko'eyu, 1999.

Hall, Christopher, *British Diplomacy and United States Hegemony in Cuba, 1898–1964*, London, Palgrave Macmillan, 2013.

Harding Davis, Richard, 'Winston Spencer Churchill', in Harding Davis, *Real Soldiers of Fortune*, New York, Scribner's, 1910, pp. 77–117.

Harrington, Peter, 'Images and Perceptions: Visualizing the Sudan Campaign', in Edward M. Spiers (ed.), *Sudan: The Reconquest Reassessed*, London, Routledge, 2013, pp. 82–101.

Headrick, Daniel R., *Ejército y Política en España, 1866–1898*, Madrid, Editorial Tecnos, 1981.

Hernández Suárez, Roberto A., *Capitanía General de Cuba: guerras de independencia en Hispanoamérica 1800–1830*, Havana, Editorial Política, 2011.

Holmes, Richard, *In the Footsteps of Churchill*, London, Basic Books, 2009.

—*Redcoat: the British Soldier in the Age of Horse and Musket*, London, HarperCollins, 2002.

Izquierdo Canosa, Raúl, *Ciego de Ávila 1895–1898: Guerra, hechos y noticias*, Santiago de Cuba, Editorial Oriente, 2012.

Jenkins, Roy, *Churchill*, London, Pan Books, 2002.

Jiménez González, Ángel et al., *Historia militar de Cuba* (5 vols), Havana, Editorial Verde Olivo, 2011.

Kirk, John, *Martí: Mentor of the Cuban Nation*, Gainesville, FL, University Press of Florida, 1983.

—and Peter McKenna, *Canadian–Cuban Relations: The Other Good Neighbor Policy*, Gainesville, FL, University Press of Florida, 1997.

Klepak, Hal P., *Cuba's Military 1990–2005: Revolutionary Soldiers in Counter-Revolutionary Times*, New York, Palgrave Macmillan, 2006.

—*Raúl Castro and Cuba: A Military Story*, New York, Palgrave Macmillan, 2011.

—'Cuba 1895: First Full Signs of the Man He Was to Become', in *Finest Hour*, No. 159 (Summer 2013), pp. 24–9.

Lawrence, James, *Churchill and Empire*, London, Weidenfeld & Nicolson, 2013.

Lee, Celia and John Lee, *The Churchills: A Family Portrait*, London, Palgrave Macmillan, 2010.

Lloyd George, Robert, *David and Winston*, Woodstock, NY, The Overlook Press, 2008.

López Jiménez, Enrique, 'El Teniente Churchill en Cuba', *Revista Ejército*, April 2013, No. 865, pp. 119–20.

McGillivray, Gillian, *Blazing Cane: Sugar Communities, Class and State Formation in Cuba 1868–1959*, Durham, NC, Duke University Press, 2009.

McMenamin , Michael and Curt Zoller, *Becoming Winston Churchill*, New York, Enigma Books, 2009.

Mahan, Alfred Thayer, *The Influence of Seapower upon History, 1660–1783*, Boston, Little Brown, 1893.

Manchester, William, *The Last Lion: Winston Spencer Churchill, Visions of Glory 1874–1932*, New York, Delta, 1989.

Marrero, Victor Manuel, *Vicente García: mito y realidad*, Havana, 1992.

Martin, Ralph, *Lady Randolph Churchill: A Biography 1854–1895*, London, Cassell, 1969.

Maurice, Sir F. and Sir George Arthur, *The Life of Lord Wolseley*, London, William Heinemann, 1924.

Mendelssohn, Peter de, *The Age of Churchill: Heritage and Adventure, 1874–1911*, London, Thames and Hudson, 1961.

Méndez Vargas, Lourdes, *Arroyo Blanco: la ruta cubana de Churchill*, Sancti Spiritus (Cuba), Luminaria, 2014.

Morales, Larry, *Máximo Gómez al oeste de La Trocha*, Havana, Editores Unión, 2003.

Morgan, Ted, *Churchill: Young Man in a Hurry 1874–1915*, New York, Simon and Shuster, 1982.

Murray, David R., *Odious Commerce: Britain, Spain and the Abolition of the Cuban Slave Trade*, Cambridge, Cambridge University Press, 1980.

Neilson, Keith and T.G. Otte, *The Permanent Under-Secretaries for Foreign Affairs, 1854–1946*, New York, Routledge, 2009.

Ovalles, Eduardo, *Churchill in Cuba 1895*, Buenos Aires, Editorial Nueva Mayoría, 1998.

Paterson, Michael, *Winston Churchill: His Military Life, 1895–1945*, Newton Abbot, David and Charles, 2005.

Pearson, John, *The Private Lives of Winston Churchill*, Bloomsbury, NJ, Barnes and Noble, 2011.

Perera Díaz, Aisnara, *Antonio Maceo: diarios de campaña*, Havana, Ciencias Sociales, 2001.

Perez, Louis A., *Cuba between Empires, 1878–1902*, Pittsburgh, PA, University of Pittsburgh Press, 1983.

Pérez Guzmán, Francisco, *La Batalla de las Guásimas*, Havana, Ciencias Sociales, 1975.

—*La Habana: clave de un imperio*, Havana, Ciencias Sociales, 1993.

—'La Revolución del 95: de los alzamientos a la campaña de la invasión', in Instituto de Historia de Cuba, *Las Luchas por la Independencia nacional, 1868–1898*, Havana, Editora Política, 1996, pp. 430–80.

—*Radiografía del Ejército Libertador*, Havana, Ciencias Sociales, 2005.

Piralta Criado, Antonio, *Anales de la guerra civil*, Vol. 6, Madrid, Editorial González Rojas, 1895.

Piñar Gutiérrez, Blas, 'Prólogo', in Piñar Gutiérrez, *Churchill en Cuba 1895*, Buenos Aires, Editorial Nueva Mayoría, 1998.

Piqueras, José A., *Cuba, emporio y colonia: la disputa de un mercado interferido 1878–1895*, Havana, Ciencias Sociales, 2007.

Pitrulla, Isaac, 'Winston Churchill en Santa Clara', *El Camajuense*, XVIII, 1997, p. 53.

Placer Cervera, Gustavo, *Inglaterra y La Habana: 1762*, Havana, Ciencias Sociales, 2007.

Portuondo Zúñiga, Olga, *Una derrota británica en Cuba*, Santiago, Editorial Oriente, 2000.

Pugh, Martin, *The Tories and the People, 1880–1935*, London, Blackwell, 1986.

Putkowski, Julian and Mark Dunning, *Murderous Tommies*, Barnsley, Pen and Sword Books, 2012.

Ranson, E., 'British Military and Naval Observers in the Spanish–American War', *Journal of American Studies*, 3, 1969, pp. 33–56.

Rodríguez, Jaime, *The Independence of Spanish America*, Cambridge, Cambridge University Press, 1998.

Russell, Douglas, *Winston Churchill, Soldier: The Military Life of a Gentleman at War*, London, Brassey's, 2005.

Sandys, Celia, *Chasing Churchill: The Travels of Winston Churchill*, London, HarperCollins, 2005.

Sarmiento Ramírez, Ismael, *El Ingenio del mambí* (2 vols), Santiago de Cuba, Editorial Oriente, 2008.

Scheina, Robert, *Latin America: A Naval History, 1810–1987*, Annapolis, MD, Naval Institute Press, 1987.

Schellings, William J., 'Florida and the Cuban Revolution, 1895–1898', *Florida Historical Review*, XXXIX, 2, October 1960, pp. 175–86.

Scott Daniel, David, *4th Hussar: The Story of the 4th Queen's Own Hussars, 1685–1958*, London, Gale and Polden, 1961.

Singer, Barry, *Churchill Style: The Art of Being Winston Churchill*, New York, Abrams, 2012.

Stafford, David, *Churchill and the Secret Service*, Woodstock, NY, Overlook Press, 1998.

Stelzer, Cita, *Dinner with Churchill: Policy-Making at the Dinner Table*, London, Short Books, 2011.

Thomas, Hugh, *Cuba: the Pursuit of Freedom*, London, Eyre and Spottiswoode, 1971.

Tone, J.L., 'The Machete and the Liberation of Cuba', *Journal of Military History*, 1998, pp. 1–28.

—*War and Genocide in Cuba, 1895–1898*, Chapel Hill, NC, University of North Carolina Press, 2006.

Uralde Cancio, Marilú, *Voluntarios españoles en Cuba*, Havana, Editora Historia, 2009.

Vidal Peláez López, José, *Winston Churchill, 1874–1965*, Madrid, Editorial Acento, 2003.

Weidhorn, Manfred, *Sword and Pen: A Survey of the Writings of Sir Winston Churchill*, Albuquerque, NM, University of New Mexico Press.

Woods, Frederick, *Winston Spencer Churchill: War Correspondent 1895–1900*, London, Brassey's, 1992.

—*Artillery of Words: The Writings of Sir Winston Churchill*, Barnsley, Pen and Sword Publishers, 1992.

Wrigley, Charles, *Winston Churchill: A Biographical Companion*, Santa Barbara, CA, ABC-Clio, 2002.

Websites

'Die, Workwear', www.dieworkwear.com, p. 43.

http://americanriflemean.org

http://www.ballisticstudies.com7x57

http://www.cubaheritage.org 'Winston Churchill, Military Observer in Cuba'.

http://www.ebay.com/itm/SS-Olivette-Built-a887-Cuba-tampa-Key-West-Mail-Steam

http://www.elsemanualdigital. Gran Cápitan, 'Churchill y la guerra de Cuba'.

www.fas.org/irp/agency/aia/cyberspokesman/99–11/history1.htm. Casey, Dennis, 'A Little Espionage goes a long way'.

http://www.Mauser+7x57+cartridge=+qs

http://QRH.org.uk/history4a.htm

http://referendumparacubaya.blogspot.co.uk/2013/05

http://www.spanamwar/spanishkrupp75.htm

http://www.ValerianGibayedodigitalhsitoryporect.com/2011/6/modern-war-correspondent-in-1895

INDEX

admiralty 23, 61, 109, 189,
        251 (en 50, 52)
Aldershot 36, 39, 72, 228,
        247 (en 29), 271 (en 6)
Alerta, gunboat 150
Alto Songo 118–9, 121
Ardagh, later General Sir John 58,
        60, 250 (en 32)
Arderíus y García, General José
        89–91, 121, 256 (en 19, 21),
        260 (en 22), 263 (en 13)
Arroyo Blanco 108, 110–1, 114,
        129, 171–2, 188, 207–8, 220,
        254 (en 3)
Australia 25, 55
Azcárraga, General Marcelo 71,
        157, 245 (en 8), 253 (en 61)

Bangalore 228–9
Barnes, Lieutenant, later Major–
        General Sir Reginald
        (Reggie)
    action and afterwards 93, 105–8,
        112, 128, 131, 135, 137, 146,
        152, 173, 206, 212, 231–2

background and personality
        48–50, 52, 81,
        248 (en 9, 10)
career 48–50, 229
decision to join Cuban
        adventure 47, 51–2, 89, 91,
        230–1, 237
departure from column and from
        Cuba 146–2, 155, 158, 216
trip 66, 76–7, 81–2, 94, 101–3,
        105, 112–3, 117, 119, 126, 170
Spanish reaction to him and
        his medal 88, 141, 152, 154,
        159–60, 223, 262 (en 51),
        271 (en 8)
support for Churchill 54, 61,
        230–2, 272 (en 22)
Benito, Father Juan Mariano 172
Boer War 39, 41, 49, 61, 92, 192,
        221, 223–4, 227
Bonham, Sir G.F., 263 (en 15),
        268 (en 4)
Brabazon, Colonel later General
        John Palmer 'Bwabs' 36–8,
        48, 53–5, 78, 229

British Army 38–9, 48–9, 56, 89,
    105, 108, 142, 160, 162, 175,
    191, 223, 230
  IV (Queen's Own) Hussars
    36–8, 48, 50, 54, 81, 175–6,
    224, 228–9, 248 (en 9, 10),
    271 (en 6)
  XVII Lancers 53, 224
  Queen's Own Oxfordshire
    Hussars 224, 271 (en 7)
  60th Rifle Regiment (and Rifle
    Regiments) 36–7, 120

Camagüey 96, 105, 115, 118, 125,
    134, 144
Cambridge, Duke of 36–7,
    56–9, 120
Canada 24, 29–30, 46, 55
Chamberlain, Joseph 63, 225, 228
Chapman, Colonel later General
    Sir Edward 60–2, 76–8,
    201, 250 (en 39)
China 45, 55, 61
Churchill, Jack 40, 45, 51, 164,
    254 (en 14)
Churchill, Lady Randolph (Jennie)
    36–40, 47, 51–4, 57, 78,
    81, 225, 246 (en 28),
    247 (en 29), 248 (en 3,
    5), 249 (en 13, 14, 16),
    250 (en 36, 38, 40),
    254 (en 15), 256 (en 22),
    261 (en 5), 262 (en 52),
    272 (en 21)
Churchill, Lord Randolph 35–6,
    38, 57, 62–3, 89, 91, 128,
    161–2, 169–70, 178, 224
Churchill, Winston
  childhood 34–5, 40, 46–7,
    63, 179

Cuba
  cigars 168–70, 239
  political analysis of 90, 99,
    135, 178–90
  1895 war military analysis
    191–221
  1895 war wider views 90,
    97–8, 103, 165–7 182–9
  return to England 164, 222
  Siesta 109–10, 239, 258 (en 5)
  travel to 81–6, 161–6
  trip to the war zone 93–4,
    101–3, 128
  views of Cuban patriots
    181–5
  views of rebel army 98,
    102–3, 127, 133–4, 183, 186,
    199–202, 207–10, 217–9
  views of Spanish Army in
    Cuba 108–15, 120–7, 136–8,
    146–8, 193–9, 212–5
  wealth 25, 96
  with the column 103–42
  decision to go to Cuba 43–6
  decision to join army and
    cavalry 36–8, 63
  education 34–5, 127
  Sandhurst 35–7, 39, 48, 54, 127,
    169, 227–8
Ciego de Ávila 104–5, 115, 215–6,
    255 (en 14), 260 (en 27)
Cienfuegos 73, 90, 99, 101, 122,
    150, 177, 180, 215
Cockran, Bourke 81–2, 91, 149,
    159, 184
Colón 93, 204
Cometa 150, 257 (en 28), 258 (en 3)
Cuba
  description 92, 96, 102, 196
  Liberation Army 101, 116, 186

insurgents (rebels) 93, 98, 102,
    113–4, 125–7, 131–4, 143,
    164, 166, 171, 181, 185, 199,
    202–7, 210, 216–7
logistics and supply 116, 172,
    189, 200,
strategy 96–8, 217–9, 233
strength 200, 204, 219,
    255 (en 7), 263 (en 9)
tactics 98, 208, 211, 216–9
weapons 31, 66, 75, 82, 97, 193,
    198–200, 204, 251 (en 49)
Spanish misgovernment of
    29–31, 92, 182–3, 203, 218
Independence War 1895–98 30,
    101, 237, 263 (en 9)

Daily Graphic 79–80, 90, 93, 101,
    103, 120, 125, 129, 138, 147,
    150, 163, 165, 180, 217, 219,
    221, 225, 234, 237–8
De Moleyns, Captain Frederick
    Wauchope Eveleigh 54–5,
    229, 231
Diario de la Marina 150, 153, 158,
    254 (en 3), 264 (en 17, 19,
    24), 265 (en 39), 266 (en 6)
Diario del Ejército 91, 154, 164,
    255 (en 8), 263 (en 10),
    265 (en 40)
Díaz Benzo, Colonel Antonio 114,
    118, 126
Drummond Wolff, Sir Henry
    62–4, 69–72, 77–8, 88, 100,
    160, 164–6, 255 (en 13),
    263–4 (en 15), 265 (en 30,
    42), 268 (en 4)

Escambray Mountains 102, 121, 204
Etruria 81, 83, 160, 222

Everest, Mrs Elizabeth 40

First World War 39, 49–50, 109,
    221, 224, 272 (en 20)
France 24–7, 46, 65, 81, 95, 127,
    156, 187, 191, 249 (en 14),
    270 (en 20)
French (language) 34, 126–7,
    260 (en 30), 265 (en 41)

García Medrano, Rosendo 208
García Navarro, General Antonio
    117–9, 121, 144–5, 148, 154,
    259 (en 16, 18, 21)
Gladstone, William 68, 128
Gollan, Alexander 69–70, 88–9,
    145, 147, 252 (en 58, 59),
    255 (en 4), 260 (en 26),
    262 (en 9)
Gómez, General Máximo 32–3,
    94–5, 100, 103, 106, 108,
    111, 115–6, 124–5, 133–5,
    138, 140, 145, 148, 150, 154,
    156–7, 160, 171–2, 183,
    197, 205–6, 213, 232–3,
    255 (en 10), 258 (en 4),
    260 (en 25, 26, 40),
    261 (en 47)
Great Britain
    Foreign Office 47, 60, 62, 67,
        69–70, 76–7, 89, 198, 238
    position in 1895 47, 59, 64, 75
    relations with Spain 47, 59, 64–6,
        76, 79, 187
    relations with the United States
        63–4
    public opinion on Cuba 47, 59,
        64, 75
    Royal Navy 23–4, 56, 66–7, 74,
        88, 251 (en 61)

Harrow 34–5, 127, 169
Havana
    Churchill in 73, 88–9, 152–8, 230
    Churchill's impressions 85–6,
        90–1, 97, 99
    description 86, 88, 180, 201–2
    history 25, 33, 85–6, 88, 193
    travel there and beyond 81, 83,
        85, 93, 149
Honorato Regiment 208
Howard, Charles James Stanley,
        Viscount Morpeth 68–9,
        251 (en 57, 58), 264 (en 35)

Iguará, Hato 108, 110, 129,
        145–6, 154, 208, 214, 230,
        258 (en 2)
India 23, 39–40, 43, 45, 49, 54, 141,
        166, 175, 192, 222, 225–31
Inglaterra, Hotel 86, 149, 154,
        170, 177

Jicotea 139, 147–9, 211, 216,
        270 (en 22)
Jubo (snake) 177, 204

Kitchener, Lord 149

La Reforma, battles of 105, 115,
        133, 136, 138–9, 143–6,
        153–4, 163, 198, 208, 214,
        218–20, 232, 261 (en 47)
Liverpool 66, 76, 81, 89
London 22–3, 39, 43, 54, 64, 71–2,
        79–80, 89, 92, 149, 160, 162,
        164, 170, 218, 226

Maceo, General Antonio 32,
        67, 94–5, 99, 106, 108,
        115, 133–4, 136–41, 143,

        145, 153, 156–7, 160, 185,
        203, 211, 214, 230–1,
        254 (en 10), 257 (en 1)
Machete 112, 134, 200, 209–10
Malakand campaign 41, 227, 231
María Isabel, Queen Regent of
        Spain 64, 68, 70, 152, 157,
        160, 231
Martínez Campos, Marshal Arsenio
        29, 33, 89, 91, 94, 100–1,
        104–5, 108, 114, 118, 122,
        124, 130, 137, 141, 144–6,
        149, 152, 159–60, 162, 184,
        188, 198, 201, 220, 232–4,
        241 (en 2), 255 (en 13),
        256 (en 25), 257 (en 2, 31),
        260 (en 27), 261 (en 36,
        46, 51), 262 (en 2, 3),
        263 (en 12, 13), 265 (en 35),
        270 (en 21)
Matabeleland 55, 229
Morro Castle 85, 201

O'Donnell y Vargas, Captain, later
        General Juan 100–1, 234
Olivette 83, 85, 158, 222,
        254 (en 17), 225 (en 22)
Oriente 29, 32, 95, 97, 105, 115,
        118, 121

Pax Britannica 21–3, 45, 66, 75
Polo 40, 50, 81, 173, 231,
        246 (en 10)

Ramsey, Lieutenant-Colonel
        William Alexander 229
Red Cross of Military Merit
        118, 151–2, 157, 172, 221,
        271 (en 4)

Sancti Spiritus 101–4, 108, 115, 117,
    122, 136, 149, 163, 204–6,
    216, 220, 262 (en 6)
Sanderson, Sir Thomas 67, 76–7,
    252 (en 52, 53, 58),
    253 (en 2)
Sandhurst, Royal Military
    Academy 34–6, 39–40, 46,
    48, 54, 127, 169, 227–8
Santa Clara 89, 91, 93–4, 101,
    103–4, 108, 118, 121–2, 145,
    151–3, 204, 216, 232, 234
Saturday Review of Politics, Literature,
    Science and Art 165–6, 179,
    185, 218, 225, 228
Second World War 110, 168, 221–4,
    237, 258 (en 5)
Spanish Army in Cuba
  artillery 120–2, 198
  cavalry
    lack of 109, 117, 122–4, 147,
    194–9, 214–5
    Pizarro Regiment 122, 124,
    126, 138
  guerrilla 122–3, 126, 198, 216
    Yero Guerrilla 122, 126, 138,
    216
  strength 198
  infantry
    description 98, 109, 117, 122,
    132–3, 148, 195–6, 210, 213
    Cazadores de Valladolid, No.
    21 119, 122, 126, 138, 148
    Regimiento de Cuba (2nd
    Battalion, No.65) 119, 122,
    137, 148
    Regimiento Chiclana
    122, 139
  Voluntarios 90, 93, 102, 123, 180,
    183, 201–3, 269 (en 9)

Spanish Navy 25, 27, 97, 104
Suárez Valdés, General Álvaro 101,
    103–8, 112, 114–5, 120, 122,
    124–5, 133, 139–41, 143–4,
    148–9, 151–4, 156–60,
    171–3, 187, 210–4, 218, 234,
    257 (en 28), 261 (en 46, 47,
    48), 262 (en 6)
Sudan (campaign 1898) 41, 223–4, 237
Switzerland 47, 127

Ten Years War 29, 31, 82, 89, 94–6,
    114, 120, 134, 145, 206, 230,
    243, 249 (en 47)
Tetuán, Third Duke of 70–2, 100, 234
Trinidad 102, 118, 147, 215, 232
Trocha Júcaro-Morón 96, 98–100,
    104, 106, 108, 111, 115,
    124–5, 135, 144, 149, 153–4,
    173, 205, 216, 220, 232,
    255 (en 14), 257 (en 28)
Tunas de Zaza 101–3, 149–50, 204,
    216, 259 (en 15)

United States 24, 27, 31, 46, 64–6,
    69, 81–4, 104, 134, 156,
    158–60, 165, 168, 181, 188,
    192, 220, 234, 238

Victoria, Queen 59, 64, 68, 74,
    249 (en 26)

Vidal, Lieutenant Félix (French
    Army) 156

Wolseley, General Lord 54–61,
    77–8, 162, 228, 230

Yellow fever 33, 69, 103, 149,
    246 (en 20), 257 (en 29)

If you enjoyed this book, you may also be interested in …

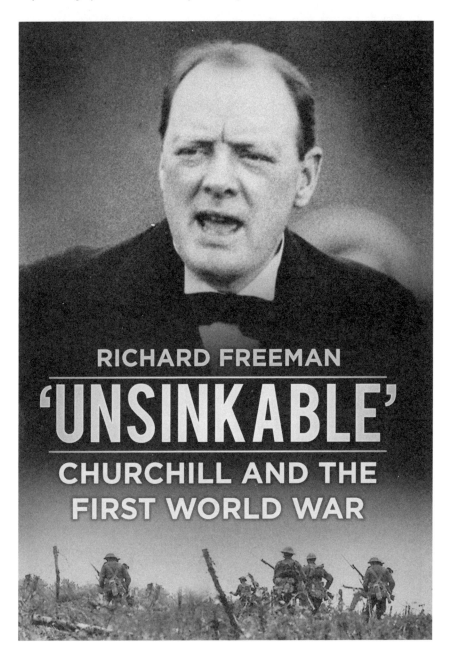

RICHARD FREEMAN

'UNSINKABLE'

CHURCHILL AND THE
FIRST WORLD WAR

9780752498898

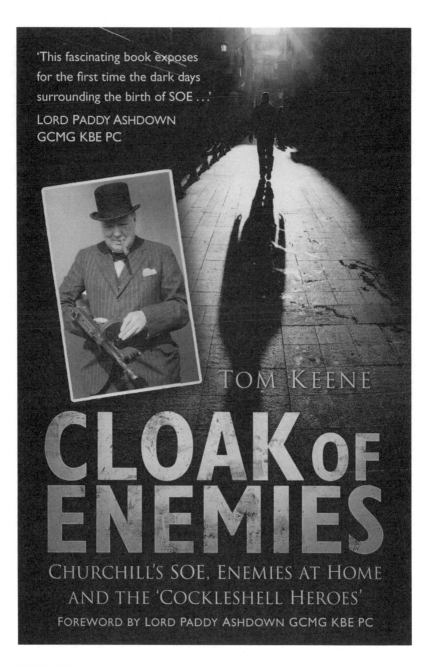

'This fascinating book exposes for the first time the dark days surrounding the birth of SOE ...'

LORD PADDY ASHDOWN
GCMG KBE PC

TOM KEENE

CLOAK OF ENEMIES

CHURCHILL'S SOE, ENEMIES AT HOME
AND THE 'COCKLESHELL HEROES'

FOREWORD BY LORD PADDY ASHDOWN GCMG KBE PC

9780752479750

Visit our website and discover thousands of
other History Press books.

www.thehistorypress.co.uk

The
History
Press